THE
CHANGING
FACE OF
WAR

THE CHANGING FACE OF WAR

Combat from the
Marne to Iraq

MARTIN VAN CREVELD

PRESIDIO
PRESS

Ballantine Books   New York

2008 Presidio Press Trade Paperback Edition

Copyright © 2007, 2008 by Martin van Creveld

Published in the United States by Presidio Press, an imprint of The Random
House Publishing Group, a division of Random House, Inc., New York.

PRESIDIO PRESS and colophon are trademarks of Random House, Inc.

Originally published in hardcover in the United States by
Presidio Press, an imprint of The Random House Publishing Group,
a division of Random House, Inc., in 2007.

Library of Congress Cataloging-in-Publication Data

Van Creveld, Martin L.
    The changing face of war : combat from the Marne to Iraq /
Martin van Creveld.
        p. cm.
    Includes bibliographical references and index.
    ISBN: 978-0-89141-902-0
        1. Military history, Modern—20th century. I. Title.
D431.V36 2006
355.409'04—dc22   2006048573

Printed in the United States of America

www.presidiopress.com

2 4 6 8 9 7 5 3 1

Book design by Fearn Cutler de Vicq

Acknowledgments

As always there are many people to thank, some of whom are not even aware of the role they played in this project. Perhaps the most important are Edward Luttwak and Joyce Seltzer, the former an incomparable writer and the latter as incomparable an editor. They taught me to go for the jugular. Forget about "parameters" and "conceptual frameworks." Don't theorize about what you are going to say; just say it. Others were my friends Professor Benjamin Kedar, who has never yet refused to read the numerous manuscripts I keep inflicting on him, and Colonel (ret.) Dr. Shmuel Gordon, who has also read this volume and with whom I have had more splendid arguments than I can remember. Among the members of my family, special thanks are due to my stepson Jonathan Lewy who, besides asking his usual incisive questions, made sure that my computer should go on working despite all the terrible things I, all unknowing, did to it. Above all, as always, I have Dvora to thank. After twenty-something years of companionship and love, my debt to her is more than I can put into words.

Mevasseret Zion,
October 4, 2005

Contents

Introduction

＊—＊＝＊—＊

A s of the opening years of the twenty-first century, the mightiest, richest, best-equipped, best-trained armed forces that have ever existed are in full decline and are, indeed, looking into an abyss. Examples of their failure abound. Almost forgotten are the days when the Israelis had fought against, and triumphed over, all the armed forces of all the Arab countries combined. Instead, having spent seventeen years vainly trying to put down the Palestinian uprising, the Israelis are even now giving up and retreating from Gaza and parts of the West Bank—to be followed, no doubt, by most of the rest. Other armed forces find themselves in a similar plight. Having spent ten years fighting in Chechnya, thoroughly demolished the capital of Grozny, and killed, injured, and "dehoused" tens if not hundreds of thousands of their opponents, the Russians are still unable to pacify that country of two and a half million. In Thailand, in Indonesia, in the Philippines, in a dozen other countries, regular armed forces are engaged in so-called counterinsurgency operations. In terms of sheer military power, all are far stronger than their enemies. None, however, seems to be making any considerable headway, and most will probably end up in defeat.

Particularly disturbing is the case of the Americans in Iraq. Whether the American decision to attack Saddam Hussein was justified will not be considered here. Suffice it to say that the United States, as the world's sole superpower, has the most powerful forces by far, with technology at its disposal that hardly any other country can match. The chosen enemy was a small third-world country with a gross domestic product so much smaller than its own that comparisons were meaningless. Twelve years earlier, that country had already lost two-thirds of its armed forces. The remainder, it soon turned out, consisted of ill-trained, unwilling levies driving a few rusting hulks. Instead of getting their aircraft into the skies, they buried them in the sand; instead of fighting, they threw down their weapons and went home. Yet no sooner had "major combat operations"—to quote President Bush's victory speech—ended than it became clear that the US forces, which had taken only three weeks to occupy a country of 240,000 square miles and capture its capital, were unable to deal with a few thousand terrorists. In early 2005, having lost ten times as many troops to those terrorists as they did during the war itself, they were still floundering. So weak had their position become that their opponents hardly bothered to shoot at them any longer. Instead, preparing for the day after the inevitable American withdrawal, the terrorists were focusing on their own countrymen.

To understand the present, study the past. Where did twentieth-century warfare come from? How did it develop from its nineteenth-century predecessor? How did it reach the point at which, at one time, the forces that waged it were capable of overrunning entire continents? When did those forces peak, why did they start to decline, and how did they reach the present impasse? Is there a way out, or are regular, state-owned armed forces forever doomed to go on losing to what are often small groups of bedraggled, ill-organized terrorists? The present volume, consisting of a short history of war over the last century or so, is an attempt to answer these questions.

In tackling this subject, perhaps the most difficult problem is deciding what to include and what to leave out.[1] Obviously any attempt to tell the story of twentieth-century warfare without reference to the political, economic, technological, and social background is as impossible, say, as describing a chameleon without taking into account the environment in which it lives. Obviously, too, any volume that tries to do all this will grow to monumental dimensions. I tried to compromise, providing enough background material to make the wars, campaigns, and battles about which I write comprehensible, but without denying military operations the center stage to which they, if the above-listed questions are to be answered, are entitled.

Another difficulty in writing about the subject at hand was that the number of available sources is practically unlimited; which, given that the library of my alma mater in Jerusalem is buying fewer and fewer books, was actually one very good reason for preferring that subject to many others. I hope I can convince people that, in addition to doing my homework and providing a brief synthesis, I do have some original things to say. Yet I did not think it necessary to read every volume produced by others or document every word I wrote. Had I tried to do so, then of course the task would never have been finished either in my lifetime or, much worse, that of my readers.

THE CHANGING FACE OF WAR

Prelude, 1900–14

1.1. States, Armies, and Navies

Around 1900, the idea that the only possible threat to a "Great Power" could come from another "Great Power" was taken very much for granted. Indeed, nowhere in the voluminous strategic literature of the period is any other possibility so much as hinted at. Depending on whether or not one included Italy, the number of Great Powers was either seven or eight. Of them, no fewer than six (or seven) were populated almost entirely by Christian people of Caucasian stock—an extraordinary fact, considering that such people formed a small percentage of the world's population. Even more extraordinary, of the seven (or eight) Great Powers in question, four (or five) were located in just one, rather small, continent by the name of Europe. Another, Russia, had its main basis firmly rooted in that continent even though it also stretched all the way across Asia to the Pacific. Only two of the powers, the United States and Japan, were geographically separated from the "old" continent. However, even those two owed their strength either to the fact that their population was of Caucasian stock or to their successful adaptation of European ideas, methods, and techniques.

The product of a series of exceptionally fortunate circumstances,[1] built up over the course of centuries, this tremendous concentration of military might enabled its owners to share almost the entire world among themselves. From about AD 1500 on, it was Europe that established colonies abroad, not the other way around. European ships were fully rigged and carried row upon row of cannon. Captained by the likes of Christopher Columbus, Vasco da Gama, and their followers, they reached the four corners of the earth. Wherever they met opposition they shot it to pieces; meanwhile, non-Europeans were able to reach Europe, if at all, only as licensed curiosities.[2]

In addition to Latin America, the only non-European countries that succeeded in staying independent were China, Thailand, Ethiopia, Liberia, the Ottoman Empire, Iran, and Afghanistan. The main reason why they did so was not their own strength but because the powers, while unable to agree on how to carve them up, did not want to go to war over them. Some were formally designated as buffer zones. Thus, Iran in 1907 was cut into three "zones of influence": a Russian one in the north, a British one in the south, and a common one in the center. In other cases, the independence in question was more apparent than real.

As so often happens, political power rested on an equally impressive accumulation of economic muscle. The Industrial Revolution had started in Britain during the second half of the eighteenth century. From there, it spread to the Continent; as of the beginning of the twentieth century, however, with the exception of the United States and Japan it had scarcely yet touched the other parts of the globe. Until 1750, according to the best available calculations, about three-quarters of all the world's manufacturing output had been concentrated in what, today, we would call the third world (Africa and Asia minus Russia and Japan). From this point, the share underwent a steady decline until, in 1900, it stood at a mere 12 percent. Conversely, by that time, Europe, the United States, and Japan together accounted for no less than 88 percent of world manufacturing output. In terms of per capita industrialization, the gap between the self-styled "civilized" and "primitive" countries was much greater still.

In 1914, on the eve of the Great War, the largest economic power was already the United States, with a population of 98 million and a national income of $37 billion. It was followed by Germany (65 million and $12 billion, respectively), Great Britain (45 and $11), Russia (171 and $7), France (39 and $6), Austria-Hungary (52 and $3), Italy (37 and $4), and Japan (55 and $2). Thus the US economy was slightly larger than those of the next four powers combined, amounting to no less than 45 percent of the total. At $377, American per capita income was also the highest by far—one result of this being that visitors to America who had been comfortable at home felt like paupers. It was followed, at a considerable distance, by Britain ($244), Germany ($184), and France

($153). On that basis, the poorest powers of all were Italy, Austria-Hungary, Russia, and Japan, in that order.[3]

At that time, five out of the world's seven most powerful armed forces, namely those of Germany, France, Italy, Austria-Hungary, and Russia, relied on some form of general conscription to fill their manpower needs. So did Japan, although in practice the country's financial penury meant that the fraction of the relevant age groups which actually saw service was much smaller. The important exceptions were Britain, whose main defense consisted of its navy, and the United States, which, feeling secure behind its oceans, hardly had an army at all.

Conscription, organized by the magistrates with the aid of pre-prepared lists of citizens, had been the normal method for obtaining military manpower both in classical Greece and during the Roman Republic. However, in the days of the empire it was abandoned, and before it was reinstituted, more than a millennium and a half had to pass. Assisted by advances in public administration, the first modern country to resort to conscription, or the *levée en masse* as it was called, was France in 1792. Other countries reluctantly followed, though not without many ups and downs that, often reflecting political battles among reactionaries, democrats, and socialists, lasted during most of the nineteenth century.[4]

Following the German triumph over France in 1870–71, most countries adopted the system of military organization developed by the victor. This system divided the armed forces into three parts. The first consisted of a core of professionals (officers and NCOs) who served on longtime contracts—in many cases, until retirement. The second was made up of a larger group of conscripts who, depending on the country in question and also on the service they joined, were usually made to serve two or three years. The two elements together might make up perhaps 1 percent of a country's population in peacetime, though in the case of France it was rather more and in those of Italy and Japan, rather less.

The third and largest part consisted of reservists who had completed their training and, having been discharged into civilian life and perhaps undergone refresher training from time to time, remained available for immediate recall in case war broke out.

By 1914, most countries expected reserves to increase their armed forces by a factor of four or five, but that did not prove the upper limit.

The best-organized countries with the shortest lines of communications were Germany and France. Ultimately, they put almost 10 percent of their entire populations in uniform and kept them for years on end; what this meant for them, and their families, we can hardly imagine.

While every Great Power, as well as most of the lesser nations, possessed both an army and a navy, most land and naval forces had developed separately over a period of centuries. As a result, few people thought of providing them with common training at any level, let alone of putting them under joint command. Instead, each service had its own ministry responsible for providing it with weapons, cannon fodder, fuel, and administrative support in everything from financial affairs to veterans' pensions. Each ministry was headed by a minister or secretary who represented it either in the cabinet or, in Britain and France, in a smaller committee consisting of key ministers.

In Germany, the only link between the OHL (Oberste Heeresleitung) and the SKL (Seekriegsleitung) was the kaiser himself, as commander in chief. Consequently, the SKL was not officially informed about the army's plans. Nor, according to one of its subsequent commanders in chief, Admiral Erich Raeder, had it prepared any plans for assisting in the invasion of Belgium and France.[5] And matters differed little in the United States. There, too, the secretary of the navy and the secretary of war (army) were insulated from each other, each answering only to the president. Beneath them, the army chief of staff and the chief of naval operations appeared to live on separate planets, a problem that, as far as procedures, signal communications, and data links are concerned, has not been completely solved to the present day. France and Britain faced the same organizational limitations, only this time the role of the missing link was played by their respective prime ministers. In effect the main difference between the military monarchies east of the Rhine and the democracies west of it was that, in the former, the chiefs of staff were entitled to address a sovereign directly. This Immediatvortrag, as the Germans called it, was nevertheless far from ideally suited for the demands of modern war to come. Yet it was only after 1945 that most countries attempted reform, setting up unified ministries of defense with a common high command for all services. By then, as we shall see, in some ways it no longer mattered.

As had been the case at least since Gustavus Adolphus showed the way early in the seventeenth century, armies still consisted essentially of the three arms of infantry, cavalry, and artillery. However, the proliferation since 1870 of magazine-loading small arms, machine guns, and quick-firing cannon was showing those with eyes to see that the days of the cavalry charge were numbered. Perhaps even more importantly in retrospect, extremely rapid technical progress during the second half of the nineteenth century had resulted in armies becoming much more articulated, leading to the creation of a host of specialist units responsible for operating the new devices. Many were offshoots of the artillery, long known as a refuge for officers who were less anti-intellectual than the rest. Among them were engineering troops, technical troops, railway troops, signal troops—soon to branch into the various flying corps—and the like; the days when 90 percent of all troops carried weapons and were expected to fight as their primary mission were coming to an end.

The first experiments in carrying troops by rail had been made in Russia as far back as the 1840s. In 1859, both the French and the Prussians used the method, the former to wage war against the Austrians in Italy and the latter to deploy their army on the Rhine. These early exercises were dwarfed by the American Civil War when both sides, but the Federals in particular, used railroads on a gigantic scale to shuttle men and supplies to and fro across the continent. However, this fact left most European observers, who were convinced of their own superiority, unmoved. Not everybody was as perceptive as Karl Marx, who, though no military expert, saw the Americans' war as "a spectacle without parallel" in history.[6] Yet it must be admitted that there was some reason behind the indifference. In 1866 and 1870–71, the Prussians gave a dazzling demonstration of what railways could do, and from then until 1914, almost invariably it was American officers who came to study German methods, not the other way around.

By 1914, the great age of railway construction was all but over. With two hundred thousand miles of track crisscrossing Europe, all powers planned on making maximum use of the lines in order to carry out mobilization and deployment. For example, the German general staff planned on operating no fewer than eleven thousand trains over a period of two weeks. Proceeding at a stately twenty-five miles per hour, their movements were calculated so precisely that even the number of axles passing over a given bridge within a given period of time was known. Then as now, in terms of carrying capacity and sheer efficiency the railways had no rival, requiring far fewer personnel and maintenance per ton/mile transported. Then as now, however, they were also inflexible and, in times of war, vulnerable to enemy action.

Moreover, railways could not be built too close to the front; as a result, many operations still had to be carried out on the backs of men and animals. A mode of transportation that the First World War did not share with any previous conflict was the automobile. In 1914, the mobilized German army had about five thousand of them, mostly impressed civilian vehicles that were unsuited to the harsh demands of war. By contrast, the number of horses used to carry cavalrymen, haul the artillery, and drag the supply wagons was estimated at 1.4 million.[7]

The newfangled contraptions did prove useful, however, in a famous episode that took place in September of that year. General Gallieni, who serving as military governor of Paris, requisitioned six hundred of the city's taxis to move troops to the front, allegedly making a substantial contribution to the French victory at the battle of the Marne.

As the First World War hammered on, automobiles became more common and were increasingly used for liaison, casualty evacuation, supply, and the like. Other vehicles, in the form of tractors, were also used to haul pieces of artillery so heavy that they could never have been moved by any other means. By 1918, the British army alone had about seventy thousand of them, including both passenger cars and trucks. Still, experience was to show that a fully motorized army needed one vehicle for every six men—a figure remarkably similar to the previous ratio of horses to men, and not even the Americans, who were much better equipped than anybody else, were able to approach it. Partly for that reason, partly because battlefields were often too difficult for mechanized transport, all major operations continued to depend, as they had for centuries, on the muscles of men and horses.[8]

If war is the father of invention, then the field of command, control, and communication had long been its unloved stepchild. Thanks to its muskets and cannon, Napoléon's grande armée could easily have smashed Caesar's legions, yet as Napoléon himself wrote, he held no significant advantage in his ability to communicate with his generals. In AD 1800 as in 44 BC, communications were moved by men, either on foot or on horseback. For short-range work, messages could be conveyed aurally by drums or trumpets, or visually by flags and standards.

For longer ranges, Napoléon did have uniquely at his disposal: the semaphore system. The semaphore consisted of moveable beams mounted on top of tall towers so as to form various combinations, indicating letters, which could be read from afar by means of a telescope. Initially there was only one line; later, the system was expanded until it linked all of the most important capital cities.[9] Owing to the need for numerous operators and observers, however, it was enormously expensive to operate. It was also fixed in place, which meant that it was unable to follow the movements of field armies.

By the middle of the nineteenth century, these age-old methods began to be supplemented by the offsprings of the new wonder of science: electricity. In the form of the telegraph, the telephone, and radio, technical progress was rapid, although by 1914 all three remained cumbersome, fragile, or both, and all of course depended on electrical power—which was not always available. As a result, the closer to the front one got, the scarcer were these high-tech marvels and the greater the use of the older, but more reliable runners, blinking lights (including rockets), klaxons, homing pigeons (discarded by the US Army only in the 1930s), and even messenger dogs.

Technological developments changed the battlefield, more or less, but it was at sea where the dramatic advances took place. The early years of the twentieth century caught the world's major navies in the midst of a major transition toward far larger and more powerful, but also more expensive and hence fewer, battleships. During the 1860s, first ironclads (sheets of iron plate over a wooden hull) and then iron-built ships had begun to take the place of the old wooden, sail-driven vessels, and in 1873, the HMS *Devastation* became the first battleship to abandon sails altogether, relying completely on coal for motive power.

By 1914, the shift from sail to coal was more or less complete. Freed from the vagaries of weather, ships were now faster, larger, more heavily armed and armored than ever. Coal, unlike wind, was exhaustible, and the need for refueling stations throughout the world authored a new chapter in the West's competition for overseas colonies. But coal, too, was being replaced by oil and reciprocating steam engines by the much more efficient turbines. In 1906 the British *Dreadnought,* the first all big-gun battleship was launched. It made all its predecessors obsolete at a stroke, compelling the other powers to follow suit.

As late as 1880, the range of naval guns was limited to three thousand yards. The crews aimed their weapons as best they could. They followed the roll of the vessel and let fly at what they hoped was the right moment; then they corrected by observing the splashes. By 1914, guns could throw shells up to thirty thousand yards, much too far away to allow gun crews to even see their target—so finding a new system to aim and track naval gunfire became imperative. Between 1900 and 1910, British and American officers did in fact put in place a system that made use of recently developed mechanical direction finders and range finders. These instruments passed their data to the chief artillery officer, who now became the third most important person aboard, after the captain and the executive officer. Perched high on the bridge—higher, in fact, than the captain, who had to content himself with the level below—he and his staff used mechanical devices to make the necessary calculations while compensating for such factors as relative speed, direction, and roll. When the moment came, it was he who pressed the firing button, sending an electrical discharge to deliver a salvo.[10]

At a time when some military wireless stations on land were still powered by soldiers furiously pedaling stationary bicycles to turn generators, electrical energy was much more readily available at sea. There, engines that could be made to drive a dynamo were omnipresent. In 1905, Japanese scouts used radio in order to warn their commander in chief, Admiral Heichachiro Togo, that the Russian fleet was approaching the Tsushima Strait;[11] by 1910, every single British vessel, military or civilian, was ordered to install a set.

For the first time in history, central headquarters, instead of issuing their admirals with letters of instruction that might or might not fit circumstances and might or might not be obeyed, was in a position to continuously monitor operations and control them. For the first time in history, messages could be sent in many directions at once without additional expense and, if in code, without entailing the risk that the craft that carried the orders would fall into enemy hands. Widely separated vessels and fleets could execute a coherent strategy, coordinate their movements, and come to one another's aid as circumstances dictated;[12] the impact of factors that used to interfere with earlier, optically based signaling systems such as fog and darkness, the position of the sun, or even the smoke from the ships' own stacks were all but eliminated.

At sea as on land, the flip side of this coin was that radio transmissions could be intercepted and, not infrequently, decrypted. Even if the transmissions could not be decrypted, the very fact that they were broadcast, their number, and the possibility of using triangulation in order to track them to their place of origin frequently provided important clues as to the whereabouts of enemy fleets, their strength, and their intentions. This was apparent even to Admiral Togo in 1905; once he had received the critical message warning him of the Russians' approach, he ordered his captains to observe radio silence as they prepared for battle. Conversely, in 1916 the first indication that the German high sea fleet had sailed toward what would develop into the battle of Jutland reached the British in the form of intercepted radio calling signals—albeit an administrative muddle at the admiralty prevented them from using that information as well as they might have.

Finally, yet another new technology with the potential to revolutionize naval warfare was the submarine. Submarines had a long history going back to the end of the seventeenth century, and a few of them had actually been used during the American Civil War. However, those early models proved as dangerous to their crews as to their enemies; it was only in 1900 that the first modern submarine, combining an internal combustion engine with an electric motor for underwater movement, was launched. An American invention, this basic design soon found imitators, but progress was slow. When the war broke out, submarines were still untried in battle, and their true potential was unknown; even the most astute naval writer of the time, Julian Corbett, thought they would be useful mainly for coastal defense.[13] With so many different new technologies emerging at sea, few people had a clear idea how they would interact and how they should be used, or what their impact would be.

1.2. Visions of War

In 1914, the uniformed military claimed a near monopoly on all things martial. It is true that the media of the day did take a lively interest in military science, but the idea of civilian think tanks and civilian university departments teaching courses on the subject remained far away. Nor did any country as yet think it necessary to have a national security council with a strong representation of civilian experts;

indeed, the German great general staff referred to the foreign ministry, which might have provided some such experts, as *das Idiotenhaus*. Though there were a few exceptions, notably in the United States and France, where the government did not entirely trust the brass, in most countries the. ministers responsible for their respective war departments were themselves former generals or admirals.

In all countries, the real experts on military science were the general staff officers, their status clearly marked by red stripes running down their pants, and the only place where military science was taught was at the staff colleges. Such institutions originated in the last years of the eighteenth century, and until the middle of the nineteenth century had been fairly obscure. However, the German wars against Austria and France (1866–71) changed the situation. While general staffs became the sole founts of military wisdom, staff colleges were the places where members of the elite were put through their paces; the importance of the role they played is suggested by the fact that key future French commanders such as Ferdinand Foch and Philippe Pétain, and their German counterparts Paul von Hindenburg and Erich Ludendorff, spent time teaching in them.

On the minus side, the system created a near-complete divorce between the military and civilian worlds—a divorce also reflected in the writing of military history, which tended to be extremely parochial. Thus the first sea lord and effective chief of staff of the British navy, Admiral John Fisher, at one point brought over Julian Corbett to lecture at the newly established Greenwich Staff College. Corbett at the time was the world's best-known naval theorist after Alfred Mahan, and though few people (other than Winston Churchill) actually read his work, most agreed that it was brilliant. One of the cardinal points he tried to put across was that, to understand naval affairs, it was not enough to know about ships, engines, cannon, tides, weather conditions, and the like. Instead, one had to refer to "the whole area of diplomatic and military effort"; today we might call this grand strategy. He was not a success, and the students, crusty sea dogs all of them, poked "good-natured" fun at his attempts to explain the actions of past naval commanders and criticize them. After all, by profession he was a lawyer, albeit one who, possessing independent means, studied naval affairs full time. And what could a lawyer know that they did not know already?[14]

Turning from the hostility of the staff colleges, the war ministries were sometimes more receptive to new ideas. Spenser Wilkinson in 1895, published his treatise on the ideas that underpinned the German general staff, just at the time when the duke of Cambridge—who as commander in chief had been blocking all change for decades—finally left office.[15] Still, most civilians—including the best-known military historian of the day, the German professor Hans Delbrueck—were contemptuously rejected. Indeed, Delbrueck's attempt to put military history "within the framework of political history" (the subtitle of his main book) was itself enough to arouse suspicion.[16] Hadn't the military always insisted that the profession was separate from, and more important than, any mere political developments? A few specialists, such as doctors and priests, received direct commissions after having attended civilian universities or schools. Apart from that, the possibility that serving officers might have anything to learn by doing so was simply inconceivable.

At the time, there were a number of recent conflicts to which those who wished could look for lessons. Never, incidentally, had the status of military history as a source of such lessons been higher. Given that the combatants on at least one side were considered barely human, the Sino-Japanese War of 1895 seemed to provide few lessons, but the Boer War of 1899–1900 was a different matter.[17] This war was waged by representatives of that highest of higher races, white, Anglo-Saxon Protestants, using the latest European weaponry. The war certainly brought home the importance of quick-firing artillery, as the small numbers of Krupp-made Boer guns were able to successfully engage the much heavier, but cumbersome and slow-firing British pieces.[18] It also demonstrated the importance of rifle fire, a lesson that the British took to heart by training their men to deliver "twelve rounds a minute, aimed," as the saying went.

Of course this experience should have led to the realization that the day of cavalry was past and that any future horsemen should fight dismounted, as the Boers did, despite being excellent riders. However, that lesson proved a bitter pill to take, and was mostly rejected. For centuries on end, officers had been horsemen first and foremost. Cavalry, the aristocratic arm, had always looked down on the poor unfortunate foot sloggers. In one German caricature, mounted officers wondered how the infantry ever succeeded in getting from one place to the next. Rulers themselves often presented themselves on horse-back. Frozen in the statues with which they adorned their squares, avenues, and streets, the ruling classes immortalized themselves upon the universal symbols of power and privilege.[19]

The man who commanded the British forces on the Western Front during most of World War I, Field Marshal Douglas Haig, was himself a cavalryman. As a young officer in 1898, Haig, along with Winston Churchill, had charged the Dervishes at Omdurman. Nine years later, having risen to become director of training, he personally was responsible for reintroducing the lance.[20] Other armies had never abolished it in the first place. Thus the cavalry of all countries rode into World War I almost as if the war in South Africa had never taken place.

To those not blinded by racism, by far the war most telling of things to come was that fought between Russia and Japan in 1904–5, but again the lessons drawn from it were wrong for the most part.[21] First and foremost was the great naval battle of Tsushima. Before Tsushima, there were thirty years of peace on the high seas, during which the transition from sail to steam had been completed and had thoroughly confused both practitioners and theoreticians. Using ancient Athens for guidance, many thought that future battles would be decided by approaching the enemy in wedge formation and ramming him, a view that the battle of Lissa (1866) seemed to confirm.[22] Battleships, accordingly, came equipped with huge rams, the power of which was illustrated in 1893 when the HMS *Camperdown* was accidentally rammed during maneuvers off Malta and went to the bottom in only a few minutes, taking along all of her crew. What a relief, then, when Tsushima put order into the confusion, proving that arrays of heavy cannon, carried by battleships arranged in such a way as to deliver the greatest firepower, continued to rule the seas as they had since the end of the seventeenth century.[23]

More foreboding was the "success" of the Japanese infantry. Wielding bayonets and supported by heavy artillery, they ultimately succeeded in breaking through the Russian lines at Mukden. However, this victory masked the fact that in doing so they took no fewer than forty-one thousand casualties. The Russian army was merely pushed back along its own line of communications and had not the tsarist empire been racked by the revolution of 1905, it could and would have fought another day. It was this belief in the frontal infantry attack, supported by artillery, that killed so many troops on the Western Front between 1914 and 1918. Perhaps the only valid lesson one could draw from the war was how hard it was to attack and take a fortified city, such as Port Arthur, from the sea. As the 1915 Gallipoli campaign was to show, that lesson, too, was not heeded.

Much worse still, the idea that wars would be short, lively, and decisive—as, given their enormous cost, they had to be—had hardened into dogma; one of those who expounded it was the German chief of staff Alfred von Schlieffen (who served from 1891 to 1905).[24] With the exception of Foch, who had some curious things to say about the matter,[25] most military experts well understood the effect that the proliferation of machine guns and other quick-firing weapons would have. They increased the power of the tactical defense, making it all but impossible for the attackers to cross the few hundred yards of beaten zone before they could close with their enemies. However, few of them were prepared to resign themselves to this fact, and understandably so. If armies could no longer attack, then obviously there would be nothing to defend against. If there was nothing to defend against, then the day would come when they would be dissolved—as some people feared and others hoped.

Instead, commanders—not just those in French uniforms, as too many historians have written[26]—looked for ways to circumvent the problem and overcome it. One way was by carrying out wide-ranging strategic movements so as to outflank the enemy lines. If keeping the cavalry had any rationale at all, this was it; yet in doing so commanders overlooked the fact that distances in Europe were much smaller than in, say, the United States, where during the Civil War cavalry had sometimes played a similar role. Another was the hope that heavy artillery could destroy the enemy defenses. Many officers even seemed to believe that if they could only train their troops to attack under all circumstances, they would be able to render them more or less bulletproof.

People, like the Jewish-Polish-Russian railway magnate Ivan Bloch, who drew the correct conclusions and predicted a long war that would be decided, if it could be decided at all, by sheer attrition, were taken to task for failing to understand "the reality of military affairs" and ignored.[27] Here and there the "frocks" and the "brass hats" changed places, the former engaging in illusions and the latter advising caution.

Take the newly appointed British minister of war, Field Marshal Herbert Kitchener. When he told his civilian colleagues in the cabinet that the war would last for years and require the creation of armies numbering in the millions, they thought he had gone mad.

By the turn of the century, all modern countries were endowed with a more or less dense network of railways as well as telegraphs and telephones. It was thought that the side that could use these instruments to mobilize and deploy the fastest would gain an important, perhaps decisive, advantage. Therefore it was only natural that the most talented officers tended to cluster in the railway departments of general staffs, drawing up plans in painstaking detail. The result was a tendency to see war itself as something that, projected from the railheads, would proceed as if by timetable. Blithely ignoring the enemy and simply using a pair of dividers, planners calculated that so and so many days were needed to reach this objective, so and so many the next. Thus, upon the signal being given, each opponent would mobilize its reserve players who would then entrain *("Marchons, citoyens, montez, sur les trains,"* as an informal variant on the "Marseillaise" had it), disentrain, march, encounter, engage, break through, outflank, encircle, kill, take one another prisoner, and be home by Christmas.

The model for much of this was neither the Russian Japanese War of 1904–5 nor the Boer War of 1899–1900, both of which had taken place in faraway lands under what many people considered less-than-civilized conditions. Instead it was the Franco-Prussian War, three decades earlier. This, it was thought, still presented the most "modern" war in history to date. Some officers, the French in particular, sought to derive lessons from Napoleonic warfare, which they studied at very great length in order to discover the emperor's "secret" as well as the immutable "principles of war." In Germany, many commanders still looked as far back as the campaigns of Frederick the Great for more insight. For example, one general wrote an entire book showing that troop movements similar to those the king had carried out with thirty-three thousand men at Leuthen in 1757 were still feasible in the modern age with its millions upon millions of troops.[28]

The universal belief in a short war had important consequences. Each country prepared to open hostilities from a flying start, so to speak. So and so many vehicles, rifles, machine guns, cannon, and their ammunition were available. For instance, Germany, as the best-prepared country of all, had about a thousand rounds per artillery barrel. Even assuming a consumption rate three times as high as in 1870–71, this should have sufficed for about two years; no wonder they entered the war with a feeling of confidence. The equipment would be taken out of the depots where it was stored and looked after, and married with the available pool of trained personnel. However, very few officers gave any thought to the need to continue, let alone increase military production after the outbreak of hostilities. The need for the organization and control of raw materials, factories, transportation arteries, and labor that would be required for the purpose could not even be contemplated. War, it was believed, would result in declining living standards and a "return to the primitive circumstances of our ancestors," including a massive rise in unemployment. Thus, for war to be of any length would be ruinous to civilization. When, a few months after the opening of hostilities, the opposite proved to be the case, everything had to be improvised.

1.3. Resisters and Enthusiasts

Some things never change, and although many a young man saw military service as the gateway to personal glory, such romantic notions were not shared by all. Even in militarist Germany, especially among the well-educated middle class, officers were ridiculed for allegedly having no higher interests whatsoever. When people claimed that the kaiser had sought the philosopher's stone and found it in the aide de camp this was hardly meant as a compliment. In Germany, as in Italy and Russia, some people emigrated specifically to avoid being conscripted, much to the chagrin of governments, which felt unable to stop them.

Perhaps more important, the period from 1899 to 1907 witnessed two successive international peace congresses being held in the Netherlands. The initiative came from Tsar Nicholas II of Russia. Personally, Nicholas was a mild character dominated by his German wife, who herself ended up dominated by that uncouth priest Rasputin. He would not have been out of place as a constitutional monarch, and might even have enjoyed acting in such a role. Ostensibly, his purpose was the purely idealistic one of saving the world from the horrors of war. However, some evil tongues claimed that what really motivated him was the realization that his country was unable to keep up in the arms race against Germany and Japan in particular.

The need to maintain face in front of public opinion forced the most important countries to send their representatives to The Hague, but not everybody took the talks seriously. For example, when the German kaiser first heard of the idea he threatened to "s_ _t" on all their resolutions.[29] The American representative to the first conference was none other than Alfred Mahan himself. Piously, he declared that "power, force, [sic] is a faculty of national life; one of the talents committed to nations by God."[30] He also opposed a ban on poison gas, opining that being asphyxiated was no worse than being torpedoed.

Perhaps the best commentary was provided by a Dutch children's song claiming that the next congress would take place at Merenberg, a well-known lunatic asylum at the time.[31] As most people had expected, this congress, as well as the next, achieved little in the way of reducing the threat of war. They did, however, produce some useful protocols concerning the ways war should and should not be waged.

Equally ineffective, if more sincere, were the various pacifist movements. The hope that "progress" would bring people to their senses and make them turn their backs on war runs through the nineteenth century like a red thread, from the economist Friedrich List in the 1830s all the way to the inventor and industrialist Alfred Nobel in the 1890s. At least one well-known peace activist, the Scottish American steel magnate Andrew Carnegie, seems to have been motivated by his desire to compensate the God who had given him so much, and his Carnegie Peace Foundation remains active to the present day.

Probably the most famous pacifist was an Austrian noblewoman, Bertha von Suttner.[32] For three decades, she toured Europe and the United States, organizing conferences, speaking, and writing about peace. Her main book, *Nieder die Waffen*, written in 1889, received much attention and was translated into several languages; it was followed by a periodical with the same title. In 1905, her efforts got her the Nobel Peace Prize, founded by the man whose secretary she had once been. Ironically, Mme. von Suttner died in June 1914 and was thus spared the horrors that followed.

This was also the time when socialist movements were gathering strength throughout the world. The socialists' objection to the military and its institutions had little to do with pacifism; rather, to them these were the mainstays of the existing regimes, the home of reactionaries, conservatives, clericalists, militarists, and imperialists—and very often this view was well justified. After all, most European countries were still ruled by monarchs, and the only army that had not begun its history as a royal guard was that of Switzerland. This fact was reflected not only on ceremonial occasions, when they were called upon to perform precisely that role, but also in the way their members behaved in the presence of the sovereign. As photographs show, ladies were supposed to curtsy and gentlemen, dressed in black, to doff their hats with bowed heads. Officers, by contrast, were expected to stand straight— no servility there—and salute with shining eyes as if meeting an old comrade. Thus the fiction that monarchs, before they were anything else, were commanders in chief who led their men to battle was maintained. Even in France, until at least 1900 most officers were probably royalists at heart and took offense at the idea of being commanded by mere civilians.[33]

In 1907, the German general staff went so far as to produce a handbook, *Fighting in Insurgent Towns*, to instruct commanders in that long-forgotten art. One of its first provisions was that, in case of need, it was the duty of every officer to strike without waiting for parliamentary approval—and if necessary to do so even against parliament's will.

Socialist leaders could not but be aware of at least some of what was going on. In places where the political system permitted them to do so, such as France and Germany, they campaigned to place limits on the influence of the military, as well as the funding. Jean Jaurès, the brilliant head of the Section Française de l'Internationale Ouvrière and a member of the French parliament, went further. He wrote a book demanding that standing armies be replaced with popular militias.[34] Electing the officers, training in their spare time, and ridding themselves of the intellectual baggage of regular armies, they would be equally effective in defending the nation; at the same time, they would be incapable of being used against it, and they might do some useful things in helping it realize its ideals. As might be expected, among military circles the book was ridiculed. Nothing came of it in any country except neutral Switzerland, and then not because of any conscious decision but simply because the militia there was already established, having a history going back all the way to the Middle Ages.

At the time when the heir to the Austrian throne, Archduke Franz

Ferdinand, was assassinated at Sarajevo, the socialist representatives in the parliaments of the various countries were within several weeks of holding their international meeting in Vienna. Like most other people, at first they expected the crisis to be resolved without bloodshed; indeed, their chief concern was that the Serb delegates might not be able to attend. As the situation became more menacing, however, they seemed to undergo a mysterious change of mind.

For years previously, socialists had talked themselves hoarse, claiming that war was the fault of the ruling classes in general and swearing to oppose it if and when it came. Now each one, blaming the ruling classes of the other country, absolved his own; it was as if they were subject to some atavistic herd instinct most of them thought they had long left behind. Next, almost to a man, they and their followers voted for the war, put on a uniform, and went off to fight much as everybody else did. Indeed to some people it seemed as if the workers, disappointed by having to wait for a violent revolution that never came, saw the war as an acceptable alternative.

As Jaurès's own fate suggested—attempting to set up a common German-French anti-war front, he fell victim to an assassin's bullet—popularity was not to be found with either the socialists or pacifists. The cue to what was socially desirable was provided by the heads of state themselves. In 1901, most of them went to London to participate in the funeral of Queen Victoria; except for the president of France, who for that reason cut a rather poor figure, every single one wore a uniform. The way was led by the German kaiser. Partly because he thought uniforms suited him, partly because he was always trying to look tougher than he really was, he rarely made a public appearance while dressed in anything else. With such an example before their eyes, no wonder it was the fondest dream of every good German bourgeois to be made a lieutenant of the reserve. After all, Bismarck himself once said that humanity started at that rank.

In every country that had it, conscription turned the military into the largest single organization by far, with all the economic and social consequences that such a situation entails. It also compelled the authorities to glorify their armed forces so as to make people willing to serve. Looking back, perhaps nothing is more surprising than the success they enjoyed in doing just that.[35] In France, which conscripted a greater percentage of its population than did any other country, there was much talk of the military as "the school of the nation," the one organization where all youngsters met and underwent the great experience that fused them together. This was even more true in Italy. As the country's founder, Benso Cavour, had once remarked, the unification of the peninsula did not automatically Italians make. The early years of the state were marked by revolts by the inhabitants of Sicily against the Piedmontese officials who had been sent to rule over them; indeed, so far apart were northerners and southerners that they could not even understand each other's dialects. Obligatory military service was seen, and deliberately used, as perhaps the most important means to correct this problem.

Military pay tended to be on the low side; indeed, in Germany people sometimes spoke of *"glaenzende Elend"* (glittering misery). Here as elsewhere, soldiers' high social status often translated itself into material benefits after retirement. Whether because the law mandated it or because of their reputation for reliability, former noncommissioned officers were frequently given preference in joining the lower rungs of the civil service including, where they were publicly owned, the railways—which in many places constituted the largest single employer of all. Officers, on the other hand, could expect to receive modest pensions and use them in order to set up house in the countryside. More senior officers might receive seats on the boards of large corporations. While the term *revolving door* did not yet exist, the phenomenon it describes definitely did.

Only in Britain and the United States, considered the most commercial of nations and hence the farthest removed from "militancy," were things somewhat different. Since these countries did not have conscription, their armed forces were relatively much smaller. They were also less influential; their governments did not have to glorify war as much as the rest did. On the negative side, their forces tended to be filled by unemployable members of the working classes. In the United States, this often meant country lads, the term *doughboys* containing more than a hint at their supposed stupidity.[36] Quite understandably, they were eager to escape from the small out-of-the-way towns and farms where they had been born and that offered them no future except for endless drudgery and boredom.

If only because there weren't many peasants left, British soldiers were more likely to come from an urban background. Shunned by respectable society, which sometimes put up signs saying SOLDIERS NOT ADMITTED, they were often described as pitiable beings, their growth stunted and their teeth rotted by a childhood of deprivation spent in the slums.

Officers in both countries enjoyed higher esteem. To realize this fact, one has only to note the impressive houses built for majors at the National War College, Washington, DC, at the turn of the last century. Still, since the forces in which they served were seen as instruments of the state rather than one of the pillars on which it rested, their prestige lagged behind that of their opposite numbers on the Continent. Churchill once claimed that the reason he attended the military academy at Sandhurst was because his father thought he was not clever enough to be a lawyer.[37]

Another factor that characterized the military of the time was the exceptionally strong tie between it and the prevailing ideas of manhood.[38] Armies, of course, had always been bastions of masculinity. Legend has it that, when he wanted to test Sun Tzu, the king of Wu ordered him to form an army out of palace women as the most difficult task of all, and the Roman military writer Vegetius in the fourth century AD had recommended that men working in "feminine" occupations not be taken into the legions. In the French Army during the middle of the nineteenth century, things were carried to the point that every officer was ordered to wear a suitable black mustache or, if he couldn't muster a real one, have one painted on his face. Historically, most armies had been accompanied by throngs of camp followers, many of whom were female. Camp followers performed many necessary functions from foraging to cooking and from laundry to nursing, but the militarization of rear services during the second half of the nineteenth century meant that they were no longer needed. Coming at the same time, the rise of the railways took responsibility for transport away from individual units. Instead it was concentrated in the hands of higher headquarters. There, experts calculated capacities to the last carriage and the last bench; as a result, field commanders were no longer able to take women on campaign as they used to do.[39]

The fact that, in the last years before 1914, armies had no women left even in semi-military positions probably helped raise their prestige, not least in the eyes of women themselves. When the call for action came, it was the fear of appearing cowardly in the eyes of women that caused many men to volunteer.[40] For their part, most women sought nothing better than to marry men who served in armies or commanded them, even if—since military pay was fairly low and the living standard officers were expected to maintain high—doing so meant supporting their husbands out of their own dowries. Even if, as on the Continent, doing so often meant spending one's life in some out-of-the-way garrison town. German papers used to joke about brides who, having wed an officer, were surprised to discover that, under their uniforms, their husbands looked and acted just as other men did.

Above everything else, this was a time of nationalist feeling par excellence. Every country now had its national anthem; many, including the "Marseillaise" and "The Star-Spangled Banner," were really marching songs and calls to arms. In every country, one very important goal of the new state-directed school system was to inculcate youth with the nation's glory, including above all military feats bravely performed. Germany had Frederick the Great and Helmuth von Moltke. France had Jeanne d'Arc and Napoléon, Italy Giuseppe Garibaldi, and Russia Alexander Nevsky; even the peace-loving Netherlands had a war hero in the person of Wilhelm the Silent. Each nation traced its origins to some noble ancestors who, after long suffering at the hands of their wicked neighbors, finally emerged from dark slavery into the glorious, sunlit present.

The importance of the military in European society could also be gauged by the popularity of voluntary civilian organizations that were modeled on the armed forces to emulate and support them. Among the more innocuous were the British Boy Scouts. Drawing their members from the middle classes, Boy Scouts specialized in tents, knots, and bicycle repair. The group was founded in 1908 by General Robert Baden Powell in an effort to train the country's youths to be useful in war.

Throughout England, in fact, it was taken as a matter of course that boys liked games. Besides "building character," the real purpose of games was to prepare for the greatest game of all; had not the battle of Waterloo been won on the playing fields of Eton? By 1910, more than 150 schools, as well as several universities, had taken up the idea, establishing officer training corps where, often supervised by retired officers or such as had been detached by the army for the purpose, students could play at war to their hearts' content. The English way of linking play with war may have been idiosyncratic, but it was hardly unique; if anything, foreign educational institutions envied the system and tried to model themselves on it. Everywhere organized sports, brought to public attention by the revival of the Olympic Games in 1896, were practiced very much under national auspices. Everywhere, too, they had a distinct militaristic flavor, allegedly serving to steel bodies and prepare spirits for the coming great struggles.[41]

Another type of organization was represented by the various army and navy leagues—although it is true that most never grew into mass movements. Even the largest, the German Wehrverein, only had about three hundred thousand members, less than one in fifty of the adult male population. On the other hand, a small, out-of-the-way provincial town such as Konstanz, on the shores of the lake of the same name, alone had a "Military Club," a "St. Barbara's Artillery Club," the "Badische Club of Guard-Grenadiers," the "Kaiser Friedrich III of Konstanz Club of One-Time Members of the 114 Regiment," a "Navy Club," and a "Cavalry Club."[42]

Officialdom was unsure whether to welcome the leagues' assistance in producing propaganda or to resent their tendency to criticize and meddle. Still, the fact that many of the more important of these organizations were headed by former generals—in Britain, the top of the pyramid was filled by a retired commander in chief, Lord Robertson— and included bureaucrats and other well-educated members of the middle classes gave them a public impact beyond their numbers. In Germany, for example, no fewer than 87 percent of the clubs were led by former officers.

One concrete thing these organizations did was to raise money. In Germany, France, and Italy in particular, fund-raising drives intended to help pay for experiments in military aviation brought in millions.[43] They also published literature, held meetings, celebrated past victories, mourned fallen heroes, engaged in field exercises, kept lists of personnel (such as physicians) who were prepared to assist the military in case of need, and published literature. Above all, they used suitable occasions in order to come out and parade in the streets. As a child in the Netherlands, one of the first songs I learned celebrated the *schutters*, or sharpshooters, of my native Rotterdam. They also, when necessary, applied political pressure, all in the name of nostalgia, patriotism, and a certain childish fascination with things martial.

During the last years before 1914, as the Jewish Austrian author

Stefan Zweig was to write ruefully before he committed suicide in 1941,[44] European cities (and their American counterparts) were visibly becoming richer. Year by year, new avenues, boulevards, squares, and streets were laid out. New sanitary systems were built, and tram and rail systems taken into service. In most countries, even the living standards of the working classes, instead of falling as nineteenth-century Marxists had predicted, began to rise. In France, for instance, real wages almost doubled between 1900 and 1914; as more and more workers came to feel like respectable petite bourgeoisie, both there and in Germany, the outcome was to split the socialist movements.

As always, much of the prosperity was linked to peace. Peace and technological progress allowed international travel, tourism, and trade to flourish as never before—not until the late 1960s, it is said, did trade again reach the relative levels it had attained in the first decade of the twentieth century. A popular nation, most prominently championed by the English writer Norman Angell, was that prosperity and the desire to ensure its continuation would banish war forever.[45]

Unfortunately, under this glittering façade dark currents were running. Having visited Europe in the spring of 1914, Colonel House, President Woodrow Wilson's adviser, wrote back that militarism was running mad and that people could not wait to cut one another's throats. Famous writers including Friedrich Nietzsche, Georges Sorel, Charles Péguy, and Gabriele d'Annunzio found peace boring. They called for bloodshed—even elementary, nonpolitical bloodshed—as the only way to cleanse a world that, the way they saw it, was about to drown in a wave of materialism and its boon companion, feminism. Each of them found some followers among the working classes. Still, most of their readers belonged to precisely that bourgeoisie that had profited most from the long years of peace.

When war finally did come, armies mobilized much more smoothly than anybody had expected. In England and Germany—the former because it only had a small professional force, and the latter because it had not drafted or trained more than part of the available manpower—they were joined by hundreds of thousands of volunteers.[46] One of the volunteers was a twenty-five-year-old would-be "architectural painter" called Adolf Hitler. In his own words, when war came he fell on his knees and thanked heaven for allowing him to live at such a wonderful time.[47] He would not be disappointed.

1.4. The Balance of Power

Of the eight world powers in 1914, the linchpin of unrestrained militarism was Germany. The reason was not so much the national character as the country's exceptional dynamism and the central geographic position it occupied; no other power combined those qualities to the same extent. A latecomer among nations, united Germany had been created by the sword in three short, limited, and decisive wars, and this was a fact that nobody either in- or outside its borders was ever allowed to forget. Had not the coronation of Wilhelm I in Versailles been a military ceremony in which Bismarck (who put on uniform for the occasion) was the only civilian present? Once it had been created, the Reich's economic development was second only to that of the United States. By 1914, it was producing more steel, the most important raw material on which military power depended, than France and Britain combined.[48]

Just as tectonic movements result in earthquakes, so Germany's growing power vis-à-vis its neighbors was ominous in itself. Bismarck himself looked at Germany as a status quo nation whose aspirations had been achieved—indeed, his chief concern was to keep the Junkers, the class from which he himself came, in power. By manipulating the other powers and refraining from attempts at overseas expansion, he managed to keep the pieces in place; however, his successors proved much less adept at playing the game.

During the last years before 1914, Germany's rulers were forever moving between saber rattling, as when the kaiser, wearing "shining armor," promised to support Austria-Hungary in regard to the latter's annexation of Bosnia-Herzegovina in 1908–9, and fear of what might happen if the powers that surrounded their country would unite against it. An antiquated political system that did not reflect the new social realities born out of economic development—in particular, the growing importance of the working classes—offered little help. Some thought that the need to escape this contradiction was the real engine behind Germany's aspirations to expand its borders, acquire colonies, and increase its power generally.[49] Others, such as the British economist John A. Hobson and an obscure Russian agitator by the name of Vladimir I. Lenin, expanded the explanation to account for not only

Germany's actions but also those of all the "capitalist" powers and, in fact, the existence of war as such.

Germany's hereditary enemy, its *Erbfeind* as the Germans themselves used to say, was France. The struggle between the ruling houses of Habsburg and Valois (later, Bourbon) for supremacy in Europe had its origins in the sixteenth century—although some would trace it all the way back to the battle of Bouvines in 1214. Though the chief protagonist on the German side now carried the name Hohenzollern and was based in Berlin rather than Vienna, the last major war that had taken place in Europe, namely that of 1870–71, was waged over just that issue. The war left *la grande nation,* as France had been known from the late seventeenth century on, truncated, humiliated, and longing for *la revanche;* "never speak of it, always think of it," as Prime Minister Leon Gambetta (1881–82) put it. In French history textbooks, the Prussian eagle was presented as swooping on the Gallic cock and tearing off his feathers.

Until the second half of the nineteenth century, France had been the most populous country west of the Vistula River, easily eclipsing both the German principalities and Britain. Since then, however, it had fallen behind in terms of both demographic and economic resources. Despite their reputation for quick-wittedness, the bulk of the French people proved remarkably conservative. They were reluctant to move from the countryside to the towns; even when they did do so, they showed a strong preference for small family firms and workshops over large-scale corporations. France's relative decline meant that the only way it could maintain its position as a great power was by looking for allies. Albeit that its regime was notoriously despotic and reactionary, geography dictated that the most likely ally would be Russia, and in 1894 the two countries did, in fact, conclude a formal treaty.

Russia's own power had grown significantly only from about the eighteenth century, during which it had swallowed most of Poland and gained outlets to the sea in both the north and south, feats that turned it from a remote, almost unknown country into an important player in European politics. As a result, it was able to assume a major role in the post-Napoleonic settlement. In 1815, Tsar Alexander I actually rode into Paris, and for more than thirty years thereafter he and his successor, Nicolas I, acted as the real guarantors of the existing European order. Nevertheless, in terms of internal development, Russia was the most backward of all the Great Powers by far, the majority of its population consisting of illiterate peasants, a legacy of serfdom that was not completely abolished until 1861.

This reluctance to modernize goes some way to explain the setbacks Russia suffered in its war against Japan, and during the earlier Crimean War—when its troops, marching on foot across the country, died in their thousands before ever reaching the theater of operations. Still, Russia was by far the largest and most populous among the European powers, and it clearly had the potential to dwarf everybody else. From the 1890s, the time when it began to industrialize very rapidly, it appeared bent on doing exactly that. During most of the nineteenth century, first Russian–Prussian and then Russian–German relations had been amicable; as also manifested by the fact that, in the period from 1909 to 1914, German-made goods formed no less than 42 percent of Russian imports. After about 1880, however, the rise of Southern Slav nationalism in Austria-Hungary, which was supported by Russia, forced Germany to choose another ally. In opting for their Austrian cousins, they drove the Russians into France's arms.

For over three centuries after 1500, the Empire of the Habsburg family with its capital in Vienna, had occupied center stage in European politics. By the second half of the nineteenth century, however, the dynastic principle on which it had been built was clearly out of date. Its decay became almost visible; some thought the only factor that still held it together was the highly efficient, German-dominated officer corps. Economically speaking, as we saw, it was near the bottom of the list, and indeed some of its provinces resembled what we today call developing countries more than they did the thriving, highly industrialized lands farther west. Another source of weakness was the fact that its access to the sea was limited to a piece of the Adriatic coast that could be blocked at the Straits of Otranto. As a result, the empire neither had overseas possessions nor any aspirations to acquire them.

Since 1813–15, when it had played a key role in defeating Napoléon and restoring the Old Order in Europe, the empire had gone from one defeat to another. In the face of the Hungarian rebellion of 1848–49, it had to be saved from collapse by Russian military intervention. In 1859, it lost a major war against France. In 1866, it took another beating at the hands of Prussia and also lost additional provinces to Italy; by that time, so accustomed to defeat had Emperor Franz Josef become that he allegedly selected his commander in chief, Field Marshal Ludwig von Benedek, for no better reason than that he could be trusted to keep the empire from collapsing altogether.

At the beginning of the twentieth century, the Habsburg Empire, though still ruled by one of the most efficient administrative systems in the world, was being torn apart by the aspirations of Polish, Czech, Slovak, Ruthenian, Romanian, Italian, and, most dangerous of all, Serb nationalists. Despite a lingering resentment that had its origins in the war of 1866, the alliance with Germany was in some respects natural and appeared to give the empire a new lease on life. At the same time it meant that, should the Southern Yugoslav nationalists continue to stir up trouble, the greatest military power in Europe would be involved.

Situated on the periphery of the system were Britain and Italy. Having been the first to industrialize, and having played a key role in Napoléon's defeat, until 1870 Britain was arguably the greatest power in the world, with an economy that dwarfed everybody else. As others—Germany and the United States in particular—began catching up, its relative position declined even though, on a per capita basis, it remained the most industrialized country by far. During the 1890s, Britain, after a series of diplomatic failures, found itself in a state of isolation that, in a typical show of arrogance, it called splendid. Nonetheless, the first decade of the twentieth century saw Britain busily mending its fences with France (over colonies), Japan (with which it concluded an alliance), Russia (which had long been considered a threat to India), and the US.

At the same time, relations between Britain and Germany, which appeared bent on dominating Europe and whose colonial ambitions were considered dangerous, worsened; in particular, the German decision to build a navy contributed to this result. Britain was in a unique position in that it controlled most of the world's strategic waterways, including Gibraltar, the Suez Canal, Aden, the Singapore Strait, the Cape of Good Hope, and, through its presence on the Falkland Islands, the Straits of Magellan. Above all, it controlled both the English Channel and the gap between Scotland and Norway. It was therefore able to cut off its enemies' trade while preserving its own.

By the dawn of the twentieth century, the smallest of the European powers was less than half a century old. Italy had been created with

French and some British aid out of a rib of the Habsburg Empire. Later, claiming that France had unfairly stolen Tunisia from it, it arrayed itself on the side of Germany and that of Austria-Hungary. When the war broke out in 1914, it nevertheless remained neutral; as the kaiser put it, Italy dropped away "like a rotting pear." Next, encouraged by British money and promises of territorial gains at the expense of the Austrian-Hungarians and the Turks, it chose sides once more, one of the most vociferous proponents of the change being a young, rather uncouth agitator by the name of Benito Mussolini.

In 1911, Italy went to war against the Ottoman Empire and succeeded in occupying Libya and the Dodecanese. These events, however, added little to the country's power and even less to its prestige, and the net result was to detract from Italy's strength, not add to it. Italy was a fairly small, fairly poor country that did not have what it took to be a Great Power in terms of either population, mineral resources, or industry. What military might it was able to develop was bottled up in the Mediterranean, which its ships could leave and enter only with British permission. The most it could do was subvert world politics to its own purposes and join one side or another in the hope of acting as the balance.

The six European powers interacted very closely, watching for the slightest change in the balance of power and reacting accordingly. This was much less true of the two extra-European powers, the United States and Japan, which formed worlds unto themselves. With the largest economy by far, the US had started building a navy second to none. The Spanish-American War of 1898 provided remarkable proof of its ability to wage war simultaneously in places as far apart as Cuba and the Philippines. The flexibility the American navy enjoyed in being able to move quickly from the Atlantic to the Pacific and vice versa, through the Panama Canal, in operation just before the outbreak of World War I, only added to its power. On the other hand its army, adapted to long years of fighting Native Americans, was so small as to nearly preclude it as a threat to any of the other world powers. And though American relations with most other powers were reasonable, a tradition dating back to George Washington precluded the United States from forming "entangling" alliances peacetime. Mutatis mutandis, the powers that faced one another in Europe felt they could deal with one another and fight one another almost regardless of what the US might say or do.

Finally, Japan was a true upstart. Long isolated from the rest of the world, it was only in 1858 that it was opened to trade, and only in 1867–68 that it adopted its first modern, nonfeudal political system. From that point on, Japan proved remarkably adept at quickly building its economy and modernizing its armed forces. Its successful war against China in 1895 brought it the respect of the world and convinced at least one other power, Britain, that a Japanese alliance was worth having. To underscore the gains in world prestige that Japan achieved, this was the first time Britain had entrusted, at least partly, the defense of its far-flung empire to the goodwill of a foreign government. Fighting Russia in 1904–5, Japan benefited greatly from its alliance with Britain, given that the latter closed the Suez Canal to the Russian Baltic fleet and forced it to sail all the way around Africa to the Far East, where it was sunk.

Among the world powers, it would be dangerous for a modern observer to conclude that international relations were any more Hobbesian than they have since become or that individual decision makers were particularly more aggressive. If anything, the opposite was the case. This was, after all, a time when Europeans were proud of their civilization, a pride that also proved useful in justifying their dominance over the rest of the world. Following centuries of intermarriage among all the leading families, many rulers were related to one another, forming a sort of international class, its members circulating freely throughout the Continent.

Crown Prince Edward VII of Britain spent much of his time in France, where he could entertain his numerous mistresses without drawing the attention of the public (and, before 1901, his mother). The July 1914 crisis found the Serb chief of staff, General Putnik, taking the waters in Bohemia—hardly something one would expect from a sworn enemy of the empire. The kaiser's brother, Prince Henry of Prussia, was on vacation in England and he himself was about to pay his annual visit to Norway. As late as July 1914, the kaiser was still corresponding with his imperial cousin, Tsar Nicholas of Russia, in what became known as the "Willie and Nicky" exchange. Both wrote in English, and both had often gone behind their ministers' backs to do so. A few years earlier in the same correspondence, "Willie" had complained about the intrigues allegedly woven against him by "my royal uncle" (Edward VII); it was as if government were still a family business.

To be sure, there was no shortage of fire-eaters. The ones perhaps best remembered by posterity were the Austrian-Hungarian chief of staff, Konrad von Hoetzendorf, and his German opposite number, Helmuth von Moltke Jr. The former's attitude, like that of his colleague Foreign Minister Leopold von Berchtold, must be judged against the clear understanding of both that the empire for which they were responsible was disintegrating and there was little they could do to halt the process. The latter lived in fear of what he saw as growing Russian military power and declared that, the sooner war came, the better for Germany. Still, such people were no more numerous than those with a deserved reputation for moderation.

One was Prime Minister Herbert Asquith of Britain, another Chancellor Theobald Bethmann-Hollweg of Germany. Bethmann-Hollweg's refusal to consider a "peace without annexations" in 1915–16 gave him bad press among subsequent historians, but there was, however, another side to his character. In 1912, the year when Moltke made his declaration in front of the kaiser, Bethmann-Hollweg said he felt "sick of war, the clamor for war, and those eternal armaments." On pain of rushing toward a catastrophe, he thought, everybody had to calm down again.[50] The following year, when the twenty-fifth anniversary of Wilhelm's accession was celebrated, the chancellor made good on his word by naming his sovereign "the peace Emperor."

Much more ominously, in Britain, Germany, and the United States, the influence of Social Darwinism was at its peak. Some, including influential writers with a desire to shock might find peace boring and long for a nice fight in which they could play out their heroics, as d'Annunzio later did; some of them came closer to anarchism than to nationalism. However, there was also a long line of thinkers, going back at least as far as Hegel, who looked at war as the supreme test by which states and nations proved their right to exist. Whether many people actually read Hegel may be questioned but there is no doubt that he found numerous followers both in Germany and abroad.[51]

Indeed, war was considered a perfectly legitimate means of international politics. True, most countries no longer actively sought territorial expansion in Europe, and apparently even the Germans were prepared to accept existing borders, provided they could dominate the continent economically;[52] but still, when it came to colonial ambitions, the gloves routinely came off. And if and when shots were fired, there would be little doubt about the righteousness of one's country, since almost everywhere fervent nationalism was considered a virtue, not a sin. The self-styled peace-loving socialist countries had not yet been born, and the day when every country replaced its war ministry with a ministry of defense was still far off. Casting an interesting sidelight upon this entire matter, members of the Japanese government around the turn of the century studied what "civilized" behavior in international relations might mean. Somewhat to their disappointment, they reached the conclusion that, among "civilized" nations, almost the only factor that mattered was armed force and the readiness to use it.[53] Perhaps this had something to do with the fact that, only a few years later, Japan attacked Russia without a declaration of war. Rulers may not have necessarily been eager to slaughter one another, but once the war started they, for the most part, did so with a perfectly good conscience.

1.5. War Plans

Compared with anything history had ever seen, preparations for war were now made on a gigantic scale. The previous war in Europe saw the combined populations of Prussia and France at around seventy million strong, and the armed forces they fielded consisted of some sixty divisions. By the twentieth century, the combined populations of Britain, France, and Russia had reached 280 million people, with combined armed forces amounting to 250 divisions. In comparison, the combined population of Germany and Austria-Hungary was 160 million, out of which they were initially able to form 140 divisions.[54] Italy accounted for another 35 million people and 30 divisions.

The United States with 98 million people should easily have been able to create as many as 70 to 80 divisions, but in fact it never got anywhere near that number before hostilities ended. And of course these figures do not include the contributions of the smaller belligerents such as Bulgaria, Romania, Serbia, Montenegro, Belgium, the Ottoman Empire, and Japan. Not for nothing did contemporaries speak of this as "the Great War."

While the various general staffs prepared their plans, the plans that have received far and away the most attention from historians were Germany's. Though not the largest—that status was reserved for the Russians—the German army was supposed to be the strongest in the world, and all others measured themselves against it. Germany, though, suffered from one critical strategic weakness: It was located between France and Russia. Thus, for the twenty years before 1914, all of its military planning was predicated on that fact. No great strategic genius was required to see that, to survive, Germany had to attack and defeat first one opponent, then the other. Deciding which opponent should be attacked first depended on many factors and was more difficult.

It was only in 1913 that Moltke finally gave that honor to France. The reason was that its smaller size, superior administrative organization, and efficient railway system endowed France with the capability of mobilizing faster, and it was hence considered more dangerous. And since it was well known that the French high command intended to concentrate its forces on the eastern border—the historic route by which its troops had invaded Central Europe—the decision to attack from the north through Belgium followed almost of itself. At first the Germans, seeking additional railway lines to transport and supply their forces, had also wanted to use the southeastern tip of the Netherlands. Concluding that they would need that country to trade in the face of a British blockade, however, the Germans thought better of it. These momentous decisions having been made, the hardest part of all was to mesh the millions upon millions of administrative, logistical, and technical details so as to form them into a coherent whole. By 1914, that, too, had been achieved.

Acting on the belief that the war would be short, other countries also prepared offensive strategies. Germany's ally, Austria-Hungary, planned to open the war with an offensive against Serbia and at the same time attempt to hold off the Russian steamroller to the northeast and keep some forces in reserve against possible Italian and Romanian moves. The Austrians also gave some thought to the possibility of mounting a combined Austrian-German offensive against the Russian forces in what is now Poland, trapping them between the pincer jaws and destroying them. The scheme was ambitious and well conceived, but it would have to wait until the fall of France freed the German forces that, following Moltke's plan, were to be deployed in the west.

In fact, both Germany and Austria-Hungary counted on one another to keep the Russians in check.

France acted much as the German general staff had expected. France, too, was committed to an offensive, and in the years before 1904 its general staff considered the idea of invading Belgium and carrying out the German plan (known as the Schlieffen Plan) in reverse. However, having been told by the politicians that such a move might turn Britain from a potential ally into an enemy, they ended up rejecting it. As a war with Italy began to look less and less likely from 1904 on, French commanders focused their field of vision until they thought of little else than an attack in Alsace-Lorraine in order to take back the provinces from Germany. Putting the center of gravity of its forces in the east meant that France would not be able to resist an invasion of its northern provinces, thus playing straight into German hands.

Keenly aware of the fate that had befallen Napoléon and, before him, Charles XII, the Russian general staff in St. Petersburg were not eager to take the strongest army in the world head-on. Had it been up to them, they would have preferred to stay on the defensive and draw their enemies into the vast, underdeveloped interior; what else was Poland, an occupied buffer state, good for? Seen from a purely military point of view, such a strategy would have made excellent sense; on the other hand, it would have meant abandoning Russia's allies, Serbia and France, to the full weight of the Austrian-Hungarian and German onslaughts. Yielding to French diplomatic pressure, the Russians made preparations for going on the offensive both in Galicia and in East Prussia (both of them, lying in today's Poland), with the former taking priority.

Britain, once it decided to enter the war (which it did only at the very last moment), aimed at preventing the Germans from overrunning France and as much of Belgium as possible. However, there had been less to this seemingly nonaligned status than met the eye. For nine years before the outbreak of war, while Whitehall closed its eyes, the military engaged in semi-official talks with the French general staff and admiralty, examining options, and allocating responsibilities, deciding that, in case of war against Germany, Britain would take responsibility for the North Sea and channel ports whereas France would concentrate its fleet in the Mediterranean where it could take care of Austria-Hungary and, if necessary, Italy. The director of military operations,

General Henry Wilson, even spent his vacations touring Belgium by bicycle so as to familiarize himself with the roads his troops might take. As a result, in August 1914 British plans for transporting the expeditionary force to the channel ports and shipping it to France, where it would form the left end of the line, were ready to the last detail.

Yet not every country prepared as thoroughly as this, and several saw their mobilization efforts attended by a lesser or greater degree of chaos. The Austrian-Hungarians in particular had a hard time of it because, making their dispositions, they had to take the ethnic sympathies of their various peoples into account—not to mention that mobilization orders had to be printed in no fewer than fifteen languages. So when the time came, Italian-speaking troops were transported across the country to face the Russians. Perhaps this explains why it took Austria the best part of two weeks to launch its offensive against Serbia, whose capital, Belgrade, was situated just across its southeastern border. As the war progressed, Austrian-Hungarian operations were characterized by confusion, and time after time its forces had to be rescued by the Germans.

Favored by newly constructed strategic railways, the Russian mobilization actually proceeded faster than most people expected. However, the country's industry and administrative bureaucracy proved insufficient; troops suffered from supply shortages that became steadily worse. As early as December 1914, food, clothing, and ammunition were all scarce.[55] Though the British tried to help, such was the authorities' incompetence that supplies, instead of reaching the front, piled up in the harbor at Murmansk. In dramatic contrast, the British were able to transport their expeditionary force to France with hardly a hitch. Such was the secrecy in which this was done that the Germans barely had an inkling of its presence before they clashed with it on the battlefield.

More important than these differences, each country had prepared its plans months, often years, in advance. The key to everything was in the railways which, as already noted, constituted a rather inflexible instrument. When hostilities broke out, the rulers of all countries tended to abdicate responsibility in favor of their senior military advisers.[56] For example, German chancellor Bethmann-Hollweg later wrote that, throughout his term of office, there had not been a single occasion when "politicians" such as he intervened in the "pros and cons" of the military situation;[57] nor would the Oberste Heeresleitung have permitted him to do so if he had tried. No ruler dared delay the moment when the button would be pressed and mobilization got under way. Nor did they dare to interfere with the mobilization plans themselves, given that any attempt to do so might reverberate throughout the gigantic, complex system and throw it out of gear.

Things came to a head in a famous encounter between Wilhelm II and his army chief of staff. An ill-written telegram from the German ambassador in Paris had made the emperor believe that France might not enter the war after all, whereupon he suggested that Germany's entire weight be turned around and thrown against Russia alone. The very idea of making the change brought Moltke to the verge of a nervous breakdown; his trust in his imperial master, he later wrote, was never restored.[58] In the event, the misunderstanding was soon put out of the way as France clarified its position. Yet, looking back, there is no question that, in insisting on greater flexibility, Wilhelm was right and Moltke, wrong. A high command less committed to its strategic dogma could and should have prepared alternative plans.

1.6. Facts and Counterfacts

Of course, many of the facts commented upon in the above pages have only become clear in retrospect. Contemporaries could not be sure who would fight whom, with what, how, and to what effect, and their guesses were often wide of the mark. In 1898, it was still thought that the conflicts most likely to lead to war would be the ones between Britain and France (over colonies) and between Britain and Russia (over access to India). One year later, the otherwise prescient Ivan Bloch thought that, in case of war, Italy would fight with Germany and Austria-Hungary against France. Indeed, as late as July 1914 the Russian general staff considered it "inevitable" that Italy would honor its commitment to the Triple Alliance,[59] and, by doing so, permit the Habsburg Empire to concentrate its forces in Galicia.

The unexpected Japanese victory over Russia that put an end to that country's threat to India made Emperor Wilhelm point to it as the "Yellow Peril." Yet with the exception of Austria-Hungary, no power was farther away from Japan, or less exposed to any "peril" it might constitute, than Germany—and in reality, nobody knew what role would be played either by Japan or, for that matter, the United States.

Just as the Germans had overestimated Russia's strength (especially its economic and social strength), once war had broken out, they underestimated the role that first Britain, and then the United States, would play. Indeed, Moltke's behavior in July 1914 suggests that Britain was of little concern to him.[60] At one point he even expressed the idea that, in return for Canada, the United States might be persuaded to join the war against Britain, but why Washington needed Berlin's permission if it wanted to overrun its northern neighbor he did not say. Whether Germany would in fact support Austria-Hungary against the Serbs (reading the Serb response to the ultimatum sent from Vienna, Kaiser Wilhelm thought there was no more reason for war) and what Russia would do also remained unclear.

Not everybody chose to ride roughshod over these uncertainties the way the German general staff, with its all-consuming passion for the fastest possible mobilization, did. For example, in favor of the much-maligned Russian general staff it must be said that they prepared two different war plans, one for fighting Austria-Hungary alone and the other for fighting Austria-Hungary and Germany together. The even more maligned Austria-Hungary prepared no fewer than four. When the moment of decision came, it could have implemented any one of them, albeit at the price of some friction that could cause the timetables to become stretched.

At the technical and operational levels, uncertainty was equally great. Given the amount of time that had passed since the last major war in Europe and the changes that had taken place since, nobody knew, or could know, which of the war plans really would succeed. Schlieffen at one point had written that military-technical progress had ended (*"Das denkbare ist erreicht"*: whatever is conceivable has been achieved).[61] That, however, was the belief of an old man. The reality was very different. Everywhere new inventions, both military and nonmilitary, were sprouting like mushrooms out of the soil; perhaps at no other time did so many possibilities, some real, some merely apparent, present themselves.

Was it true, as some claimed, that modern military science (with aid of new communications technologies) reduced war to "cool mathematical calculations"?[62] Or was it true, as others feared, that armies had grown too large and too cumbersome to be commanded at all? How would the numerous technological innovations transforming naval warfare act and interact? Was a revolutionary invention that would make all existing weapons obsolete just around the corner? After all, as early as 1914 a British writer, H. G. Wells (who had received a solid scientific education before turning his talents to fiction), was able to predict the introduction and use of nuclear weapons. All this made it really difficult to decide which of the daring new ideas and technologies would be truly realizable and worth investing in.

Recalling the events of 1801, when the British had annihilated the Danish fleet for fear it would fall into Napoléon's hands, the Germans thought that their fleet might be "Copenhagened"—a fear that, since it had been informally considered by Admiral Fisher,[63] was not without a certain foundation in reality. Across the channel, their worries were reciprocated by quite a number of writers, including some intelligence officers, who spun tales about the coming German invasion(s) of Britain. Some provided ingenious answers to the little problem of dealing with the British navy. Others simply ignored it; either way, they proved to be nonsensical. Yet at the time, they were considered threatening enough to make Edward VII worry lest his temperamental imperial cousin one day present himself with an army and, promising to do away with British socialism, take over.[64] When war finally did break out, road signs were removed all over the isles lest they help the kaiser's troops find their way.

In the end, perhaps the most interesting vision of the future was presented by that archetypical if fictional character, Josef Svejk. A resident of Prague, Svejk was a Czech—a member of an "oppressed minority" bent on asserting its national rights. Nevertheless, like millions of ordinary people of the day, he was a good Habsburg subject who avidly followed the news by reading the papers in the beer houses. By his lights, responsibility for the assassination of Archduke Franz Ferdinand rested on Turkey, and Austria-Hungary was certain to declare war against it. The Germans (whom he of course considered "low scum") would stand by Turkey and declare war on Austria-Hungary; France, Germany's enemy, would come to the aid of Austria-Hungary. The critical point to remember is not that all this turned out to be totally wrong, but rather that, when it did turn out to be totally wrong, instead of thinking twice Svejk cheered, waved his crutches (he had gout), and went to fight anyhow.

The pacifist German sculptress Kaethe Kollwitz took her soldier son to the railway station and gave him a copy of Goethe's *Faust* as a parting present; the young Austrian philosopher Ludwig Wittgenstein insisted on going to the front even though he could easily have obtained a discharge owing to a stomach complaint. Millions of others acted likewise.

World War I, 1914-18

2.1. Opening Moves

Considering the very great uncertainties described in the last chapter, the really surprising thing about the early weeks of the war is that things went more or less as planned, although this was by no means evident at the time. For example, as late as 1913 the decision to extend conscription from two years to three had led to riots in France. Hence it is scarcely surprising that the authorities feared a national failure to respond to the call for mobilization and, just to make sure, had even prepared lists of "anarchists" to arrest. But instead, the vast majority packed their meager belongings and tamely went to the mobilization centers and the railway stations, most encouraged by their womenfolk.

The German high command had worried lest the crucial bridges over the Rhine might be blown up by French saboteurs.[1] This did not happen, and the gigantic deployment proceeded like clockwork.

Once the railheads had been left behind, too, operations developed more or less as expected. Enormous columns of troops marched across frontiers hitherto considered sacrosanct, often cheering as they did so; simply to pass over a single point might take a field army a week or more. These columns advanced, wheeled, united or separated, as their commanders dictated. With a quarter million troops, more than had been concentrated on any European battlefield to date, the Austrian-Hungarians invaded Serbia from two separate directions. With about the same number, the Serbs, proving a tough nut to crack, resisted and within two months succeeded in repelling the invaders. The French commanders in Alsace, in Lorraine, and in the Ardennes obeyed their instincts and attacked. At one point, they succeeded in occupying

Mulhouse, but later they, too, were repulsed with vast losses. The British also did what they had expected to do, embarking their expeditionary force and sending it to the French channel ports. From there, they marched east practically unopposed until they finally met the Germans at Mons.

Meanwhile, in southern Poland, about a million Austrian-Hungarian troops clashed with a somewhat larger number of Russians. At first, fortune favored the Austrian-Hungarians in the northern part of the front, the Russians gaining in the south as battles named for such obscure Polish towns as Kasnik and Zamosc-Komarow came and went. The equilibrium did not last. By late September, the Russians had surrounded the great fortress city of Lemberg, occupied part of the Carpathian Mountains, and inflicted losses numbering in the hundreds of thousands. These were defeats from which the Austrian-Hungarians never completely recovered, and from this point on, whenever they wanted to achieve something notable either on the defense or on the offense, they first had to call on the Germans for aid.

With 6 million men under arms, the Russian army was the largest in Europe, and even as it fought the Austrian-Hungarians its commanders still felt strong enough to meet the request of their hard-pressed French allies and launch more than half a million troops into East Prussia. After achieving some initial successes, they found themselves opposed by German forces under the command of two soon-to-be-famous German generals, Paul von Hindenburg and Erich Ludendorff; the fact that, incredibly, the Russians sent their radio transmissions en clair did nothing to help. By the end of September, the invaders had been heavily defeated in the battles of Tannenberg and the Masurian Lakes. The threat to East Prussia having been removed, Hindenburg and Ludendorff were able to send their forces south so as to defeat a Russian attempt to exploit their victories over the Austrian-Hungarians and invade Silesia. The Russians were defeated at Lodz and forced to call off their invasion. In early December, the fronts were frozen.

As most people had expected, the most significant operations of all were those carried out by the Germans on the Western Front. The total number of front-line German troops in this theater was about a million and a half, divided among seven field armies (only one army, the Eighth, had been left to defend East Prussia). The greatest concentration of all consisted of about seven hundred thousand troops who formed the

First, Second, and Third armies on the right wing. Moltke's critics have often blamed him for not making his right wing stronger still by adding to it the new divisions that had become available in the last years before the war. Worse still, he took away two army corps in mid-campaign and sent them to East Prussia. And while it is true that Moltke's nerves were not among the strongest, his resignation on September 14 being accepted in favor of the minister of war, General Erich von Falkenhayn, these criticisms overlook two points.

First, by refraining from violating Dutch neutrality and allocating far fewer troops to the investment of Antwerp than Schlieffen had wanted to use, Moltke saved at least as many forces for carrying out the plan as he took away from it. Second, the Belgian network of roads and railroads was already congested. Had additional troops been fed into the country, then surely the only result would have been growing supply difficulties and monumental traffic jams.[2]

The Belgian fortifications at Liège were the strongest in the world, holding up the advance for a few days until the country was finally forced to capitulate when the Germans brought in the heaviest artillery used by any army in history. With its fall, a steady, if not quick, advance into the interior began, and for the first three weeks it went very well. Strangely, under the so-called Plan XVII, the French deployment was the mirror image of the German, with most of their troops concentrated on *their* right wing. This was put into operation even though the French high command was aware of the Germans' intention to go by way of Belgium. Facing such a juggernaut, the Belgian army was brushed aside, its remnants retreating into the fortress of Antwerp where they were joined by a British brigade hastily shipped over from England. The British, whom the German Second Army encountered at Mons on August 23, were also pushed back. These were not inconsiderable successes, yet some German officers were disturbed at the ease of it all. If the French were indeed being defeated, then there should have been masses of prisoners, guns, and other trophies; in fact, however, the number of those taken was very small.

Considering the distances the troops had to cover and the difficulties in supplying them as they did so, the original German plan for enveloping Paris from the west may have been megalomaniac—and all the more so because the main French railways, radiating from the city, ran across the German supply lines and thus could not be used to support such a movement even if they were captured intact. In any case the commander of the First Army on the right, General von Kluck, felt that he could not risk losing contact with the Second Army on his left, which, confronted by the British and some French units, moved forward more slowly than his own. On August 20, acting on his own initiative, he changed the direction of his advance from southwest to southeast, thus turning his right flank toward Paris and leaving a growing gap between himself and the channel farther to the west.

The German movement was discovered by a French aviator who reported on the gray columns "gliding" in the new direction—an early example of aerial reconnaissance at its best. The French chief of staff at this time was a wine-drinking, imperturbable general by the name of Joseph Joffre, and by an astonishing feat of staff work he and his subordinates were able to bring up troops from Lorraine, form them into a new army, and direct them at Kluck's rear. By an even more astonishing feat of staff work, Kluck was able to turn his columns around, make them cross their own communications, and counterattack on the Ourcq River. It was at this point that additional troops, always assuming that they had been available and that they could have been supplied, might have played a decisive role. In their absence, Kluck's maneuver, though brilliantly executed, caused the gap between him and Second Army to reopen. Into the gap moved the British expeditionary force, which had rallied after the setback it suffered at Mons.

As the Second Army began to retreat, a lieutenant colonel by the name of Hentsch arrived at Kluck's headquarters on September 9. Hentsch had been sent by Moltke, who, isolated in his Luxembourg headquarters, had little idea of what was going on and was desperately trying to find out. On his way, Hentsch had passed through the headquarters of the Second Army and learned that it was about to retreat. Together he and Kluck made the decision that the First Army should retreat as well.[3] With that, the French had won the so-called battle of the Marne, and the initial German plan had failed.

Had the war ended that fall, it would have met expectations, more or less. That it did not was due to several factors, and first and foremost was that the meaning of the term *battle* was changing.

As the combination, in many languages, of the terms *battle* and *field* shows, from Marathon in 490 BC to Gettysburg in AD 1863, commanders preparing for the former had sought to concentrate as many forces as possible at a single point. From Rafa in 217 BC to Sedan in AD 1870, the troops in question hardly ever numbered more than a quarter million or took up a front longer than ten miles. Thus even the largest armies formed mere specks in space. Once they had been defeated, often there was little to back them up. When Napoléon spoke of "battles that decide the fate of states, nations and crowns," he knew what he was talking about.

Over the next half century, things changed. On the one hand, the growing numbers of support troops meant that those on the front line comprised a diminishing fraction of all armies. Whereas, as late as the American Civil War, perhaps nine out of ten men had been combatants, in 1914 only five were. On the other, the advent of modern levels of firepower forced the troops who were deployed at the front to disperse until, on the average, each man occupied up to twenty times as much space as had his Napoleonic predecessor.[4] Meanwhile, armies had grown until they numbered not tens or hundreds of thousands but millions, far outpacing the capabilities of the railways on which those armies depended for transportation. With the transport problems and supply difficulties that such masses implied, the very possibility of concentrating one's "main" forces to give "battle" in a single "field" was lost. Conversely, even a dramatic victory on the front lines meant no more than that only a fraction of the total opposing army was defeated.

This fact was reflected in the number of casualties and the way they were distributed over time. Until the middle of the nineteenth century, a few hours of intensive slaughter on a field such as Wagram (1809), Leipzig (1813), or Solferino (1859) could sometimes account for as many as 20 to 30 percent of the total number of troops on either side. However, in the years from 1914 to 1918, the above factors meant that the "main" forces of either side were rarely if ever present to oppose each other. However powerful the weapons and however great their effect now was, the rate of casualties suffered even on the bloodiest occasions was lower by far—to the point that any day on which more than 1 or 2 percent of an army was lost was considered a disaster.

Acting as the grand introduction to twentieth-century warfare, the battle of the Marne reflected these realities. Nothing like it had ever been fought before, and the absolute number of casualties on both sides was staggering. The German figures have never been published and, by now, are probably lost. This, however, was a roughly symmetrical struggle in which neither side enjoyed any particular technological or tactical advantage. Relying on what intelligence they could obtain, both sides advanced and retreated and wheeled and turned and countermarched. Neither fought from fortified positions, and both were simultaneously on the offense and on the defense; hence it would be surprising if German losses were very different from those suffered by the French, which amounted to eighty thousand men.[5] Surely the deaths of 160,000 men is monstrous, yet compared with the 9 million men that Germany and France had under arms at this point it carried little weight. As Churchill was to write to his wife not long thereafter, entire "avalanches of men"[6] were preparing to take the place of the dead and the wounded.

Thereafter, almost without pause, the first battle of the Aisne, the battle of the Yser, and the first battle of Ypres came and went. So heavy were German losses at Ypres that the battle acquired the nickname *Kindermord,* the massacre of the innocent. Yet, in all the slaughter, a decision did not result. Having reached the channel at Ostend on October 15, the Germans kept almost the whole of Belgium except for a small corner in the southwest where the Belgian army, having broken out of Antwerp, succeeded in maintaining a toehold. The French in their turn retained control over their channel ports, without which continued British participation in the war would have had to be routed through Brittany and the Gulf of Biscay and made considerably more difficult than it was. More important from our point of view, the stalemate led to the opening of trench warfare.

2.2. From Movement to Attrition

Trenches have often been used in siege warfare, some of the most recent instances in early-twentieth-century memory being the siege of Richmond in 1864–65 and that of Plevna (Bulgaria) in 1878. More ominous was the role trenches had played at the battle of Mukden in 1905, where the Japanese only overcame them after suffering horrific casualties. Still, siege warfare was the last thing most commanders expected, so it is scarcely surprising that the first trenches were dug simply on the initiative of individual troops seeking to escape the hail of bullets and artillery shells directed at them. Soon the high command on both sides made the practice of digging official, creating order out of chaos by issuing instructions, supervising the works, and allocating so and so many yards of front to corps, divisions, and regiments. Back home, training soon came to include using the spade as well as the rifle. Within months, on both sides, vast networks of zigzagging trenches appeared, until it became theoretically possible for a soldier to walk from the channel coast all the way to the Swiss border without once having to show his head above ground.

Most trenches were up to ten feet wide and about eight feet deep. This enabled people to walk upright in them, but required steps so that they could fire and often ladders so they could sortie and attack. Almost from the beginning, they ran in zigzags, the idea being to provide better cover from shell fire and ensure that resistance could continue in case 'part of the system was invaded by enemy troops. Most trenches were open to the sky, but here and there parts of them were covered both against the weather and to provide shelter against weapons such as trench mortars and hand grenades. Some trenches had boardwalks for keeping out the mud, but the majority did not. Access was provided by communications trenches that, becoming shallower as they ran to the rear, zigzagged across the terrain in a similar way.

The first systems were simple and consisted only of a single line. As early as 1915, however, both sides began experimenting with fortified belts consisting of layers of parallel trenches. First came the forward line, shallow, thinly held, and serving mainly for observation. Next came the main fighting line, located, if possible, on the reverse slope of a ridge—in Flanders, anything more than a couple of yards high constituted a ridge—so as to be out of the enemy's sight and harder to target. Partly because they took better care of their men, partly because they spent most of the war on the defensive, the Germans invested more in their trenches than did the British and the French. Much of the credit on the German side was due to expert miners who directed the construction of deep dugouts (Stollen). Most Stollen housed a platoon or so, providing them with very good protection against anything but a direct hit by a heavy shell. All that was left above ground was a small number of lookouts. As soon as the barrage lifted, they would alert their comrades, who would seize their weapons and race outside as fast as they could.

Some systems also included a third defensive line, located out of range of all but the biggest guns and intended mainly to serve as shelter for troops as they assembled in preparation for the counterattack. By the middle of the war, most systems probably varied between four and six miles in depth. Also at this time, most systems were more or less continuous as far as the topography allowed. In 1917–18, however, the Germans started experimenting with individual strongholds. Each stronghold might be manned by a force of company strength. Each was independent of the rest, and each one was so designed as to be capable of defending itself not just to the front but in all directions, the rear included. The idea was that they should act as breakwaters, continuing to resist even after they had been surrounded or bypassed, causing the attack to disperse and peter out.

Whatever their precise form, all trench systems were completed by the laying of millions upon millions of mines—suitable for protecting a pre-selected battlefield—as well as miles upon miles of barbed wire to entangle attackers and expose them to defensive fire. At places, the wire could be dozens of yards thick. In others, it was left deliberately thin so as to entice attackers into killing grounds; the more numerous the directions from which the defenders could bring fire to bear, the greater the slaughter they could commit. Between major offenses, when the times were quiet, life in the trenches was uncomfortable and dangerous. Sniper fire, sudden artillery bombardments, attacks from the air, one's own raiding activities, and the raids launched by the enemy in response all resulted in a steady trickle of casualties. No major battle took place on the Western Front between December 1915 and June 1916, and yet six thousand British soldiers were killed. Between January and April 1916, during a period of relative calm, the Austrians lost fifteen thousand.[7]

According to a rule of the thumb used by the German army, at any given moment one out of twelve soldiers would be absent owing to sickness. Unhygienic conditions caused untreated wounds to fester and often caused intestinal problems. Cold and damp led to pulmonary diseases and trench foot. Conditions tended to be more tolerable in summer—but even then the trenches were hellish.

Fighting had always been the most stressful of all human activities by far, but hitherto combat had usually lasted hours or, at most, a few days. This was no longer true in 1914–18, when many battles, such as Verdun, the Somme, and Ypres, lasted for weeks, even months. Imagine a continuous concussion of exploding shells, the very air filled with screaming pieces of metal and noxious fumes from cordite or gas, the sound of screaming wounded, and the smell of dead comrades (a horrible mixture of rotting flesh and excrement) left where they fell, perhaps weeks before.

The outcome was the appearance, apparently for the first time in history, of masses of psychiatric casualties. In the German army alone, about one in twenty soldiers was affected.[8] These were men who, though their bodies appeared to be uninjured, displayed a variety of symptoms, from stammering to bed-wetting, trembling, and paralysis. Many of the symptoms resembled those that, before the war, had characterized females of the middle and upper classes (lower-class women were regarded as more or less immune).[9] Accordingly, those suffering were classified as suffering from either neurasthenia—weakness of the nerves—or hysteria; the latter, despite the fact that they had no uteruses.

On pain of disintegration, armies could not afford to treat their soldiers as leniently as hysterical women were. Some men, judged to be malingerers, were tried and punished. Most were summarily treated by being given a strong sedative that put them to sleep for a few days. After waking, they would be subjected to an additional few days of military-style exercises before being pronounced "cured" and returned to their units. Those, however, were the fortunate ones. Patients who still showed symptoms were taken to rear-area hospitals. There, hard-faced doctors subjected them to electrical shocks, some of which were so severe as to amount to real torture; either they "recovered" or they did not. For example, in Britain after the war, sixty-five thousand veterans drew pensions because psychological injuries made them unfit for work, and of them nine thousand had to be hospitalized.

While the junior officers, up to and including captains, lived and fought with their men under deplorable conditions, the same rarely applied to the remainder of the leadership. Senior commanders and their staffs usually took quarters in country houses situated up to thirty miles from the front. They lived in comfort, not seldom as their hosts' table guests; the fact that they brought their own food with them usually secured them a warm welcome. Except for the occasional air attack, they were almost entirely out of harm's way. On the other hand, the most senior commanders virtually carried their countries' weight on their shoulders, often for years on end. To avoid breaking under the strain, they were compelled to develop regular, punctilious habits that made them appear cold-blooded, aloof, and insensitive.[10] Hindenburg slept soundly before the battle of Tannenberg, after the battle of Tannenberg, and, wags claimed, *during* the battle of Tannenberg. If the commander's first task is to keep up his subordinates' confidence at all costs, then to that extent, even sleeping during a battle may have its uses.

Compared to the troops serving at the front, the situation of those positioned along the lines of communications was much more comfortable. Legally or otherwise, the rear-echelon troops had first access to whatever the homeland could send its heroes, at the same time often enjoying the amenities of towns and villages. Among them were bathhouses, movie houses, coffeehouses, and women who, especially in occupied territory, often sold themselves cheap. For every professional prostitute, there was the amateur in search of a little food, warmth, and, perhaps, human kindness as well; such encounters have been described in the memoirs of Ludwig Renn and Carl Zuckmayer, among others.[11] These marked differences in living-conditions, not surprisingly, tended to cause tensions between front and rear. For example, German troops spoke bitterly of *Frontschweine* (front-line swine) as opposed to *Etappenhengste* (rear-echelon studs).

At the time the war broke out, two-thirds of the ground forces consisted of infantrymen, and of those the overwhelming majority carried bolt-action, magazine-loading rifles. Four years later, the percentage of infantrymen had declined to slightly under half, and many of them no longer carried rifles but rather were assigned to machine-gun crews. These fearsome weapons, each of which developed firepower equivalent to that of a platoon and a half, were efficient defensive weapons but did have an offensive component. In attacks, they provided cover for advancing infantrymen by forcing the other side to keep their heads down, a tactic used by a young German company commander and future field marshal, Erwin Rommel, in his famous 1917 attack on the Italian Front. On defense, when fired from pre-prepared, carefully sited, and if possible enfilading positions, the results of their use could be horrific. When French troops were mown down in Lorraine early in the war, the Germans themselves were appalled by the results.

These early machine guns tended to be clumsy and on the heavy side, which was one reason why most armies, instead of distributing them among the infantry, had originally considered them artillery weapons. Most models were water-cooled and required crews of two or three men to carry the weapon, cooling equipment, and ammunition, as well as to aim, fire, and feed the ammunition belts. And even if they could be carried forward on the assault, these qualities made machine guns unsuitable for the next phase of an assault, the fighting in the trench. Here even rifles, measuring a little over four feet even without bayonets, were not ideally suited for fighting in the restricted space trenches provided. As a result, 1915–16 saw limited use of the first experimental submachine guns in the form of the German Bergman and the French Chauchat. Another weapon that made its appearance in these years was the mortar. Also sometimes known as Coehorns, after their inventor, mortars had a long history dating back to the seventeenth century when they were used against besieged cities; now that all warfare had turned into a gigantic siege, they again came into their own.

Mortars differed from ordinary artillery in that the trajectories on which they fired their bombs were much steeper than those permitted even by howitzers. Accordingly, they did not need a complicated recoil mechanism but were supported by a detachable base plate lying flat on the ground. The smallest models could be disassembled and carried by two or three men; others were put on wheels so that they could be pulled or pushed. Under the conditions of trench warfare, mortars gave the infantry just what it needed most: the ability to lob explosives from above. Their principal disadvantage was relative inaccuracy, but even that could be overcome by a well-practiced crew.

The greatest killer of the time was, of course, artillery. In the years before 1914, preparing to fight one another in the open, armies had acquired large numbers of field artillery pieces, the most famous of which was the French seventy-five-millimeter gun. Thanks to its recoil mechanism, which made it unnecessary to reaim after each round, the "75" and its counterparts in other armies could fire almost as fast as a rifle could. Thus, in 1870–71, over a period of five months each German gun had only fired two hundred rounds on the average; but now there were periods when more than that number was fired on a single day. So enamored of "madame soixante-quinze" were the French that they regarded it as a solution to almost any problem. They used it to equip some of their early tanks. They fired it over open sights so as to serve as an anti-tank weapon, and they even provided it with curious contraptions so as to make it point skyward and use it to shoot at aircraft. All this was well and good as long as operations proceeded in the open field. However, the 75 and its equivalents quickly turned out not to have the power for dealing with trenches, raising the cry for much heavier guns.

In 1914, having planned on breaking through heavily fortified perimeters, the side best provided with such guns was the Germans; they alone possessed easy-to-transport, quick-firing 105-, 150-, and 210-millimeter howitzers. Later, the others caught on. Concentrated in the hands of divisions, corps, and, in the case of some superheavy models, armies, the guns were normally positioned a mile and a half to two miles behind the front. Artillery used defensively would shoot up enemies as they tried to cross no-man's-land. Offensively, it was used to demolish the enemy trenches and then change to a creeping barrage behind which the infantry could shelter and advance; indeed, the longer the war, the more true it became, as the saying went, that "Artillery conquers, infantry occupies." The list of standard missions was completed by providing harassing fire, intended to make life on the other side more difficult, and counterbattery fire, employing any range advantage to take out the other side's guns.

Operating the guns required brains and brawn, with highly intelligent and mathematically knowledgeable officers directing parties of sweating, grunting, often half-naked men to haul the ammunition and swab the barrels. Yet survival rates among gunners were higher than among the infantry, with the result that many a junior artilleryman of the First World War made it to a high command position by World War II. Among them, to list but three examples, was the British chief of the imperial general staff, Field Marshal Alan Brooke; and, on the other side, the chief of the Wehrmacht high command, Field Marshal Wilhelm Keitel. Another was the chief of the army general staff, General Franz Halder, who, as a result of his specialty, was taunted by his Fuehrer for knowing nothing of front-line service.[12]

To augment the effect of artillery, beginning in the spring of 1915, both sides began experimenting with poison gas, though the Germans were the first to actually use it. At first gas was released from cylinders laboriously brought to the trenches, put into position, and opened when the wind was favorable, that is, blowing toward the enemy, a chancy operation even under the best of conditions. A better solution was to put the gas in heavy artillery shells capable of delivering it where commanders wanted it, at the time they wanted it, for the purpose they wanted it.[13]

The first gas attacks caused much excited denunciation in the press of the receiving side (who happened to be the British)[14] as well as a short-lived panic among the troops subjected to the attacks. Later, though neither side exactly liked the idea, both increasingly came to regard gas as a normal weapon of war. They prepared their troops accordingly, providing them with masks and filters, and set up decontamination facilities. All of this proved to be fairly effective. Considering the evil reputation gas later acquired, it is an interesting fact that, even after the more effective mustard gas and phosgene replaced hydrochloride, only 3 percent of all fatalities were caused by gas; yet the number of shells that were filled with it rose from just 1 percent in 1916 to as high as 30 percent in 1918.[15] This might explain why, in 1935, at least one participant in the Geneva Disarmament Conference (who had been gassed himself) considered gas a rather humanitarian weapon.[16] Thus the real logic behind the use of gas was that, being heavier than air, it would settle onto the lowest points on the battlefield, forcing the men on the receiving end to leave their trenches. Once they had done that, hitting them with conventional artillery became all the easier.

Apart perhaps from the early phases of major offensives, when the battlefield would be filled with line after line of men attempting to run forward, stumbling, falling down, seeking shelter, and rising again (if they had not been killed or incapacitated), it was curiously empty. Yet less than half a century had passed since, on fields such as Chancellorsville and Gravelotte, vast formations of colorfully dressed troops had gathered as if on parade. Whether these men were on foot or on horseback, whether they had advanced, retreated, wheeled, or maneuvered, weapons were displayed in full view, discharging white clouds of smoke and revealing positions as they did so.

As always, the key to everything was intelligence and in every army, the intelligence officer was among the most important of all. Both sides relied on prewar estimates and material, which they received by way of neutral countries, to answer basic questions concerning military geography, the enemy's demographic and economic reserves, production and transport capacities, and the like. Both used lighter-than-air devices and aircraft for taking a look behind the enemy front—indeed, many of the early air-to-air battles resulted precisely from attempts to gather intelligence or prevent it from being gathered. As the magnificent collections of surviving pictures in archives and military museums show, over the years probably every single inch of the principal fronts was photographed not once but many times. Toward the war's end, interpreting aerial photographs, which proved much harder than anybody had anticipated, was already turning into a specialized craft, as was the art of camouflaging targets to disguise them and blend them with their surroundings.

At the front, the principal methods for obtaining intelligence consisted of direct observation, raids, the interrogation of prisoners, listening in on the other side's telephone and telegraph lines (as well as radio transmissions), and, for technical purposes, the examination of captured equipment. Spies also played a role in the war; a Russian spy gave his handlers the plans of an Austrian fortress. But this was a conflict of vast scale, and when compared with the massive day-to-day collection and collation of information from many sources, not even the best-placed spies were in a position to know much; most of them were probably of minor importance. For every spy who provided sound information, there were several who, acting in good faith or bad, came up with the most fantastic ideas. For example, agents working for Russia in 1916 reported that the Germans had plans for attacking targets as far apart as Egypt and Finland.[17] The most famous spy by far was a Dutch-born, Indonesian-trained dancer and demimondaine named Mata Hari whom the French secret service caught and executed. In vain, as it turned out, for almost certainly she had never spied on anyone at all.[18]

Transmitting intelligence as well as other kinds of information also presented a problem. As long as the formations stayed in place, and as long as messengers were not prevented from moving by heavy shelling, communications could function tolerably well. However, any advance would at once cause the most important signals apparatus—wirebound telegraphs and telephones—to be left behind. Troops on the attack could, and often did, lay out wires behind themselves. However, the resulting communications tended to be makeshift, spotty, and unreliable; trying to solve the problem by burying the wires only resulted in making them less mobile still. Particularly difficult was the problem of coordinating artillery fire with the movements of infantry on the attack. Without good portable radios, there was only so much that forward observers, including those who operated from aircraft, could do.[19]

To this problem, two opposing solutions presented themselves. On one extreme, the British at the Somme in 1916 tried to solve the difficulty by holding both the infantry and the artillery to rigid timetables so that communication between them would not be needed at all—a system that often led to lost opportunities and unnecessary casualties as battlefield dynamics were ignored in favor of keeping to schedule. On the other hand, the Germans during their great 1918 offensives decentralized the command system while providing the infantry with special, lightweight artillery and machine guns so that it could be pushed far forward to deal with any opposition on the spot. Most armies positioned themselves somewhere in between these extremes, resorting to such things as signals from aircraft (klaxons, wing waving, dropped messages), boards laid by the infantry on the ground (to signal to the aircraft), or colored rockets fired into the air. Although none of these solutions was satisfactory, and indeed they often led to friendly casualties, judging by the 1991 Gulf War, such casualties are a problem that no technology, no matter how sophisticated, may be able to eliminate.

What was true of information was equally true of supplies. Taking the war of 1870–71 as its base, as late as 1896 a famous book claimed that, compared with the quantities of food and fodder needed, all other logistic requirements were "as nothing."[20] In fact this had been the received wisdom since the beginning of the world, and indeed, between 1914 and 1916 the estimated weight of supplies needed to keep a standard infantry division operational tripled from 50 to 150 tons a day.[21] Most of the increase consisted of ammunition for quick-firing weapons (both artillery and machine guns), spare parts, and the construction materials needed to keep the trenches in shape. As motor vehicles and aircraft multiplied toward the end of the war, fuel would be added as a necessity; by 1918, the German air service alone was consuming seven thousand tons of gasoline each month.

As long as the front remained stationary, the system of supply—though extremely demanding in terms of manpower—could work tolerably well. Indeed, at least one senior officer compared it to the functioning of a great city.[22] But as soon as the front shifted forward, very great difficulties appeared as the distance between it and the railheads increased. The fact that newly occupied ground would often be found to be churned up by bombardment (Flanders was a sea of mud) did nothing to help. The more successful an advance, the harder it was for the supply columns to catch up and keep up.

Having advanced, armies attempting to exploit a breakthrough would usually find that the retreating enemy had demolished the railway net, although as the American Civil War had shown, repairing track wasn't too difficult and by 1914 most armies had set up units of specialist troops for that purpose. However, opening blocked tunnels, restoring demolished bridges, and repairing collapsed viaducts was a different matter. Using such means, a well-conducted retreat was capable of reducing the pursuers to an ant-like crawl. Sooner or later the front, whether it had been torn open or merely bent back, would be reinforced and restored.

These factors gave the defense an advantage that was probably unequaled at any other time and place—to the point at which it led some to conclude that, in modern war, a good defense was the best form of attack.[23] Between late 1914 and early 1918, the only time the Western Front shifted more than ten miles in either direction was when the Germans carried out a voluntary withdrawal in the spring of 1917. Neither the great German offensive at Verdun, nor any of the numerous Allied "pushes," could do more; most of the time, they did considerably less. Even the large, well-planned, innovative German offensives in the spring of 1918 only forced the British and the French to retreat forty miles. Though the tactical problem of carrying out a breakthrough might be solved, that of turning a local victory into a strategic one remained as intractable as ever.

The situation on the Italian Front was similar. Italy having entered the war in May 1915, the fighting with Austria-Hungary lasted for three and a half years. In that entire period there were only two breakthroughs (one by the Austrian-Hungarians and Germans at Caporetto in 1917 that ended by petering out, one by the Italians at the very end at Vittorio Veneto) but no fewer than twelve offensives on the Isonzo; all of which ended in bloody failure. Likewise on the Gallipoli Peninsula, months of stalemate that were the product of the Turks' stubborn resistance finally forced the British and the French to reconsider and evacuate their forces. Indeed the Gallipoli campaign might almost serve as a model of the war as a whole. It was started in the hope of bringing a decision; over six months, all it produced was stalemate and corpses.

When it comes to the Eastern Front, Palestine, and Mesopotamia, these considerations require some modification. First because of the vast distances and considerably lower number of railway lines to square mile of land, the second and the third because they were, after all, mere sideshows, had this in common that troops and supplies were relatively thin on the ground. For example, in late 1916 a typical German division in the east was responsible for three times the length of front its opposite number in the west covered—something that was made possible, of course, only because the Russians were almost equally thinly stretched and less well equipped than either the British or the French. In proportion to the length of the front, the Austrians had six times as many infantrymen in the Tyrol as they did in Galicia. Whereas, in the east, both sides combined had sixteen thousand guns, in the west the figure was twenty-nine thousand.[24] Considering that the eastern front was twice as long, the real difference was four to one; which among other things explains why German veterans of the Western Front tended to look down on their "Eastern" comrades as if they had hardly fought at all.

Less firepower on the ground meant that, on both sides, breakthroughs were easier to carry out and more common than on the Western or Italian fronts. Thus, in 1915 the combined German and Austrian-Hungarian offensive at Gorlice-Tarnow pushed the Russians out of Poland; in the next year, another combined offensive succeeded in overrunning Romania. Long after they had disappeared from the Western Front, large formations of massed horsemen continued to played a role, as in the offensives mounted by the Russian general Brusilov in 1915 and 1916[25] as well as British General Allenby's advances to Beersheba, Jerusalem, Megiddo, and Damascus. Still, such was the discrepancy between the size of armies and the means at their disposal that, in the east as elsewhere, breakthroughs rarely led to decisive results before the front was restored. As attrition set in, factors other than operations on land began to play a decisive role.

2.3. The War at Sea

Had the war been as short as most people expected, then presumably it would have been fought almost exclusively on land. In the event the fact that it was prolonged meant that resources had to be sought from all over the world, which helped turn it into a vast naval struggle as well. Just as military strength on land was calculated in terms of army divisions, so strength at sea was calculated in terms of Dreadnoughts.

The original Dreadnought was a new and very powerful type of battleship with an armament consisting exclusively of heavy guns. It was first launched by Britain in 1906. All other powers were forced to follow suit, so that henceforward the largest fighting vessels were classified into pre-Dreadnoughts, Dreadnoughts, and Super-Dreadnoughts. The trouble with Dreadnoughts was that each belligerent possessed only a relative handful of them—a little under thirty in the case of Britain, far fewer in that of the other powers—so that the scarcity value of Dreadnoughts, plus their role as symbols of power, meant that the loss of any one of them was considered a minor national disaster.

In the last few years before the war, Britain, thanks to its alliance with Japan, was able to concentrate in European waters a force of Dreadnoughts about equal to that of the next two powers combined, basing them on the newly built port at Scapa Flow in the Orkney Islands. The basing of Royal Navy ships at Scapa Flow itself reflected an important change in strategy. Throughout the long period of Anglo-Dutch and Anglo-French wars between 1655 and 1815, British fleets had been based first on East Anglia and then on the channel ports from Dover to the west. This permitted Britain to exploit its dominant geographic position vis-à-vis its enemies, blockading them and interfering with their trade. The navies of the time depended on the wind for propulsion. Since it blew from west to east more often than the other way around, Britain was favored twice.

Traditionally, blockades were a matter of containing enemy ports, effectively shutting them down. However, such methods were rendered out of date by modern technology. The closer any capital ship ventured to the enemy coast, the more exposed it was to mines as well as to the action of smaller, swifter, more maneuverable, and, last but not least, more expendable destroyers, submarines, and even motorboats.

Carrying torpedoes as their main armament, light vessels—provided they took advantage of appropriate conditions such as darkness and mist—stood a reasonable chance of approaching their larger enemies by virtue of agility or stealth. The conclusion was that the days of such "close" blockades were past.

From Scapa Flow, the British navy blocked the German fleet from approaching the Straits of Dover, thus allowing the transport of troops to France to proceed in safety. At the same time, by closing the gap between Scotland and Norway, it would leave the German navy only the North Sea and the Baltic to operate in. Finally, Malta, which they had occupied in 1798, enabled the British to bottle up the Austrian-Hungarian surface fleet even more securely than they did the Germans.

As early as September 1914, the pattern was set. The British successfully imposed a blockade—which, since the German admiralty had been singularly incompetent, led to the immediate loss of many German merchant vessels caught outside the ring or else anchored in neutral ports. From that point on, the only German ships that succeeded in operating outside the North Sea were a handful of commerce-raiders, most of which were converted merchantmen, well armed, and like the Flying Dutchman, forever on the run.

Relying on stealth to both avoid the Royal Navy and approach their victims, they would drop their camouflage and hoist the flag at the last moment. In this and some other ways, they were the successors of the old-time pirates and buccaneers. As in the case of the pirates and the buccaneers, there grew around them an entire literature that celebrated their exploits and their chivalrous behavior. Chivalrous they had to be, given that practically every one of them could expect to be cornered sooner or later so that the fate of captain and crew depended on their previous record. Their exploits were often spectacular, and the search for them could tie down considerable resources. In 1914, the three-month search for one ship, the Emden, drew no fewer than eighty British vessels. Still, in relation to the war as a whole they amounted to mere pinpricks. From 1914 to 1918, all the German blockade-runners combined accounted for only 323,000 tons out of a total 15,000,000 tons of Allied shipping sunk.[26]

Unlike blockade-runners, submarines had the armament to take on not only merchantmen but also warships of all sizes. Thanks to their low profile when surfaced, they were hard to spot and could always dive in their approach or to make their getaway. Their great disadvantages were their slow submerged speed and the limited time they could spend underwater owing to their need to replenish their batteries, an issue even when they were operating at periscope depth. Finally, the range of World War I submarines was limited by their fuel-carrying capacity, which with few exceptions, caused their operations to be confined to the waters surrounding the British Isles and the Mediterranean Sea.

In 1914, the laws of maritime warfare, as codified most recently in 1899, permitted the sinking of enemy merchantmen only after provisions had been made for the safety of passengers and crew, and in the case of neutral ships, it was necessary to first stop and search the vessel for contraband. This system of board-and-search, though eminently suitable to the age of sail in which it originated, was not fit for submarines which, having surfaced, could be rammed, and the crews of which were too small to carry out searches on any but the smallest vessels. So severe were these problems that the Germans, calculating they could win the war by this weapon, decided to ignore the rules. No less than three times during the war, they declared unrestricted submarine warfare, meaning that any ship entering certain designated waters could be sunk without warning. Twice, surrendering to pressure, they changed their policy. The third time, failing to do so, they brought down American intervention on their heads.

Whereas overseas trade had played a role in the economies of all the belligerents, nowhere was this more important than in Britain. Without food for its population, raw materials for its factories, and, most recently, fuel oil for its warships, Britain would have had to surrender within a matter of months. In fact, it is arguable that only German shortsightedness saved it from this fate; had the imperial navy spent less money on battleships, it could have started the war with many more than the twenty-nine effective submarines it actually had. This tiny fleet, of which no more than seven or eight boats could be on station at any one time, was a ridiculously small force with which to confront an empire whose navy and merchant marine were the largest in history and whose trading interests spread from Canada to New Zealand.

From 1915 on, surface vessels began to be equipped with hydrophones for locating submarines and with depth charges for destroying them once they had been located. Both, however, were still fairly primitive devices that did not prove adequate for dealing with the menace. Apart from their own technical capabilities, which kept improving, the most important factors governing the submarines' success were their numbers and the policy decisions that dictated whether or not they would disregard international law. By February 1, 1917, the number of German submarines in service was around one hundred, although maintenance requirements and the distances at which they operated from base still meant only a third were on station at any one time. However, unlimited submarine warfare created a situation in which the rate at which vessels supplying Britain were sunk threatened to exceed the pace at which new ships could be built.[27]

Going back at least as far as the sixteenth-century Spanish "silver fleets," historical experience in protecting merchantmen was readily available and still applicable. The answer to submarines, as to earlier generations of surfacebound commerce raiders, was in the convoy. The convoy took advantage of two realities of submarine operations. First, the fact that submarines sat low in the water and were relatively slow when submerged, meant that armed prey had to venture pretty close to be spotted and then successfully intercepted. This forced the tactic of stationing submarines far apart from each other so as to increase the chances of encountering the enemy.[28] Second, the number of torpedoes each submarine could carry was strictly limited, hence after an attack, the vast majority of ships would always get through. And the larger the convoy, the more true this was.

Surprisingly, the admiralty resisted the tactic of the convoy. Its argument was based on the best-known naval theories of the day: namely, those propagated by Captain Alfred Mahan in his famous 1890 book, *The Influence of Sea Power upon History*. Convoying, the admirals argued, violated the principles of war, the most important of which were concentration of force and aggressive action. Instead, it would disperse the navy's smaller vessels over large parts of the sea, committing them to defensive operations, depriving the main battle force of its eyes and ears, and all but paralyzing it if and when the opportunity for a decisive fleet action occurred. Their arguments were rejected by the new prime minister, David Lloyd George.

Once the tactic was adopted, the results of convoying could not fail to impress. Whereas, in April 1917, almost 873,000 tons of shipping were sunk, in June sixty merchantmen crossed the Atlantic in convoy without a single loss. Subsequently, out of 1.1 million American troops sent across, only 637 were drowned.[29]

But how about the long-expected fleet action between the surface forces? In 1914, along with their concentration of ships on the North Sea, the Germans still had squadrons based in other parts of the world. Twice, at Coronel and at the Falkland Islands, these squadrons clashed with their British pursuers. The first of these engagements was a tactical victory for the Germans. In the second, however, they were faced by superior forces and defeated with the loss of four warships; with that, any possibility of major surface actions being fought outside the North Sea came to an end. Considering their numerical inferiority, the only way the Germans could risk such an action was by somehow tricking the British into fighting the entire high seas fleet with only part of their own. Doing so would be hard enough under any circumstances; unknown to the Germans, the fact that the British had come into possession of one of their codebooks and were reading their radio communications made it harder still.

In 1914 and 1915, there were several small engagements at places such as the Dogger Bank and Heligoland but none that was anywhere near decisive. Nor did German shelling of the coast of East Anglia amount to anything more than a slap.

When the great meeting of naval forces finally came about on the last day of May 1916, it was as if the battle of Jutland had been designed to illustrate all the factors shaping World War I–type naval warfare. Indeed for years afterward the British navy, in an attempt to justify the way the battle had been conducted, took extraordinary care to explain those factors. This is how the battle unfolded.

The Germans, commanded by Admiral Reinhard Scheer, were the first to leave port in the hope of catching part of the grand fleet with the whole of their own. The British, having received intelligence that the Germans had sailed, followed suit with their entire force. Partly as a precaution, partly because they hoped to draw their enemies and take them by surprise, both sides sailed with their lighter vessels leading the way and the heavier ships drawn up behind.

At 1600 hours on May 31, the British vanguard under Admiral David Beatty ran into a much stronger German force. In the subsequent exchange of fire, he lost several ships, then turned tail in the hope of leading the Germans into a trap. The ruse worked as expected; two hours later, with the battleships of the home fleet appearing over the horizon, it was the Germans' turn to be surprised. Several German ships were hit by heavy shells, but whereas British vessels tended to catch fire and explode, excellent armor and damage control saved the German ships from sinking. Next, a well-executed maneuver enabled the Germans to turn away and save themselves.

As dusk came, both sides found themselves groping about in the smoke and mist. Both possessed electrical searchlights developed a few years earlier; however, any ship that switched them on would automatically be a target. In the murk, a confused, more or less accidental series of maneuvers ensued, which finally created a situation whereby the British stood between the Germans and their bases. Considering himself out of danger as he ran for home, Scheer suddenly found himself in the worst conceivable situation, both greatly outgunned and outnumbered by the entire grand fleet—which literally covered the horizon—and with his escape blocked. His response was the only possible one: namely, to send his light vessels on a near-suicidal charge against the British battleships while most of his own heavy ships, by means of a second brilliant maneuver, were able to extricate themselves and disappear.

Critics have often blamed the British commander, Admiral John Jellicoe, for being too fearful of the German light vessels and torpedoes. It is certainly true that Jellicoe had a well-ordered, meticulous mind tending toward caution.[30] It is also true that the belligerent whose main naval forces he commanded had so much more to lose as to make almost any kind of risk taking foolhardy; besides, this was probably the first time in more than two centuries that the British navy faced an enemy whose ships and training were superior to its own. During the night of May 31–June 1, Jellicoe may indeed have missed a chance to destroy the German high sea fleet. On the other hand, since that fleet never ventured out of port again, the result actually achieved was almost equally good.

Considering the stalemate that had developed on land, Jutland was the one great battle that might have knocked a major belligerent out of the war in short order, and perhaps decided it in favor of Germany and its allies. Once it had ended as it did, the only thing that remained was attrition, as both sides were now given more time to mobilize their resources and throw them into action. In this way, a struggle that was already the largest ever waged was destined to become much larger still.

2.4. A Continent in Flames

At the outbreak of war, the daily production of French factories stood at 13,600 shells, which was just enough to allow each gun to fire four times a day. Within less than a month, Joffre was screaming for four times as many,[31] and a year later production had risen to a hundred thousand per day. Preparing to go on the offensive in Champagne in September 1915, the French were able to stockpile eight hundred thousand shells—at that time, about a week's production. That, however, was just the beginning. At the Somme in 1916, the British fired 1.2 million shells, a total weight of twenty-three thousand tons. But the peak was reached at Ypres in the fall of 1917, when the British fired 4.3 million shells with a total weight of over a hundred thousand tons. Taking over from the tsar at about the same time, the Bolsheviks inherited no fewer than eighteen million shells, and by the last year of the war the Germans alone were consuming as many as three hundred million rounds of small-arms ammunition per month. Yet ammunition was just the tip of the iceberg; even before the Americans came in, the total number of major-caliber guns deployed by both sides on the Western Front alone was over thirty thousand.[32] To focus on just one country, between 1914 and 1916, British annual production of cannon went from 91 to 4,314. That of tanks went from zero to 150, that of aircraft from 200 to 6,100, and that of machine guns from 300 to 33,500.

This, then, was a war not just between armies but also between factories. Nothing like it had been foreseen in the prewar plans, and indeed very often those plans ran at odds with what was actually to take place. For example, French military authorities, in calling up workers to serve, caused employment at Schneider-Creusot to drop by half; yet this was the firm that manufactured more artillery pieces and more shells than any other.[33] Their counterparts in other countries were no more prescient. Britain, the country of free trade par excellence, went to war with the idea that business could and should continue as usual, and throughout the war there was a tug-of-war between the army and industry as to who should obtain the available manpower. In Germany, the early months of the war led to the giant chemical firm Bayer losing almost half of its eight thousand employees, causing production to fall by a similar amount.[34] The tendency to look at war as an activity in itself, the almost complete separation between military and civilian education, and the expectation of a short conflict all contributed to this outcome.

As so often in this period, the model for what followed was provided by the railways. Not only were railways absolutely vital to the war effort, but they were also among the largest enterprises of all. In service since the middle of the nineteenth century, most railways had originally been privately owned, though in some countries they were later taken over by the state. Even in countries where they remained in private hands, special legislation empowered the authorities to take them over and run them for the benefit of the public—read: the military—in case of a national emergency. Now, though no state went so far as to nationalize its factories outright, the same system was extended to other parts of the economy.

Step-by-step, arms-manufacturing plants (to the extent that they were not already government-owned), the energy supply, and the raw materials that fed them were brought under government control. In this way, it was government officials rather than factory owners who decided how resources would be allocated, what would be produced, by whom, with what tools, under what conditions, and, very often, at what prices as well.

Those who worked the system at the top were often prime ministers such as David Lloyd George—who, not accidentally, had taken up his post after serving as minister for munitions. Under them, the controls were entrusted to existing or newly established ministries. Day-to-day regulation and supervision were normally exercised by businessmen who were the only people with the requisite hands-on experience to establish such giant systems and make them work.[35] Serving them, in turn, were vast, often newly raised armies of clerks with budgets to match. The obstacles to the establishment of governmental control were mainly political as neither manufacturers' associations, nor trade-union leaders, nor consumers necessarily liked the restrictions that were placed on their freedoms. Many of them engaged in active, if necessarily sporadic, resistance, quietly sabotaging the state's efforts by striking, and engaging in black-market activities.

Whereas manufacturers felt the effect of controls over production, ordinary people, to the extent that they had not been conscripted, experienced the heavy hand of government mainly through its mobilization of labor. Among the countless prewar predictions, one of the few that did come true was the expectation of increased unemployment as living standards and, with them, demand for nonessential items fell. As early as 1915, however, the situation reversed itself as the roaring armament factories, the mines that provided them with raw materials, and the transportation arteries that served them grew rapidly. Thus in Britain, France, and in Germany, the armed forces began exempting men so that they could return home, take up work, and produce what was needed. By the last months of the war, for example, the number of German men who enjoyed this privilege stood at two and a half million. Among them, just over half were classified as K.v. *(Kriegsverwendungsfaehig,* fit for field duty).[36]

Far removed from the trenches, and often earning very good wages, workers who gained exemptions had excellent reason to bless their luck. On the other hand, the very fact that they had been exempted meant they were placed under a certain kind of discipline; they could always be recalled to duty, either in a military emergency or because of insubordination. Other means by which governments tightened their grip on labor included increased working hours; abolishing restrictions on shift work, night work, and dangerous work; and attempts to restrict workers' freedom to move from one employer to the next. They also tampered with training standards so as to permit less skilled labor to be used, regulated the pay scales, and prohibited strikes. A tremendous propaganda effort did what it could to make workers redouble their efforts, though it was not always effective.

As dramatic as these changes were for labor on the whole, the effect the war had on the women's labor force was less severe than one would first guess. Taking Britain as our example, when everything is said and done women's contribution to the war effort remained limited. Total female employment went up by about 1.5 million, from 3,276,000 in July 1914 to 4,808,000 four years later. However, these figures probably overestimate the change that took place. They mask the fact that, before the war, many women working as household servants or else in small, unregistered sweatshops failed to be included in the statistics. Now, provided with the opportunity to earn more, they simply changed from one job to another.

Even at a time when more than four million British men were on active service and wore army or navy uniform, six out of ten people in the British workforce remained male. As the government recognized, the fields of economic activity absolutely essential for the country's survival were coal mining, merchant shipping, and food production. Of the three, the first two were among the most dangerous, so the near-complete absence of women from them is hardly surprising. As to the third, an attempt was made to meet labor shortages by setting up a Women's Land Army; however, it met with resistance and never got off the ground.[37]

Of the eight principal belligerents, only two, Britain and the United States, permitted women to join the military. This probably had something to do with the fact that these countries, before the war, held the military in the least esteem. From 1916, Britain allowed women to enter either the army or the navy. Later the United States made similar arrangements. To prevent what people today would call sexual harassment, then known as "corruption of morals," women were formed into their own separate corps and put to work in a very great variety of fields such as nursing, communications, administration, food preparation, as drivers, and so on.

The total number of women who wore uniforms was not large; they certainly did not comprise more than 1 or 2 percent of those who did.[38] What distinguished them was the fact that, coming from a middle-class background, they tended to be better educated than either the female population as a whole or their male comrades. This may help explain why they generally performed their functions quietly and efficiently. Besides, being both volunteers and women, in case they did commit an offense it was always easier to get rid of them than to discipline them. As the American Secretary of the Navy, Josephus Daniels, wrote when his subordinates wanted to punish a woman: "one cannot deal with women as with men."[39]

Whether or not one was in the workforce, the factor that brought the war home to practically every citizen of the belligerent countries was food rationing. There was, of course, nothing new about rationing cities under siege. Still, based on the administrative capabilities of the modern state, this was probably the first time in history when an attempt was made to apply it to entire countries. Whether because imports had been reduced (Britain), or because the supply of fertilizer was interrupted (Germany), or because so many men had been called up that farm work had to be done by women and youths (all countries), the war led to food shortages. The primary objective of rationing was to counter those shortages by preventing waste and making sure that the available stocks would be utilized as efficiently as possible. At last on paper, another one was to cope with rising prices. In all countries wartime expenditure, which was only partly covered by taxes and loans, led to inflation. In all countries, inflation could easily create a situation where available stocks would be bought up by the well-to-do, shortchanging the majority and leading to social unrest in the form of demonstrations, strikes, etc. Rationing was supposed to put everybody on an equal basis. In addition, it permitted the available stocks to be distributed in ways that adjusted consumption to the nutritional needs of various groups of people such as the very young, the old, workers engaged in hard labor, etc., as calculated by experts.

The system worked better in some countries than in others.[40] In all countries, there existed people—large property owners, war profiteers, and the women who, with or without marriage, depended on them—who could buy whatever was on offer at whatever prices and whom rationing left untouched. In all countries, the combination of rising prices with food-scarcity hit urban residents more than it did villagers. While the latter usually had enough to eat, the former did not. Often they had to trek to the countryside so as to sell their possessions and obtain food; in this way the modernizing process, which tends to concentrate wealth in cities, was to some extent reversed. Inflation also hit members of the middle classes harder than it did workers, some of whom actually found themselves entitled to buy and consume more and better food than they had been able to afford before the war. Furthermore, whereas middle-class incomes remained fixed, workers were often able to make more than before by leaving their jobs and moving into the armaments factories. As a result, in Britain at any rate living standards among the working classes probably rose rather than fell.[41]

Historians writing before 1990 or so have generally claimed that the German and Austrian-Hungarian mobilization-systems were less effective than those of Britain and France and tried to blame authoritarianism, conservatism, and militarism for that "fact." Since then, relying on an analysis of enemy troops killed per unit of currency spent, at least one well-known historian has claimed that they were more effective.[42] However, this overlooks the fact that, instead of having to rely on long lines of naval communication, the "Central" Powers were operating on internal lines. Be this as it may, the really decisive factor was that the Central Powers lost their overseas trade, largely because of the blockade, but also because, unlike Britain in particular, they did not have any considerable overseas assets that they could have used to pay for what they bought. Hence they were unable to substitute imports for domestic production; hence real shortages developed and some people starved.

Worst of all was the situation in Russia. Before the war, in spite of its generally very low living standards, Russia had been the largest European producer of food by far (in fact its output, 68,864 thousand metric tons, was triple that of the remaining countries combined). Though the war caused farms to be neglected and the production of wheat to fall by about 12 percent (1917 figure), the drop was partly balanced by curtailed exports due to the fact that trade routes through the Baltic and the Dardanelles were blocked.[43] What really did the Russians in were not any absolute shortages but a combination of very high inflation with the difficulty of imposing efficient administrative controls on a huge, underdeveloped country with a relatively meager railway system and a largely illiterate population. Inflation gave farmers every incentive to hide their production in the hope of obtaining higher prices later on. Inefficiency prevented the state from extracting those products against the farmers' will, a feat finally achieved only by the Bolsheviks who used ruthless methods that included starving millions to death. As Bloch had predicted twenty years before, the outcome was hunger, strikes, and revolution.

When it comes to Russia, few will doubt that hunger, strikes, and revolution played a key role in bringing about defeat—as is also reflected in the fact that, even before October 1917, the rouble had lost more of its value against the dollar than any other currency.[44] The evidence in regard to Germany and Austria-Hungary is less clear. That the civilian population of both countries suffered grievously there is no doubt and indeed by the last year of the war German official rations only allowed seven pounds of potatoes, 250 grams of meat, and less than 100 grams of fat a week. That these factors led to considerable dissatisfaction and social unrest during the last year of the war is likewise not in doubt, though it is arguable that France and Italy had encountered similar difficulties in 1917 and, in the end, succeeded in overcoming them. It is also certain, though, that the last weeks before the armistice saw these countries' armies, as well as their Ottoman and Bulgarian allies, being defeated in the field and pushed back. When Hindenburg, who in 1916 had been promoted army chief of staff, went to see the kaiser on the 2nd of October to demand that hostilities be ended, it was this fact he had in mind. Writing to his sovereign later on the same day Ludendorff, Hindenburg's second in command and arguably the most powerful man in Germany, took the same line. It was the inability of the army to sustain the fight that made further sacrifices on the part of the civilian population pointless, not the state of the civilian population that demanded that the army lay down its arms.[45]

In summary, the superiority of the defense over the offense generated attrition on practically every front where armies were sent in the hope of producing a decision. While attrition meant that naval operations played a greater role than expected, its most important effect was to give the belligerents what they needed to bring about a change in the nature of war: time.

Previously, war had consisted very largely of the employment of force against force—a fact reflected in the military literature of the time and which explains why military and civilian education had been kept almost completely separate. Now it turned into a vast exercise in coordinating all national resources—from factories to labor and from raw materials to machine tools—until, in theory and to some extent in practice as well, not a screw could be produced nor a calorie consumed without official permission.

Though the beginnings were often confused, all the expertise at the disposal of the modern state, all its administrative capabilities, all its means of communication and transportation, were thrown into the effort. With the notable exception of Russia, a semi-developed country that had only started flexing its industrial muscle some two and a half decades earlier, most of the belligerents probably mobilized their resources about as efficiently as they could. Putting aside the United States, which thanks to geography and the fact that it was only in the war for eighteen months had an exceptionally easy time, in the end it was the belligerents that both escaped blockades and devised efficient production, manpower-allocation, and rationing systems that won the day.

2.5. Technology Takes Over

The prolongation of hostilities that enabled the belligerents to mobilize their economic and social systems also gave them the opportunity to experiment with new weapons and weapons systems. Though military and technological innovation has a long history, before the nineteenth century true innovation was a relatively infrequent occurrence. It is certainly not easy to argue that the French, Prussian, Russian, Austrian, and British armies emerged from the Seven Years War (1756–63) considerably better armed than they were when they entered into that conflict. However, with the spread of the Industrial Revolution after 1815, new breakthroughs in technology, instead of appearing more or less accidentally and more or less at random, were now the products of systematic research and development.[46] Technological progress would accelerate to such a rate that weapons could be obsolete within a decade.

In August 1914, each of the principal belligerents possessed several hundred aircraft as well as a small but dynamic military-industrial establishment that produced them.[47] After hostilities opened, aircraft were at once pressed into undertaking reconnaissance missions, or they were planned to do so before the war. Almost immediately, pilots began carrying pistols or carbines, taking potshots at one another in the air. As was inevitable at this early stage, here and there oddities appeared. Some pilots were even issued with incendiary darts in the hope of setting alight the canvas of which aircraft fuselages and wings, as well as balloons, were made.

By 1915, the favored weapon for air-to-air fighting had become the machine gun. Firing machine guns forward, however, risked hitting the propeller—which, being made of wood, would disintegrate as a result of the stream of bullets—and forced designers to experiment with all kinds of improvisations. Some entrusted the weapon to a separate crew member who would fire to the side and rear; others mounted a gun on the top wing, where it fired by means of a rope tied to the trigger. By 1916 the problem was solved by adding a device that synchronized the gun or guns with the propeller, enabling the pilot to shoot straight forward and making it much easier to aim. Though the invention itself was Dutch, the first to use it was Germany. Since aircraft of both sides were constantly being forced down over enemy territory, it was only a matter of weeks before it was copied.

Air-to-air combat was an entirely novel field to be mastered by a process of trial and error. The objective was always to place one's own aircraft in a position where one would be able to shoot at the enemy without that enemy being able to shoot back. Most of the time this meant coming in from behind, either from above or from below, and in such a way as to have the sun shining in the enemy's eyes. To do this, pilots also had to master the opportunities that the weather provided, such as by darting out of clouds when the opportunity presented itself, or into them when danger threatened. By 1916, most of the necessary maneuvers had been mastered, as is evident from the fact that, to this day, several of them are named for World War I pilots.

Fought far from the madding crowd, man against man, at enormous risk (the first parachutes were only introduced late in the war), air-to-air combat was spectacular. Pilots tended to come from the well-to-do, and some, having shot down numerous opponents, were turned into popular heroes, being fêted by the authorities from the kaiser down and getting countless offers from women who wanted to sleep with them with or without marrying them first.

Less spectacular, but equally important, were airpower's other missions such as liaison, artillery observation, and strafing (flying low while firing their machine guns into enemy columns or trenches). The last was a particularly dangerous task; some aircraft were modified with light armor for protection.

Along with reconnaissance, the very first days of the war saw the first air bombardments, improvised affairs as pilots tried to hit targets by tossing grenades at them. Later, aircraft equipped with special apparatus for dropping bombs were developed, and clear differences began to appear between them and lighter, more agile types.

The first "strategic" bombardments—strategic in the sense that the attacks were directed at targets far to the rear, rather than at the front— were carried out by the Germans in 1915, using lighter-than-air airships. Still, given the primitive state of technology, when used as bombers, aircraft could not be said to have played a decisive role in the war. As auxiliaries, however, they were becoming indispensable, and this was reflected in the fact that, taking Britain, France, and Germany together, the total number of aircraft produced between 1914 and 1918 was about 150,000.

Whereas a few aircraft had taken part in war even before 1914, the tank was an altogether new invention. This armored box capable of moving about on the battlefield only first became practical in the early 1900s following the invention of the internal combustion engine on the one hand and of the caterpillar track on the other. The first experimental machines, designed to cross trenches while providing shelter to the soldiers who followed them, were built in Britain in 1915. Following somewhat different ideas as to what they should look like, the French began to build them at about the same time. Compared with the machines that were to follow during the interwar years, early tanks were large and heavily armed, with some carrying two six-pounder cannon, one on each side. They were, however, intended for action against enemy infantry rather than other tanks.

Tanks received their baptism of fire at the Somme in 1916. Underdeveloped, and suffering from teething problems, there were also too few of them to make a difference. They *did* make a difference at Cambrai in November 1917, when five hundred of the monsters, preceded by a short but intensive bombardment from a thousand guns, helped tear open a section of the German Front.[48] As was almost always the case, the Germans were able to contain the breach by bringing up fresh troops and launching a counterattack. Still, from this point on the importance of the tank grew until it became a first-line weapon in every major French and British offensive launched in the remainder of the war. The Germans, partly because they failed to grasp the importance of tanks, partly because Ludendorff did not think them worth the resources,[49] built very few of them. Those they did build tended to be overmanned (with crews of up to eighteen soldiers), unstable, vulnerable, and ineffective, to the point that they preferred using captured Allied tanks to their own.[50]

The first tanks to appear on the battlefield caused a panic among the defenders, yet countermeasures, in the form of ditches wide and deep enough to stop the machines, appeared almost immediately (and were in turn countered by tanks carrying fascines). So did special rifles provided with ammunition able to penetrate their armor and artillery firing over open sights.[51] Other factors that prevented the first tanks from turning into really decisive weapons were their short range, low speed, mechanical unreliability, and extreme discomfort. Besides suffering from noise and being bumped about in their unsprung vehicles, crews were always in danger of being asphyxiated by the exhaust gases from the tank's engine. To these problems were added difficulties in command and control of the vehicles. A small, spark-operated radio set was available, but this only worked as long as the tanks were stationary with their engines shut down, and then only to a range of two hundred yards. Painted metal disks waved through portholes were even less reliable. As legend has it, crewmen as well as troops accompanying the tanks were sometimes provided with hammers, to the former to knock one another on the helmet and to the latter in order to do the same on the vehicles' sides.

At the time the war ended, attempts to combine aircraft with tanks in joint operations capable of doing more than breaking through a line of trenches were still in their infancy. In his plans for 1919, Foch, the supreme Allied commander on the Western Front, looked forward to employing no fewer than ten thousand tanks, but whether his thought reached far beyond the front line is not clear.[52] Way below him in the chain of command, the chief of staff of the British Royal Tank Corps, Lieutenant Colonel J. F. C. Fuller, was developing some radical ideas on that subject.[53] He called for a combination of heavy and medium tanks to be used not only for forcing a breakthrough but also for striking at command and communications targets in the rear, all to be followed by a pursuit "of at least 20 miles per day for a period of five to seven days."

Whether the technical means of the time were really up to such an ambitious scheme is not clear. In spite of the fame it later acquired, Fuller's "Plan 1919," was more of a general declaration of principles than a detailed attempt to explain who should do what, how, in what order, and to whom at a specific time and place. In the event, the transformation of siege engines into armored cavalry, their organization into divisions, and their coordination with airpower so as to make them capable of deep operations had to wait until the 1930s. When these changes finally came, it was the Germans and not the British who were in the lead.

In all of this, perhaps the most impressive thing was how fast armored technology developed. In the three years after they first appeared, British tanks went through eight model changes, some of which came in several variations. They were already starting to fall into two basic types, heavies for breaking through trench systems and medium tanks for exploitation and pursuit. The experimental "Tritton" of 1915 had an engine developing 105 horsepower and was capable of a speed of 3.7 miles an hour. Three years later, the Mark D had an engine three times as powerful and a speed of twenty miles an hour. Even the so-called funnies, special machines developed in World War II for a variety of purposes, already had their counterparts in 1917–18. Some tanks came with hooks for tearing up wire, whereas others dragged sledges loaded with supplies.

The evolution of aircraft was faster still. In 1914, a French observation aircraft such as the Blériot XI weighed less than a ton. It was powered by an engine that developed 70 horsepower, had a ceiling of 3,300 feet, and flew at a maximum speed of 66 miles per hour.[54] Three years later, a Nieuport 28 fighter weighed slightly less but came with 160 horsepower, a ceiling of 17,000 feet, and a maximum speed of 122 miles per hour. The very first specialized bombers were built in France in 1915; taking as our example the Voisin 5, it weighed just over a ton, had a single engine developing 150 horsepower, and was capable of carrying 130 pounds of bombs to a distance of about 100 miles before dropping them and returning to base. Four years later, the Italian Caproni Ca.46 weighed over five tons, was propelled by four engines developing 300 horsepower each, and was capable of carrying almost a ton of bombs to a distance of almost 200 miles. By that time aircraft had reached the point where, in terms of both speed and load-carrying ability, they were superior to lighter-than-air machines. After a few years, almost the only remaining use of lighter than air devices was to hoist aloft cables for anti-aircraft work.

As always during periods of rapid innovation, designers, pressed to produce results quickly, sometimes cut corners. On other occasions, they failed to test their products properly. For example, the first British tanks were equipped with glass-covered vision slits that splintered into crewmen's eyes when they were hit. And far more projects were conceived on the drawing boards than ever left the factories. Among those that did leave the factories and reached the battlefield, quite a few proved to be stillbirths and had to be scrapped. Thus, the British toward the end of the war built a giant six-engined bomber, the Tarrant Tabor, which was so badly designed that it crashed during its first test flight. The Germans built two monster tanks weighing 160 tons each, a performance they were to repeat during World War II. The Americans, unhappy with the available internal combustion engines, experimented with a steam-powered tank.

Even when designs were competent, quite often countermeasures emerged so quickly that a weapon's net impact was practically zero. Against the background of the ongoing slaughter, though, it was hardly noticed.

2.6. The Beginning and the End

Whether Germany could have won the war—for example, by overcoming the French at the Marne or by building fewer battleships and more submarines with which to starve out Britain—will never be known. What is known is that, considering the two coalitions that waged it, the war was won neither by the side with the better armed forces nor by the one with the political system better able to harness its population. Instead, victory went to the one that, possessing the larger demographic and economic resources and operating on exterior lines, set up the most battalions and armed them with the largest number of serviceable, though perhaps not revolutionary, weapons.

Counting those killed in action, wounded, and taken prisoner, the total number of military casualties on both sides stood at just under thirty-three million. Of these, almost nine and a half million were killed—four times as many as during the French Revolution and Napoléonic Wars, which lasted six times as long. The country with the largest absolute number of dead to mourn was, as so often, Russia with its unique combination of a huge but backward population, economic underdevelopment, and incompetent leadership. The country that, relative to its population, suffered most was Serbia. Counting only the Great Powers, the number of those killed ranged from one per thousand of the population in the United States to thirty-four per thousand in France. In relation to the 50 percent of the population that was male, the losses were, of course, twice as high. In Serbia, better than one in five men of military age (generously calculated as fifteen to forty-nine) died. In Scotland, the equivalent figure was one in ten; in France, no less than one in seven.[55]

Among the prewar visionaries, the ones who probably came closest to foreseeing what actually happened were Ivan Bloch and Julian Corbett. Both, not accidentally, were civilians. As such, they tended to take a rather wider view of conflict than most of the military men of the time, considering not only weapons technology and operations but economics and politics as well. Thanks to his extensive reading in the military literature, Bloch knew as much about weapons as most officers did, but still he missed some of the most important technical innovations such as the advent of heavy artillery and mechanization. He also underestimated the ability of the modern state to dominate its citizens; yet his main prediction of a long war of attrition with all the attendant consequences, down to the ultimate collapse of entire countries, did come true. By contrast, Corbett's greatest insight was his realization that sea power, used less to fight climactic battles than to keep communications lines open, would be decisive.

Had it not been for sea power, Britain could not have come to the aid of France, and Germany, whose resources were greatly superior, would probably have won the war within a matter of months, as happened in 1870–71. Likewise, had it not been for sea power, no British or French aid could have reached Russia, which might have collapsed earlier than it did. A fortiori, it would have been impossible for the United States to bring its superior resources to bear even to the rather limited extent it did so while the war lasted. Conversely, it was only sea power, this time in the form of submarines, that could have prevented that development from taking place. Sea power also permitted France and Britain to open up numerous secondary fronts in places as far apart as Macedonia, Gallipoli, Palestine, and Mesopotamia, though some would say that doing so did more to disperse resources than to produce victory. More importantly, it enabled them to maintain communications with their empires from which much of their raw materials (including oil) and some of their manpower came. Had it not been for this factor, Allied trucks might have been equipped with steel tires as were German vehicles.

In early 1918, with Russia compelled to sign a separate peace and Italy having suffered a heavy defeat at Caporetto, it looked as if the Central Powers had finally reached the point where victory was within their grasp. On both sides, the war industries turned out equipment at a previously unimaginable rate. Having been armed by countless new weapons and having learned to wage modern technological war, the armed forces themselves would have routed their 1914 predecessors almost as easily as if the latter had consisted of colonial levies. Still, the factors that for three years prevented a breakthrough on the all-important Western Front remained. The great German offensives of spring 1918 were the most successful since 1914, yet they failed to knock either France or Britain out of the war. Meanwhile, fresh American forces were arriving, and by the time of the armistice there were more than a million doughboys in France. Partly because their commander, General John Pershing, refused to scatter them among the British and the French forces, and partly because of inexperience, their contribution to the actual fighting was limited,[56] but it was the promise of many more to come that convinced Ludendorff the war had to be brought to an end.

Perhaps the really surprising thing about all this is that, when the end came, it happened, almost simultaneously, on all fronts. As late as July 1918, the German armies were again on the offensive, moving toward Paris, and by means of the so-called Paris gun, with its seventy-mile range, Germany was able to threaten the city as it had not done since 1914.

Then, in August, the tide turned. On the eighth of the month, "the Black Day of the German Army," coming under attack by British tanks near the city of Amiens, the defending forces broke and ran. They rallied in the end, but by that time they had lost seventy-five thousand men, and of those no fewer than thirty thousand were prisoners—a proportion that had been unheard of previously, at least on the Western Front. Thereafter the Allies advanced steadily, although there would be no decisive victory and, on the German side, no sudden collapse.

Instead it was the allies of Germany that went under first. The Austrian-Hungarian army, the Bulgarian army, and the Ottoman army were all defeated within a period of less than three weeks. It was as if a chain reaction of falling morale and alarm had been set loose. Bulgarian troops believed that their country's alliance with Germany was only effective for three years and was about to lapse.[57] With Turkey defeated in Syria, it was thought Bulgaria could not hope to hold out, and with Bulgaria defeated, Austria-Hungary would surely collapse. Finally, with Austria-Hungary gone, Germany would be deprived of its last remaining ally.

Yet even as the crow flies, the distance from Syria to Berlin is over two thousand miles, much of it through rugged Anatolia and Bulgaria, presenting any number of favorable defensive positions. At the time of the armistice, one of the original members of the Entente, Russia, lay in the dust. By contrast, Germany still retained control over parts of France, almost all of Belgium, and huge parts of Eastern Europe including Poland, the Baltic countries, and the Ukraine. Yet from one moment to the next the fight went out of the Oberste Heeresleitung like air escaping from a pricked balloon. When Foch, many years previously, wrote that no battle could be lost until the commander conceded it to be lost, perhaps he had more right on his side than some subsequent critics of his cared to admit.

The Twenty Years' Truce

3.1. Powers, Aspirations, and Attitudes

Though World War I resulted in the collapse of no fewer than four empires—the German, Austrian-Hungarian, Russian, and Ottoman—at a deeper level it brought about surprisingly little change. Only one Great Power, Austria-Hungary, was permanently taken off the map; the seven remaining still monopolized almost all the military power available on earth, as well as the economic capacity to generate more of it if and when needed. Though Germany lost its empire, the colonial possessions of Britain, France, and, to a much lesser extent, Italy, Japan, and the United States expanded; seen from the point of view of the occupied peoples it was a question of changing masters, not getting rid of them altogether. The only country that became independent as a result of the war was Ireland. However, even there the events that led to liberation had their origins in the years before 1914.

As previously, five of the seven powers continued to be located in, or chiefly oriented toward, Europe, which thus retained the greatest concentration of military power by far. The defeats suffered by Russia and Germany proved temporary. The breakup of Austria-Hungary and the establishment in Eastern Europe of a whole string of small successor states would strengthen Germany's position. Britain and France certainly profited from the war in expanding their overseas empires in the Middle East (at the expense of the Turks) and Africa (where the Germans lost their colonies), although France, in particular, was barely able to mask its continuing relative decline. Finally Italy, despite Mussolini's grandiose pretensions and aggressive posturing, was still the smallest and weakest power of all. Faced with limited raw materials and energy sources, and having a relatively small industrial base to support its armed forces, the country remained firmly enclosed within its Mediterranean prison.

Outside Europe, too, the geopolitical change that nine and a half million dead soldiers bought was limited. The greatest powers were, and continued to be, the United States and Japan. The former had done much to pay for the war. As a result, it became a creditor nation for the first time, and its economy was able to lead the world. In 1929, America's share of world manufacturing output stood at no less than 43.3 percent. Ten years later, with the US in the grip of the Great Depression and after Germany and the Soviet Union had fully recovered from the war, it still accounted for 28.7 percent—a figure almost equal to those of the other two combined.[1] In other ways, though, the United States seemed to return to its previous geopolitical stance. As had been the case after the Spanish-American War, Washington all but dismantled its wartime army and relied almost exclusively on the navy for defense, occasionally sending the marines to places few people had ever heard of.

Japan's involvement in the war was marginal, with the result that the human and material losses it suffered were even smaller than those of the United States. Yet for its efforts, it was able to gain some fresh colonial possessions in East Asia (at Germany's expense)—and was clearly bent on acquiring even more. The British decision, made under American pressure, to terminate its alliance with Japan should perhaps have suggested caution. In the event, so incompetent did the civilian and military leaders in Tokyo prove that, within a decade and a half, they had quarreled with all their major neighbors both in Asia and across the Pacific: China, the USSR, and the US. Only in September 1940 did Japan, by joining the Tripartite Pact, find itself new allies in the form of Germany and Italy.

After the war, the powers, being powers, continued to do what powers always did. They intrigued, allied themselves, armed themselves, and, perhaps most importantly, felt afraid of one another almost to the exclusion of anything and anybody else. During the 1920s, Britain's greatest concern was preventing the Continent from coming too much under the domination of its own former ally, France. Germany formed a sort of quasi-alliance with the new Soviet Union from which both sides drew great benefits, the former by being allowed to build up clandestine forces, the latter by gaining access to military-technical expertise.[2] Much as had been the case before the war, France sought to contain Germany by means of an alliance system while also preparing to resist Italian pretensions in both Europe and Africa. The United States withdrew from Europe and focused mainly on Japanese attempts to expand in the Pacific and East Asia. The US Navy in particular soon became obsessed with the need to prepare for war in the Pacific, including, until at least 1932, plans for action against the Royal Navy.

Of course the sums spent on defense declined very sharply, in most cases to less than 5 percent of GDP. As a result, the international market was flooded with huge inventories of surplus weapons, some going to the scrap yards, some to second-rate militaries in Europe, Asia, and Latin America, and a few into the hands of anti-colonial resistance movements from Morocco to Burma. Germany was compelled by the victors to all but dismantle its armed forces.[3]

Meanwhile, the United States and Britain returned to their prewar military systems:[4] strong navies and small, professional ground forces that depended on volunteers to fill their ranks. The armed forces of France, Italy, and Japan remained largely intact. Finally, no sooner had the worst damage resulting from World War I, the Civil War, and the Soviet-Polish War been put aside than the Red Army began to be rebuilt, and by the late 1920s was again the largest in Europe, though its quality left something to be desired.[5]

If in 1914 most people welcomed the war, nowhere was the change in public opinion after 1918 more evident than in Britain.[6] There, the replacement of the Liberals by Labor in 1919–20 was accompanied by the emergence of a powerful anti-militarist, anti-imperialist sentiment. And once the initial euphoria of victory had passed, the middle classes, too, turned their faces against anything vaguely resembling militarism. Writing from personal experience, authors such as Siegfried Sassoon and Robert Graves described the war as an exercise in futility filled with endless suffering, vain slaughter, and generals so obtuse that they sent hundreds of thousands to die in muddy swamps they had never even set their eyes on. From interviewing shell-shocked soldiers, Rebecca West presented the war as a mad episode that generated more madness. By 1933 Oxford students, hardly the kind of people from whom one would expect revolutionaries to emerge, were solemnly promising one another not to fight for king and country. The idea of appeasement was well on its way. Should it be any wonder then that, when Neville Chamberlain returned from Munich waving a piece of paper and promising peace in our time, he was given a hero's welcome?

In the United States, the decision to enter the war soon came to be regarded as a huge mistake,[7] brought about by the nefarious machinations of industrialists and bankers. Worse still, and even though Germany and Austria-Hungary had been defeated, the war had failed to bring about the kind of better world President Woodrow Wilson had promised. Feeling that their idealism had been betrayed, most Americans wanted nothing more to do with Europe. The Neutrality Laws of 1936–39, which prohibited the sale of weapons to belligerents, capped the process. Far from being the handiwork of a few politicians, isolationism was so popular that when the time came to reverse course, doing so proved anything but easy.

Partly because the hereditary enemy had finally been brought down, and partly because the war led to the return of Alsace-Lorraine, such regrets were less often expressed in France. During the first years after the armistice, people celebrated the victories and the sacrifices that had led to war, holding parades and listening to speeches. At this time, the French army was the largest and most powerful in the world, a fact that itself made for a certain reluctance to consider change.

Yet by 1925, the popular mood began to change. In terms of both people and material, French losses had been devastating. Whereas other countries recovered, in France a declining birthrate did not permit these losses to be made good. Perhaps this had something to do with the fact that, during the interwar years, a higher proportion of women worked than in any other country.[8] Female or male, most French citizens came to think of war as an evil necessity at best, a horror to be avoided at almost any cost at worst.

During the 1930s, as the German threat increased, the rise to power of the left-wing Popular Front created a rift between the armed forces and the population. At the same time, the strongest supporters of the military in French society, the conservative right, became alienated from the Republic. As the slogan went, "Better Hitler than [socialist prime minister] Blum." Thus both ends of the political spectrum, each for its own reasons and in its own way, became firmly committed to pacifism, setting the stage for the "strange defeat" of 1940.

Russia, now transformed into the Soviet Union, entered the 1920s in a state of weakness. First World War I, then the Civil War, left the economy devastated, society in tatters, and the country subject to a new and entirely unprecedented form of government. Communist leaders, even more than their socialist comrades, had spent their entire apprenticeship denouncing armed forces as instruments of militarism, imperialism, and every other wicked cause they could think of. Now, seeking to emphasize their own uniqueness, they hit on the idea of calling themselves "peace loving." Unlike France, though, the Soviet Union, by its sheer size and by using the most brutal means imaginable, had what it took to pull itself up by its bootstraps. It resumed its march toward Great Power status and, in the end, emerged much stronger than before; as a result, its retreat from militarism also proved temporary.

Perhaps the most interesting cases were those of Italy, Germany, and Japan. Italy emerged from World War I as one of the victors. Although it did not succeed in realizing its territorial ambitions in Anatolia, it was the only belligerent to gain territory in Europe that had never previously belonged to it—a fact that might have turned it into a "satisfied" nation. This, however, did not happen, and the Italians soon decided that they had been betrayed by their allies—all fuel for the fascist regime that seized power in 1922.

During the first eighteen years of his rule, Mussolini threatened to wage war against virtually the entire world, sometimes citing reasons, sometimes simply because he believed, or professed to believe, that fighting was a nice way to spend one's time.[9] However, as World War II was to show, the slogan *"Credere, ubbidire, combattere"* found an echo only among a very small number of adventurous youths. Neither the aristocracy, which remained loyal to the king, nor the settled bourgeoisie, whom Mussolini called "slipper wearers," nor the broad masses were persuaded by his propaganda.

Germany entered the postwar world by undergoing a revolution of sorts, doing away with the kaiser but leaving power, for the most part, in the hands of the center and the moderate right. Once conditions had settled down, and influenced by best-selling writers such as Erich Maria Remarque and Ludwig Renn, much of German society seemed to retreat from war in the same way Britain had. Yet Germany differed from Britain in that, even during the heyday of the Weimar Republic, it had a number of right-wing, powerful, and politically very active veteran organizations with a membership in the millions. They did not content themselves with celebrating the past, assuring each other of the horrors of war, and promoting their members' interests. Instead they called for a war of revenge—Germans often spoke of "the Day"— to reverse its consequences, including both disarmament and territorial loss.

In Germany, Erich Maria Remarque's *All Quiet on the Western Front* was a huge best seller, but it was also an exception; far more numerous were writers, the most famous of whom was Ernst Juenger, who relished war and glorified it. Nowhere else was willingness to engage in paramilitary activities and nostalgia for the so-called *Schutzengraben-kameradschaft* (comradeship of the trenches) as strong. Hitler himself built on these feelings, dressing in the uniform coat of a simple soldier with only one decoration and thus separating himself from his entourage of generals with their glittering arrays of epaulets, ribbons, and medals. Making full use of the German tendency toward discipline, the Nazi attempt to remilitarize society made use of every available medium to send the message, including painting, sculpture, and film.

Japan had been ruled by a military caste for centuries, and its social values, trickling down from the top, had prepared it for war. Though the Meiji Restoration of 1868 terminated Samurai rule, the new Japanese system of government was in many ways modeled on the German one and created a situation where only the emperor (or, since he did not meddle in day-to-day affairs, those who claimed to act in his name) commanded the army and the navy. This arrangement, as well as the series of military successes the country enjoyed from 1895 on, enabled the armed forces to play a decisive role in social and political life (though still not sufficiently so for some extremists who, in 1932 and 1936, attempted to mount mini coups).[10] Japanese leaders tended to be self-effacing—then as now, it was the collective that counted, not the individual. They were also less given to military display than their German counterparts. Still, in 1941, the year when the American political scientist Quincy Wright published his massive *Study of War*, he ranked Japan as the second most "aggressive" nation of all.[11]

In summary, compared with the years before 1914, the situation that prevailed between 1919 and 1939 showed both continuities and change. Practically all the armed forces on earth still remained in the

hands of seven so-called Great Powers. Of the seven, six were populated by Caucasian people professing Christianity (even though one,
the USSR, no longer acknowledged religion) and five were located in,
or focused on, Europe. Taking various factors such as economics and
politics into account, some of the powers were becoming relatively
stronger, others weaker. However, the nature of relations among the
Great Powers remained essentially as it had been, a fact that neither the
creation of the League of Nations nor the Kellogg-Briand Pact of 1928
was able to change. The great difference lay in that the rulers who had
seized power in the "totalitarian" countries were neither aristocratic,
nor cosmopolitan, nor moderate. As self-declared have-nots, these countries openly announced their dissatisfaction with the status quo and
their determination to alter it even at the cost of all-out war. Still, there
is little doubt that, in 1939, not even Hitler's minister of propaganda,
Joseph Goebbels, was able to make the majority of his fellow Germans
show much enthusiasm for the renewal of hostilities. If anything the
spirit was one of resignation, a hope for some miracle that might save
them at the last moment.[12]

The Soviet Union purged its armed forces (one of the Bolsheviks'
greatest fears had always been "Bonapartism") and at the same time rebuilt and reequipped on an impressive scale, glorifying the military as
the workers' bulwark that would one day liberate the earth from its nefarious capitalist exploiters.

Finally, the great democracies' retreat from any kind of enthusiasm
for war proved permanent. In 1939–41, and to a very considerable extent thereafter, they went to war only reluctantly and expected the
worst.

3.2. The Military Thinkers

Throughout history, all too often the conclusion of one armed conflict has served as a prelude to the next. Never was this more true than
at the end of World War I, which, although it was sometimes described
as "the war to end all wars," provided only a temporary respite.
Scarcely had the guns fallen silent than people started looking into the
future on the assumption that the Great Powers of this world had not
yet finished fighting one another. Which gave rise to the question:
How was this to be done?

To virtually all of those who tried, the point of departure was the need to avoid attrition, reopen the way toward decisive operations, and reduce the number of military casualties on the battlefield. The casualties themselves had been the direct result of the superiority of the defense as brought about by modern firepower, hence the most pressing problem was to find ways to bypass or overcome it. One of the first serious theoretical treatises to look at the problem was written by an Italian general, Giulio Douhet. An engineer by profession, during the early years of the century Douhet had become fascinated with the military applications of the internal combustion engine. A little later he was also found dabbling in futurist ideas concerning the spiritual qualities allegedly springing from those two speedy new vehicles, the motorcar and the aircraft, claiming that they possessed the ability to rejuvenate the world and Italy in particular.[13]

As a staff officer in 1915–18, he was in a position to observe, and reflect on, the twelve abortive offensives the Italian army had launched across the River Isonzo. Surely there had to be a better way of doing things—one that, in fact, he had already promoted during the war itself, arguing in favor of the creation of a massive bomber force and its use against the enemy. His masterpiece, *Il Commando del Aereo* (the command of the air), was published in 1921 and, as the title suggests, tried to do for the air what Mahan had done for the sea. In his own words, "the form of any war . . . depends upon the technical means of war available." In the past, firearms had revolutionized war; then it was the turn of small-caliber rapid-fire guns, barbed wire, and, at sea, the submarine. The most recent additions were the air arm and poison gas, both of which were still in their infancy but possessed the potential to completely upset all forms of war so far known.[14]

Douhet surmised correctly that as long as war was fought only on the surface of the earth, it was necessary for one side to break through the other's defenses in order to win. However, those defenses had become stronger and stronger until the ability to maneuver past them and take strategically important targets such as cities and industrial areas became impossible. Sheltered by this reality, the civilian population carried on almost undisturbed. As we saw, it was by mobilizing that population that the belligerents were able to produce what it took to wage total war and sustain the fight for years on end.

The advent of aircraft changed this situation. Capable of flying over battle lines and natural obstacles, and possessing a comparatively long range, aircraft were free to attack centers of population and industry. Because no effective defense against such attacks was possible—given that the air could be traversed in all directions with equal ease and there was no predicting which target would be hit next—any war would have to start with a massive attack on the enemy's air bases so as to establish "command of the air."

That having been achieved, and extrapolating from the events of 1916–18, Douhet suggested that forty aircraft dropping eighty tons of bombs might have "completely destroyed" a city the size of Treviso. A mere three aircraft, he calculated, could deliver as much firepower as a modern battleship in a single broadside, whereas a thousand aircraft could deliver ten times as much firepower as could the entire British navy—counting thirty Dreadnoughts—in ten broadsides. The kicker was that the price tag of a single battleship would buy about a thousand aircraft. As Douhet pointed out, moreover, even these calculations failed to take account of the fact that the science of military aviation had just begun and that aircraft capable of lifting as much as ten tons of bombs would soon be built. Carrying Douhet's views further, investments in armies and navies would by necessity come to a halt, and given that the new weapon was inherently offensive in nature, most of the aircraft ought to be not fighters but bombers. And instead of being grafted on to the army and navy, such air fleets would be formed into an independent air force. At the outbreak of the next war, that air force would be launched like a shell from a cannon. Having obtained command of the air in this sense by destroying the enemy's airfields, the attackers would switch from military to civilian objectives. Using gas as the principal weapon, the aim should be not merely to kill but to demoralize. Leaping over the enemy's ground defenses, a war waged by such means might be over almost before it had begun. By minimizing the casualties of both the attacker and the defender (whose population, feeling the effects of war directly, would force the government to surrender) represented a humane alternative to an endless battle of attrition. To carry out the air offensive, Douhet proposed a comparatively small force made up of elite warriors, a vision that meshed well with the anti-democratic, fascist ideas he also entertained.

The dream of avoiding warfare by attrition was also alive in the great prophet of mechanized land warfare, John Frederick Fuller.[15]

Even as a young officer, Fuller had given evidence of a formidable intellect expressed by an interest in everything from Greek philosophy to Jewish mysticism. In the years before World War I, he made great effort to discover the principles of war, of which he settled on nine: direction, concentration, distribution, determination, surprise, endurance, mobility, offensive action, and security.[16]

In numerous publications—Fuller was a prolific writer who, however, often tended to overstate his case—he argued that war, like every other field of human life, was decisively affected by the progress of science. Like Douhet, he considered the most important fruits of science to be the internal combustion engine (on which depended the airplane and the tank) and poison gas. For him, future warfare on land would center on the tank and the mechanization of artillery, reconnaissance, engineering, signals, supply, and maintenance units. Fully mechanized, an army would enjoy almost as much freedom of movement as did ships at sea. Now armies could once again maneuver against each other, concentrating against select sections of the enemy front, breaking through, and bringing about victory at comparatively low cost.

In the debates about tanks and mechanization, his views, coming as they did from an ex–chief of staff of the most advanced mechanized force in history, commanded particular respect. Yet even barring his most extreme ideas—say, that armies should consist of tanks alone and every infantryman provided with his individual tankette—many of his suggestions have come to pass. Considering himself not merely a military reformer but a philosopher as well, Fuller went on to spin an immensely complicated network of intellectual propositions on the nature of war, life, history, and whatever. Combining all these different strands, many of his historical writings were decidedly brilliant. However, much of his theorizing was decidedly half-baked, tied as it was to his interest in mysticism and the occult.

In the history of twentieth-century military thought, Fuller's name is almost always associated with that of his younger contemporary and friend Basil Liddell Hart.[17] Unlike Fuller, Liddell Hart was not a professional soldier, but rather studied history at Cambridge before enlisting, received a commission, and fought in France. Gassed at the Somme, Captain (throughout his life he enjoyed emphasizing the military rank he had attained) Liddell Hart spent the rest of the war in England training infantry recruits. It was in this capacity that he first started thinking seriously about the best way to prepare for, and wage, armed conflict.

Concerning his intellectual development, two points are worth noting. First, like so many of his generation who were educated in public schools, Liddell Hart was brought up on the notion that war was akin to sport and games. In his memoirs, he explains that he was good at football—not because his coordination and technique were in any way outstanding, but because he could envisage all various combinations of play and foresee where the ball was likely to end up. Second, and again like so many of his contemporaries, Liddell Hart ended the war as a fervent admirer of the British military establishment, which after all had just fought and won the largest armed conflict in history to date.

However, within a few years he reversed himself, joining the then fashionable trend of disillusionment with the war in general and with its conduct at the hand of the British high command in particular. In criticizing that conduct, his stature as the popular journalist he became after the war and interest in sports were to come in handy. Like Fuller, Liddell Hart concluded that sending men into the maws of machine guns had been the height of folly, the origin of which was to be found not in simple bloody-mindedness but in the writings of the greatest of all military philosophers, Carl von Clausewitz. To Liddell Hart, this was the prophet whose clarion call had misled generations of officers into the belief that the best, indeed almost the only, way to wage war was to concentrate the greatest possible number of men and weapons and launch them straight ahead against the enemy.[18] In 1914–18 the "Prussian Marseillaise" had borne its horrible fruit.

To restore the power of the offensive and save casualties, in his early writings Liddell Hart recommended "the indirect approach." Rather than attacking the enemy head-on, he should be thrown off balance, achieved by combining rapidity of movement with secrecy and surprise, with attacks carried out by dispersed forces (so as to conceal the true center of gravity for as long as possible), coming from unexpected directions, and following the least expected route, even if this meant overcoming topographic obstacles. Above all, every plan had to possess "two branches"—drawn up in such a way as to keep the opponent guessing concerning one's true objectives. Any plan should also be sufficiently flexible to enable an objective to be changed if it turned out to be too strongly defended.

All such maneuvers were to be carried out in two-dimensional space, along lines of communications, overcoming all natural and artificial obstacles, while trailing "an umbilical cord of supply," and against an enemy who presumably was both intelligent enough to understand what was going on and capable of engaging in countermaneuvers. War, consisting essentially of movement, was presented almost as if it were some kind of sophisticated game played between opposing teams. This was particularly true of Liddell Hart's mature work. The older he became, the more pronounced his tendency to give tactics a short shrift. Other subjects such as mobilization, logistics, intelligence, command, communication and control, and questions of killing and dying were also lightly skipped over. Reading his most famous and oft-reprinted book, *Strategy: The Indirect Approach,* one might be excused for thinking war was about operational movement and very little else.

During the early 1920s, Liddell Hart also became interested in mechanization, and in this so much of his thinking was "borrowed" from his mentor, Fuller, that their friendship suffered for it.[19] Thus it was little surprise that Liddell Hart's vision of mechanized armed forces, as set forth in his *Paris, or the Future of War* (1925) as well as *The Remaking of Modern Armies* (1927), employed a combination of aircraft, tanks, and poison gas as weapons with which defenses could be skipped over or overcome, resulting in the war brought to a swift and cheap, if violent, end.

What prevented Liddell Hart from making a detailed forecast of the Blitzkrieg, with its characteristic combination of armored divisions and tanks, was his abiding revulsion for the horrors of World War I and his determination, which he shared with so many of his generation, that they not be repeated. From about 1931 on, this caused him to switch from attempts to devise more effective ways to win toward thinking about less costly ways to avoid defeat. Following Julian Corbett without bothering to acknowledge the master, he now claimed that the "British Way in Warfare" had always been to stay out of massive Continental commitments. Instead the kingdom had relied on its navy to keep the enemy at bay (and harass and weaken him by means of well-directed strokes at selected points) and on Continental allies to deliver the coup de main. By 1939, Liddell Hart had convinced himself that "the dominant lesson from the experience of land warfare, for more than a generation past, has been the superiority of the defense over attack"; even in the air, as experiences in Spain had shown, "the prospects of the defense are improving." Therefore, instead of Britain repeating its World War I error—which had led to so many casualties—it could safely trust the "dauntless" French to stop the Germans. Britain itself, its armed forces thoroughly modernized and mechanized, should revert to its traditional strategy, relying primarily on blockade on the one hand and airpower on the other. This had the additional advantage that it would make universal conscription and mass armies unnecessary—a preference for small professional forces that Liddell Hart, a liberal, shared with some thinkers like Douhet.

Compared with Douhet, Fuller, and Liddell Hart, Erich Ludendorff was a towering figure. Much more than the first two, he understood what modern war was like from the top, and unlike the last-named he did not regard it as some kind of field game; "the war has spared me nothing," he would write, having lost two sons. On the other hand, and again unlike Liddell Hart in particular, neither did he shrink from its horrors.

At first, Ludendorff was perhaps no more bigoted than was required of a German officer of his generation. Indeed, during the war he once opened a proclamation to the Jewish population of occupied Poland with the words, *"Meine liebe Jidden."* In the 1920s, however, influenced by his second wife, he started dabbling with anti-Semitism, anti-Catholicism, and anti-freemasonry (he could never make up his mind which of the three international forces posed the greatest danger to Germany). He also took a part in the 1923 Nazi Putsch; for all this he has been rightly condemned. However, this should not obscure the fact that his vision of future war was more nearly correct than any of the rest.

Having spent more than two years in charge of Germany's war effort, Ludendorff did not believe that a first-class modern state could be brought to its knees rapidly and cheaply by aircraft dropping bombs, or by fleets of tanks engaging in mobile operations, however brilliantly. In part, his *Der Totale Krieg* merely continued the work of some pre-1914 militarist writers, such as Colmar von der Goltz and Theodor von Bernhardi, who had advocated total mobilization and mass armies. And up to a point, his book recounted his own experience, which by attacking many of his less cooperative colleagues sought to explain why Germany had lost the war. Yet whatever the book's precise origins and purpose, Ludendorff's main thesis was that the developing technologies of production, transportation, and communication made modern war into much more than merely a question of armed forces maneuvering against one another for mastery of some battlefield. Instead, war would now demand a nation's total effort, and therefore a total devotion of all resources to its execution.

To be sure, the next war *would* make use of all available weapons, including poison gas. Both civilians in their cities and soldiers in their trenches would be targeted, and the resulting casualties, destruction, and suffering would be immense. Therefore, by necessity, as important as the total mobilization of material resources would be the spiritual mobilization of the people—a point on which, as Ludendorff and many of his countrymen saw it, imperial Germany with its old-fashioned, authoritarian system of government and its neglect of the working classes had been sadly deficient.

The implication of such mobilization was an end to democracy and the liberties it entailed, including not only freedom of the press but workers' rights and capitalist enterprise as well. For either industrialists or union leaders (during the war, Ludendorff had had his troubles with both) to insist on their own privilege was intolerable. Along with the entire financial apparatus available to the state, they, too, were to be subjected to a military dictatorship. And having experienced the process firsthand, Ludendorff was under no illusion that the nation's spiritual and material mobilization could be improvised. Hence the dictatorship he demanded, and for which he no doubt regarded himself as the most suitable candidate, was to be set up in peacetime and made permanent.

The next war would be a life-and-death struggle to be won by the belligerent with the greatest resources and the strongest will to mobilize and deploy them—which incidentally disposed of any childish illusions concerning small, professional, and highly mobile, let alone chivalrous, armed forces. Anything that did not serve the war effort would have to be ruthlessly suppressed. Politics would, in effect, be swallowed by the war. Ludendorff was never one to mince his words. "All of Clausewitz's theories should be thrown overboard. . . . Both war and policy serve the existence of the nation. However, war is the highest expression of the people's will to live. Therefore politics must be made subordinate to war."[20] Or else, to the extent that this did not happen, treated as superfluous and, indeed, treasonable.

In the decades after 1945, Ludendorff's military ideas were often attacked by featherweight commentators[21] who mistook their world—in which nuclear weapons had made total warfare as he understood it impossible—for his. During these years, it was Liddell Hart and Fuller who, whether rightly or not,[22] were celebrated as the fathers of the Blitzkrieg. Nevertheless, the fact remains that it was not their vision of World War II but Ludendorff's that turned out to be only too horribly true.

To be sure, fleets of aircraft, though they did not drop gas, did fly over fronts and bombed cities on a scale that, had he been able to envisage it, might have made even Ludendorff blanch. The combination of airpower, armor, mobility, and wireless restored operational mobility, laying the groundwork for some spectacular campaigns in which countries the size of Poland and France were knocked down at a single blow. The Second World War also demonstrated the reestablishment of the balance between defense and offense, although events were to show that both tanks and aircraft were equally as capable of preventing a breakthrough as they were of helping one take place.

Where Ludendorff proved most correct, however, was in his insistence that the Second World War—a term, of course, that he did not use—would be broadly like the first, and like its predecessor would develop into a gigantic and prolonged struggle. As was the First World War, it would be waged on many fronts, at sea and in the air as well as on land. Like its predecessor, it would both demand and make possible the mobilization of all resources. He was also proved right in that even democratic Britain found it necessary to curtail the role of politics by setting up a national coalition government—which meant that, as long as the conflict lasted, there was no parliamentary opposition, and elections were postponed. Ludendorff's posthumous triumph may, indeed, be seen in the fact that, by the time the war was over, a continent had been devastated and an estimated forty million people lay dead.

3.3. Innovation: From Theory to Practice

At the beginning of the twentieth century, the idea that systematic research and development could result in a never-ending stream of new inventions had become firmly established, and indeed perhaps never before in history had the belief in "science" been stronger and more widespread. Book after book extolled the great inventors as well as the benefits they had bestowed on humanity; some public opinion surveys even pointed to Thomas Edison as the most important person of all. Militarily speaking, the principal innovations took place in the field of mechanized warfare, air warfare, and naval warfare, where the development of the aircraft carrier and amphibious landing vessels during the interwar years was especially dramatic. These elements were tied together by a vast array of communications and other electronic devices that, in retrospect, may have been the most important of all.[23]

By the time the First World War ended, the country with the greatest experience in mechanized warfare was Britain, where development of tanks continued with the Mark C (on which Fuller, preparing Plan 1919, had relied) being canceled in favor of the Mark D. This was a truly revolutionary machine. With a range of two hundred miles and capable of speeds up to twenty miles per hour, it wore enough armor to proof it against armor-piercing bullets, and was topped by a very modern revolving turret that carried twin machine guns. As if all these marvels were not enough, the suspension was sprung, with the result that the crew could survive the ride without being thrown around too much. This, however, was only the beginning. Originating either in official orders or in private initiatives, almost year by year new, experimental, models made their appearance—light, medium, and heavy. Some were armed with two-pounder cannon, others merely with machine guns; quite a number had more than one turret. Some were considered successes, but most were not.

In parallel with the tank's technological development, theories concerning the way tanks should be employed abounded. Some, Fuller included, thought they were analogous to ships at sea, and pressed for an army made up exclusively of the new machines, with heavy tanks providing the impetus for a breakthrough supported by medium "cruiser" tanks to exploit the breach. While these ideas were vindicated by World War II, others, such as small, one-man tankettes for use in guerrilla operations, were destined to be forgotten until the advent of suicide car bombers realized them in a somewhat different form. The operations of armored forces were often compared to those of heavy cavalry, a view that eventually proved more correct than any of the others.

Year by year on Salisbury Plain, the machines and their supporting vehicles—trucks for carrying supplies, motorcycles for liaison and communications, and large, open staff cars for accommodating commanders—were put through their paces, often in the presence of senior officers and their ladies who saw the event as an occasion for a picnic. By 1927, the British had created the world's first experimental mechanized force; however, the army never got to the point at which a firm commitment was made to expand its units so that all forces would be mechanized.[24]

This was in part due to entrenched conservatism—many cavalrymen, afraid lest their status would suffer, refused to give up their horses—and in part to sheer financial penury. At the time, it was assumed that there would be no major war for ten years to come, and by the order of secretary of the exchequer, Winston Churchill, the "ten years' rule" was automatically extended from one day to the next.[25] Hitler's coming to power in 1933 ought to have sounded the alarm and made a difference in the pace of modernization. Instead, by an accident of history, only one year later the post of chief of the imperial staff was taken over by a more than usually conservative officer, Field Marshal Montgomery-Massingberd who held the position of many top commanders that Britain should never again send an army to the Continent.[26] As a result, most officers continued to play polo or, if stationed in India, stick pigs as if nothing had changed since 1900. As a result, it was only in 1939 that Britain finally got its first armored division.

French and American attempts at mechanization were hardly more successful. Inspired by Foch, who at long last had concluded that no offensive was likely to succeed unless the enemy's firepower was neutralized,[27] France put its hopes on the so-called methodical battle, employing a combination of all arms and advancing on a wide front so as not to take undue risks. Essentially this was a rehash of the combats of summer and autumn 1918. There was in it a role for armor, but no more than a subordinate one, with tanks providing fire support for the infantry. When World War II broke out, most of the French tanks were still the small, lightly armored machines introduced in 1935. There was also a much heavier, better-armored type, the Char B. However, like its smaller compatriot it was undermanned, which meant that it could not fire its gun fast enough. In addition, it could carry only enough fuel for fifty miles, and since French tanks were not equipped with radios, command and control of armored forces was extremely difficult.

American developments were even more limited. In 1917–18, the Americans had begun building copies of existing French and British tanks, but few could be completed before the war came to an end. Yankee technical ingenuity also led to all kinds of curious experiments including the above-mentioned steam-powered tank, a gas-electric tank, a steam-wheel tank (basically an armored box mounted on steel wheels), and even an unarmored "skeleton tank."[28] However, in the person of William Christie the United States had a designer whose ideas were as advanced as those of anyone else, among them the fastest tank built to that time and an amphibious tank. Unfortunately, here, too, conservatism and inertia played a part, and all he was allowed to do was produce a few experimental models. The underlying reality was that the US Army was just too small to set up and test large formations, armored or otherwise, scattered as it was in penny packets all over a huge continent.

This left the Soviets and the Germans, and during the 1920s the two pariah states worked together, reviving the close relationship they had enjoyed during most of the nineteenth century. They built experimental vehicles and tested them in Kazan, until Hitler's rise to power brought such cooperation to an end, much to the regret of some German officers. Left to their own devices, the Soviets made their share of mistakes, coming up with their own designs and also buying foreign models that they tried to copy. They certainly were not alone in producing monstrosities; one heavy tank design featured no fewer than five turrets. However, in their next step they committed an error opposite to the British, French, and Americans. Whereas the Western countries came up with a very large number of experimental designs, most of which either went nowhere or were produced in only very small numbers, the Soviets settled on a single, basic design as early as

1933 and began mass-producing it.[29] By 1939, they had nearly twenty-five thousand vehicles—far more than the rest of the world combined.

The Red Army tanks were organized in no fewer than four armored corps, fifty tank brigades, four armored car brigades, twenty-six tank regiments in cavalry divisions, eleven tank regiments in armored schools, and an unspecified number of tank companies in infantry divisions. Yet they were used only in support of the infantry. There were no armored divisions; nor were tanks expected to operate independently. Worse still, by the time the design, called the T-26, went into action against the invading Wehrmacht, it was obsolete and easily dealt with. Modern fighting vehicles, such as the heavy KV-1 and the magnificent T-34, made up only a very small percentage of the total, and even those were not properly employed.

The case of the Germans was unique. First, they had been defeated, which made them better prepared to experiment and innovate. Second, by the beginning of 1918 they had developed a new organization, a new doctrine, new techniques, and some new weapons—which, as the events of March through July proved, were capable of breaking through the strongest fortified fronts that then existed. Company-sized, decentralized battle groups, supported by short but intensive artillery bombardments, armed with an assortment of weapons up to and including light cannon, pushing forward into nooks and crannies while bypassing centers of resistance and leaving them behind, accomplished the trick.[30] Except that the available technical means still prevented the groups from bringing up supplies and maintaining easy communications with one another and with the rear, there was no question that the toughest problem of all—gaining superiority over the defense—was finally being mastered.

As was the case elsewhere, not every German commander was enthusiastic about armored warfare. Another factor was the Treaty of Versailles, which prohibited Germany from building tanks; in the end, it required Hitler's personal intervention to get things moving.[31] No later than 1935, the Reichswehr had its first three armored divisions. By the time the war started there were eight self-contained divisions, each made up of tank units, artillery, motorized infantry, anti-tank troops, a headquarters, signal troops, and an organic supply component equipped with trucks. These early units, however, proved to be tank-heavy, and after the victory over France the number of tanks in each division was cut to two hundred or so, which has remained standard for tank divisions to the present day.

When unleashed on first Poland, then France, the results were devastating. But what made these formations so powerful was neither their number (never during the war were more than 20 percent of all German ground troops motorized), nor the quality of the tanks themselves, which in 1940 were hardly better than their French opposites.[32] It was instead the way they were organized and grafted onto the pre-1914 strategic doctrine, which emphasized mobility, simultaneous attacks coming from several directions, outflanking, and the *Kesselschlacht* (the tactic of surrounding the enemy in a cauldron or pocket).[33]

Impressive as these developments were, they would never have grown as successful as they did had it not been for the simultaneous rise of airpower. By the close of World War I, though both sides were already launching "strategic" bombardments, air forces remained very much ancillary to their respective armies and navies. Later, most countries followed Britain's lead in creating independent air forces, so that the aggressive promotion of airpower was driven partly by the new air forces' attempts to preserve their independence, expand it, and gain additional financial resources in order to do so.

There were sharp differences in the expression of that aggressiveness, however. In the United States and Britain, island powers both, advocates of airpower insisted that it should be used for launching attacks on civilian, demographic, and industrial targets in a Douhet-like fashion.[34] In Germany and the USSR, the insistence was rather that it be used either to attack military targets at the front (this came to be known as close air support, or CAS) or else to interdict lines of communications. The two opposing points of view struggled and intermingled, but they were never really reconciled. In the US Air Force this remains true to the present day.

This debate as to the best use of airpower had important repercussions in the field of technology. True to their doctrine, the United States and Britain invested fortunes in the development of heavy, four-engined bombers, thus establishing an important technological lead that they never subsequently relinquished—and which later, incidentally, translated into the production of commercial passenger aircraft. On the other hand, finding ways to make the most effective use of these forces proved much more difficult than Douhet and his followers had anticipated, and several more years had to pass before the problem was really solved.

In the case of France and Italy, failure to build such large aircraft was more a result of financial penury than anything else. After all, the money needed for building a heavy bomber could buy several light, twin-engined bombers and single-engined fighters. And if the outcome was a large order of battle that would impress dilettantes such as Mussolini and Hitler, then all the better.

Planning for a war in the Pacific, Japan focused on carrier-launched aircraft, with the result that heavy bombers were never in the cards. Finally, the Soviet Union produced a few gigantic aircraft for demonstration purposes. However, its commanders never abandoned the idea that the real purpose of airpower was to act as flying artillery.[35]

As so often happened during this period, the most interesting case was presented by the Germans. Commanded by Hermann Goering, Hitler's corpulent deputy and ex-World War I fighter ace who claimed that "everything that flies belongs to me," the Luftwaffe was as jealous of its independence as any other air force. Since there had been no air force during the Weimar Republic, though, most of its commanders were ex-army men, who consequently understood the importance of joint operations better than their British and American colleagues. Whenever such operations were planned, it was German practice to put an air force general in charge. Like the Soviets, the German Luftwaffe was not organized by type of aircraft—bomber command, fighter command, and so on—but divided into air divisions, air corps, and air fleets, each including machines of all types with organic ground support. Accordingly, they could be moved from one theater of war to another without any need for reorganization. All that was needed was to build the physical infrastructure, and even for that, the Luftwaffe was able to rely partly on its own resources.

As in several other countries, one reason behind the German failure to build heavy bombers was the desire to create a large, impressive-looking order of battle in the face of fiscal reality. Another, though could be connected to a doctrine that began to be developed in the mid-1930s. Unlike the Red Air Force, the Luftwaffe never allowed itself to degenerate into mere flying artillery—or, as one of its commanding generals put it, to become "the hand maiden of the Army."[36] Insofar as the Luftwaffe planned to start any campaign with a devastating attack on enemy air bases, it owed more to Douhet than is usually realized. However, in the form of the famous Stuka dive-bombers, it acquired a superb instrument for providing close support—sometimes almost literally at the feet of the ground troops. This required excellent air to ground cooperation, and air officers had to possess a good understanding of the ground battle. Here, again, the fact that many Luftwaffe officers had started their careers in the army helped. Only during the later half of the war did the Western Allies finally begin to equal the Germans in these respects.

Another field in which the Germans acquired a commanding lead was airborne operations. Beginning around 1930, the armed forces of many countries toyed with the idea of delivering troops either by parachute or by glider and developing the necessary units, equipment, and doctrines to do so. Because they were taking the offensive, however, the Germans were the first off the mark. Fearless men dropping from the sky, including a former world heavyweight boxing champion, Max Schmeling, played a spectacular part in the invasion of Norway as well as the Netherlands, Belgium, and Crete. On the other hand, such operations proved enormously expensive. This was true in terms of both matériel and personnel. Besides being vulnerable during the approach flight, even under the best conditions many gliders and aircraft had to be crash-landed and could not be reused. And since the troops could not carry any heavy weapons, they were sometimes slaughtered by their better-equipped opponents, which is what happened to US paratroopers at Arnhem in 1944. As a result the entire technique, spectacular as it was, proved something of a cul-de-sac. After 1945, it was only rarely employed and then only on a relatively small scale against very light opposition, as for, example, when the US 101st Airborne operated in Iraq in 2003.

For millennia, the ability of fleets to identify and track their enemies had depended essentially on lookouts. From perches high on the swaying masts of ships it was the straining human eye that had to do the job, day and night. Once flying craft had been introduced, it did not take long to appreciate that their use at sea could greatly extend the range of observation. The earliest experiments in this direction were made just before World War I. By 1918 British aircraft were logging thirty thousand miles a month over seas surrounding the Home Islands on submarine patrols.

Owing to their need for takeoff and landing surfaces, aircraft were more difficult, and so took longer to deploy at sea than balloons. Aircraft equipped with floats (hydroplanes) could be lowered into the water by means of a crane, take off, and, having performed their mission and landed, be recovered. It was, however, soon discovered that doing so was a dangerous operation practicable only in calm seas. To really draw the benefit from sea-based airpower, it would be necessary to construct a specialized ship equipped with its own airfield so that wheeled, high-performance aircraft could be launched and recovered. The first such ship, the British *Argus*, entered service in 1918.

As usual, the attitudes of the powers toward what would become known as the aircraft carrier varied. France, the Soviet Union, Germany, and Italy never built or completed carriers. In the case of the first three, this was because they were, or considered themselves, primarily land powers. In that of the last-named, it was because Italy itself was a giant carrier jutting into the Mediterranean—or so, at least, Mussolini (who was always right) said. This left the island nations of Britain, Japan, and the United States, all three of which depended on the sea to project their power, and the first two could not survive for long if their naval communications were cut. During the 1920s, all three had already established a separate naval air arm and were busily experimenting with its use. All three commissioned a number of carriers and produced the specialized aircraft that could fly from their decks. Armed with torpedoes, naval aircraft soon turned into a formidable threat to ships, and indeed the time was to come when any fleet operating without air cover was as good as lost. On the other hand, it took decades after the end of World War I for carriers to be able to operate aircraft with sufficient power and range to have a significant influence on the land battle.

A debate between the advocates of airpower and the supporters of battleships went on throughout the interwar years. Many exercises were held, but they did not resolve the matter, given that they were seldom entirely realistic and that they were often rigged to suit one side or another. Compared with carriers, battleships enjoyed the advantage of being much better armored and capable of delivering more sustained fire on target. Moreover, as time went on, battleships were able to somewhat neutralize the threat of air attacks by sprouting batteries of anti-aircraft guns, as well as large "blisters" of dead space on the sides of their hulls to protect against torpedoes. In 1938, a British blue-ribbon commission, put together specifically to study the matter, did not reach any firm conclusions. Even the Japanese, who were as committed to carriers and naval aviation as anybody else, still found it necessary to lay down two gigantic battleships, the *Musashi* and the *Yamato*.

Another field that revolutionized naval warfare during the twenty years' truce was amphibious operations. If our interpretation of the Bayeux tapestry is correct, special ships for transporting and landing horses had been used at least as far back as 1066 when William the Conqueror landed on England's southern shores. And while it is true that the 1915 Gallipoli landings had ended in failure, the war did see a few successful opposed landings made by the Germans against the Russians in the Baltic, as well as British amphibious raids against German submarine bases in Belgium. Still given their geopolitical position as well as their concentration on airborne operations, it is scant wonder that the Germans did not proceed very far in developing an amphibious force. The Italians did even less, and in planning an invasion of Malta in 1942, the two Axis partners had to call in Japanese experts for help.[37]

The British attitude is more surprising. Throughout the interwar period, though the various sea lords commissioned many paper studies, amphibious warfare was given low priority, and as of 1938 the number of available landing craft was exactly eight. Interservice rivalry, manpower constraints, and insufficient financial means all contributed to this outcome. If these factors explain the failure, they can scarcely excuse it.

In this way, leadership in the field fell to the Japanese and the Americans. Japan drew experience from successful amphibious operations against China (1894), Russia (1905), and the German colonies in the Pacific (1915), although none of these was carried out in the face of a determined modern enemy. With Japanese planning shifting to the possibility of occupying American possessions in the Pacific, it wasn't until 1932 that the Imperial Japanese Navy identified the essentials of a successful landing operation, the most important being transport of the expeditionary force by means of submarines, surface ships, and aircraft; seaborne artillery capable of demolishing coastal fortifications;

and motorized landing craft capable of rapidly discharging troops by day and by night.

Like their opposite numbers elsewhere, the Japanese army and navy proceeded separately and not without considerable interservice rivalry. The army designated no fewer than three divisions as "amphibious" but lacked the necessary sea transport. The navy built battalions of marines but did not go for larger formations. It was also the Japanese navy that came up with the world's first specialized landing craft as well as the first amphibious assault ships. The landing craft not only allowed troops to be discharged rapidly but also possessed the necessary shallow draft, a requirement that was particularly important in the Pacific with its many reefs and lagoons. However, the assault ships were real technological marvels. In addition to carrying landing craft on derricks, they were provided with a deck that could be flooded; as two stern doors opened, the landing craft would sortie like piglets from a sow. Another deck was also provided with doors, thus enabling motor vehicles to proceed directly from the ship onto piers—a principle adopted much later by the US Navy as well.

The war with China from 1937 provided the army and navy with opportunities to test both doctrine and equipment, doing so with considerable success, but only within limits. Most landings took place at night, involving forces no larger than a battalion, and were more or less unopposed. However, the psychological impact such assaults had on the defenders was a significant reason for the successes.

Until and through World War I, the US Marine Corps was a minuscule organization. It reached its nadir in 1919 when it numbered just 1,570 officers and men, and its demise seemed imminent. Originally the marines' task had been to guard ships in port, hardly a glamorous job, nor one that left them much time to practice the rifle drill for which they are famous. Throughout the nineteenth and early twentieth centuries, they also set up small landing forces that went ashore at obscure, weakly held places from the Halls of Montezuma to the Shores of Tripoli—which, incidentally, is how they acquired their modern mission of guarding embassies. In 1919–20 the navy's Plan Orange, which for the first time envisaged a major war against Japan, finally created the conditions that were to catapult the Marine Corps into prominence.

The commandant at the time, a mere major general by the name of John A. Lejeune, quickly grasped the opportunity the plan presented, both for the country and for his corps. Separate from both the army and the navy, but nevertheless coming under the Navy Department, the marines, having found their mission in life, were able to maneuver between the two. Throughout the 1920s and 1930s, they busily wrote doctrines and conducted exercises, often borrowing navy ships and asking for the participation of army troops where their own number did not suffice. By the late 1930s, in the words of one modern historian, they had "experimented with about every imaginable amphibious approach allowed by their equipment. They tried day and night land-ings, smoke screens, varieties of air and naval gunfire support, concen-trated assaults and dispersed infiltrations, the firings of all sorts of weapons from landing craft, and an array of demonstrations, feints, subsidiary landings, and broad-front assaults."[38]

While naval aviators sought new ways to wrest command of the sea, and amphibious warfare enthusiasts were looking for better ways to project sea power onto the land, the submariners faced the problem of perfecting the art of sinking warships and cutting sea-lanes. Despite their technical limitations, submarines were one of the great success stories of World War I. German submarines sank no less than 11.9 million tons of Allied shipping. When comparing the number of sub-marine sorties with submarine losses, the kaiser's submariners did about three times as well as Admiral Karl Doenitz's "wolf packs" did in 1939–45. Indeed, it was only the belated adoption of the convoy sys-tem that saved Britain from abject surrender.[39]

In 1939, submarines still depended, as many do to the present day, on a diesel-electric propulsion system. But in the twenty years be-tween the wars, boats grew considerably faster and dived deeper. They also grew larger, which meant that they could carry more torpedoes for a longer range—the more so since some submarines were designed as tankers and were thus able to replenish other boats at sea. Yet another innovation was a new optical target-acquisition and tracking mecha-nism introduced by the Germans. It enabled submarines that were at-tacking on the surface—as they often did—to calculate the firing data for up to five torpedoes simultaneously. The resulting salvos were much harder to evade. Probably the most important innovations, how-ever, were sonar and radio. Sonar, which reached fruition during the interwar period, was originally developed to locate submarines; however, it also allowed submarines to actively hunt for ships at much greater ranges than previously possible. Radio permitted submarines to work closely with one another as well as with surface ships and aircraft, and receive updated commands from central headquarters.

At the outbreak of World War II, the leading countries in the development of the submarine were Britain, the United States, and Japan. By contrast, Germany was a latecomer; the Treaty of Versailles prohibited the Reichswehr from having a submarine arm, with the result that experimentation and development had to be carried out in secret. While lessons were drawn and doctrine continued to be written, the construction of new vessels was moved outside Germany's own borders and depended on foreign countries placing orders. These measures allowed the German navy to keep abreast of intellectual and technical developments, but they did not permit it to gain practical experience or train crews. No sooner did Hitler come to power than he violated the treaty. By 1939, Germany once again had a strong, well-organized, capable submarine arm; albeit it did not and could not have the kind of support from surface vessels and aircraft that its enemies, Britain and the United States, considered crucial for success.

Both on land and at sea, short-range communications had always depended on visual and auditory signals. Long-range traffic had to be carried either by (usually mounted) messengers or by dispatch-boat. Both were slow and expensive; both were also subject to interference either by nature or by enemy action. It was only the advent of the electric telegraph and telephone during the nineteenth century that changed this situation. Telegraphs, however, were hard to move from place to place even on land; whereas at sea they were entirely useless. The invention of radio changed all that. For the first time in history, a device became available that, in theory, made possible coordinated action on land at sea; messages could be sent and received regardless of distance, relative movement, topographical obstacles, weather, or time of day.

In the interwar years, advances in technology were dramatic, but nowhere more obvious than in the field of aviation, especially combat aircraft. At the end of World War I, the most advanced types were still made of wood, fabric, and wire. Twenty years later, they were made of stressed aluminum, which incidentally turned production of that metal into a critical requirement for any country that sought to build military airpower and put it to use. Taking just two examples, the British Sopwith 7F.1 Snipe World War I–era fighter weighed less than one ton, had an engine capable of developing 230 horsepower, could reach a speed of 121 miles, and was armed with two machine guns. In 1939, the supermarine Spitfire Mark I was two and a half times as heavy, had an engine four times as powerful, was almost three times as fast, and carried no fewer than eight machine guns. Other fighters, such as the German Messerschmitt Bf 109, were already being armed with twenty-millimeter cannon.[40]

By this time, any air force that lagged more than a year or two behind the most recent developments found itself in a hopeless situation. Indeed, almost the only thing that can be said in favor of the men of the French air force is that they recognized this. When the time came in the spring of 1940, afraid their aircraft would be shot out of the sky, they took care to disperse them to airfields so far away that they were unable to participate in the battle.[41]

3.4. Civilized Wars

Though World War I saw the Great Powers tear each other to pieces, it failed to diminish their collective dominance over the rest of the world, and after hostilities ended some embers left over from the war were still burning. The Russian Civil War and the Soviet-Polish War together spanned the period 1918–20, and to some extent, the latter was a direct continuation of the former. Early on, the Poles, of whom contemporaries said that *"les Polonnais ont devenues des Napoléons,"* tried to exploit Russia's internal difficulties by advancing into their eastern neighbor's territory. They were thrown back almost to the gates of Warsaw, but, risking everything and launching a daring counterattack against the enemy's rear, they reasserted themselves at the last moment and in the end succeeded in establishing an independent state that reached far into present-day Belarus and Ukraine.

Both armed conflicts were waged almost exclusively on land by fairly large, but also fairly disorganized, armies that in the case of the Russians, had gone through the chaos of revolution, and of the Poles, had to be created almost out of nothing. The most powerful new weapons to emerge from World War I, such as heavy artillery, aircraft, and tanks, saw only extremely limited use; neither was either belligerent nearly up to date in respect to transportation, logistics, and signal communications.

In many ways, these wars were lesser versions of the titanic struggles that had taken place on the Eastern Front in 1914–18. In the broad-open spaces of Russia, the Ukraine, and Poland, old-fashioned cavalry charges were attempted, the riders brandishing their swords or lances and shouting "hurrah," like something straight out of Tolstoy. Both Poles and Cossacks, after all, had long prided themselves on their prowess as horsemen. The consequences became evident in 1939 when the Poles tried to use horses against the German tanks, and also in 1941 when Stalin's choice to defend the Ukraine fell on his Civil War–era crony, the cavalryman Semyon Budenny (who even had a breed of horses named after him). Given such primitive tactics, it did not appear as if there was much for the rest of the world to learn from these conflicts. The Poles, after all, modeled their army after the former Austrian-Hungarian army and partly after the French. The Soviets struck a course for which there was no precedent and precious little guidance. Many of their commanders were jumped-up corporals with little formal training and even less education. They did not carry rank insignia, but came under the control of political officers. No wonder that the Soviet system found few admirers and fewer imitators. Even inside the Soviet Union, Sergei Gusev, head of the political directorate of the Red Army, solemnly warned that the new force, "in the form it has currently taken, is powerless against mighty imperialist armies."[42]

Unfolding simultaneously with the wars in Eastern Europe were the operations of the German Freikorps. The Freikorps were set up by the ministry of defense in order to carry on the war in the parts of Germany that, according to the Treaty of Versailles, were to be transferred to Poland. In size, they were not impressive. The total number of men who participated at one time or another was no more than two hundred thousand; this, against more than ten times as many soldiers who fought in the Red Army alone. In theory the largest Freikorps unit was the brigade, but in practice most were much smaller. Most were ill organized, and heavy, crew-operated weapons were noted chiefly by their absence since the forces rarely possessed what it took to keep them in working order. Still, the Freikorps, perhaps building on the experiences of the Stosstruppen who had broken through the British and French lines in March through July 1918, did set afoot an important innovation. Traditionally, European armies had selected their officers from members of the higher classes, the only ones considered loyal to the sovereign, even to the point that the availability of such personnel did as much to govern the size of the prewar German army as any other factor.[43] In it and other armies, military discipline was enforced from the top down; indeed, the term *Fuehrung* itself referred not so much to leadership as to the conduct of operations at all levels.

Though they themselves were veterans of the old imperial army, the officers who commanded the Freikorps could not operate in the same way. Their troops, instead of being conscripts, were volunteers and stayed with their units only as long as it suited them. Many were rough types who had fought in World War I and found civilian life unattractive; certainly they did not distinguish themselves by following the rules of war. The units operated on a precarious, semi-legal basis, often in lands that had never been part of Germany, such as in the Baltic or else in the provinces that were about to be transferred to Poland under the Treaty of Versailles. Consequently, their commanders had to develop a new form of leadership. It was based less on formal discipline and more on personal influence or, to use that much-abused word, charisma—a fact also reflected in their units' names including Erhardt Brigade, Rossbach Brigade, and the like.[44] It is probably no accident that 1922, the year that saw the dissolution of the Freikorps, also saw the publication of a book that extolled the new style of leadership. Its title was *Der Feldherr Psychologicus* (the psychologist-commander), the author a retired army captain by the name of Dr. Kurt Hesse. The volume quickly turned into a national best seller; here, indeed, were the seeds of the future.

Later, some former Freikorps personnel were taken into the new Reichswehr. Others ended up in the armed formations of the Nazi Party,[45] where they could give free reign to their anti-Semitism and tendency toward rowdiness. The Nazi regime itself proclaimed its adherence to the so-called *Fuehrerprinzip*, leadership principle. At the same time, it was in some ways anti-authoritarian, insisting on the *Volksgemeinschaft*, or people's community, at the expense of the old, class-bound traditions. As noted by the American war correspondent William Shirer in the heady days immediately after the fall of France: "There is a sort of equalitarianism. . . . The German officer no longer represents . . . a class or caste. . . . They fell like members of one great family . . . in cafés, restaurants, dining cars, officers and men off duty sit at the same table and converse as men to men."[46] Thus, paradoxically, the one country that exchanged the strongest authoritarian tradition for one of the most totalitarian regimes also developed a novel, quasi-democratic style of leadership—one that, when combined with "the old Prussian goose step, the heel clicking, the 'Jawohl!' of the private when answering an officer" (Shirer again), was to make its power felt in ways that made the world hold its breath.

As the various peace treaties came into effect, Europe finally calmed down. The next war on the Continent wouldn't begin until 1936, and it was not an international conflict but an internal one fought with some external support. The Spanish Republic was but five years old when Francisco Franco, the youngest general in the Spanish army, led his colonial troops in a revolt against the elected, left-wing government that had just taken power in Madrid. Italian aircraft were sent in and flew some of Franco's advance units from Spanish Africa to the homeland, the first operation of its kind. Franco's hopes for a rapid victory did not materialize, however, and soon enough the two sides were engaged in a massive civil war in which entire Italian and German units, as well as organized and disorganized volunteers from many countries, also participated.

Geographic conditions dictated that the war would be fought not on one front but on several simultaneously. Most of the time, this fact prevented the forces on either side from being used en masse, creating vast gaps that were almost entirely unoccupied. By Great Power standards, the number of troops involved was not very large; nor did Spain, at that time a semi-developed country, have the industrial-logistical infrastructure that modern armed conflict requires. Practically every heavy weapon and motor vehicle, as well as most of the spare parts they required, had to be imported. For these reasons, most operations in Spain could not bear comparison to what occurred in World War I, let alone what actually took place in World War II. Yet the timing of the conflict, and the appearance of weapons from the newly militarized Nazi Germany, meant the war would be intensely studied by the future belligerent nations.

This was particularly true in respect to those twin new instruments of war, armor and airpower, although the attempt to use tanks turned out to be a disaster. On the republican side, coordination between the Russian crews and the Spanish and international infantry they supported proved very difficult. The fact that the crews themselves were insufficiently trained didn't help matters. A proper organization, a proper infrastructure, and a proper doctrine were all lacking.[47] As a result, the Soviet armored forces, instead of being formed into independent units, were reincorporated with the infantry,[48] suffering a setback that was to cost them dearly when the Germans invaded in 1941.

On Franco's side, tanks were operated by the Italians, who would establish here their reputation for battlefield timidity. Air operations were largely conducted by the German Condor Legion with its five thousand men and one hundred aircraft, on the one hand and Soviet aircraft, flown by Soviet volunteers (but not organized as a separate Soviet unit), on the other. On the whole, the Germans, whose aircraft were superior, emerged victorious. Thus the freshly minted Luftwaffe was able to gain experience on almost every kind of mission, from reconnaissance and air-to-air combat to close support and interdiction, and even "strategic" bombardment.[49] Returning home, the personnel were used as instructors to teach what they had learned.

Apart from the use of amphibious operations, the Sino-Japanese War had little of interest to offer the military specialist.[50] While it is true that the Japanese set an example by using their airpower to bomb China's coastal cities, their operations went largely unopposed. The conflict that took place farther north, in Manchuria, was another matter. Throughout the second half of the 1930s, the Japanese leaders had been divided as to the direction in which their country should expand. The generals pressed for Northeast Asia. Opposing them, the admirals preferred to go in the opposite direction: the American-occupied Philippines and the rich colonial possessions of Britain, France, and the Netherlands. In the spring of 1939, it was the generals who, at least for a time, gained the upper hand.

Border clashes between Soviet forces and the Japanese in Manchuria multiplied, culminating in a full-scale battle at Khalkin Gol. The Soviet commander on the spot was a general named Georgy Zhukov. From a shoemaker's apprentice, he had made his way to the top—a feat almost entirely inconceivable in any other army at the time. With seventy thousand men, an armored brigade (which he employed as a concentrated force against the dispersed enemy tanks), and several hundred aircraft, he inflicted a crushing defeat on forty thousand Japanese troops. Tokyo was compelled to abandon its plans in Northeast Asia and redirect its efforts to the south, as the navy had demanded. In April 1941, it even signed a nonaggression treaty with the USSR, ensuring that the latter had its rear covered when the Germans invaded just two months later.[51]

Finally, the last "civilized" conflict, fought even while World War II was gathering steam, was the Russo-Finnish War.[52] It began when Stalin, aware that Hitler would attack him sooner or later and worried about how close Leningrad was to the Finnish border, demanded that the Finns make territorial concessions. When these were refused, he sent in his air force, bombing Helsinki and other targets but failing to get the results that Douhet had predicted and Guernica seemed to prove.

For four months the Finns fought on in the snow, using skis to maneuver and silently surround and eliminate Red Army infantry columns. So effective, incidentally, was the assistance that the Finnish troops received from the Lottas Women's Organization that Hitler later summoned its commander to Berlin and presented her with a medal.[53] Although, in the end, the Finns were forced to surrender, the impression left by the Red Army was of a blunt instrument, incompetently commanded. That impression, in turn, played a role in Hitler's decision to invade the USSR a little more than a year after the so-called Winter War had ended.

Compared with what had taken place in 1914–18 and what was about to take place in 1939–45, the "civilized" wars during the twenty years' truce were neither large nor militarily significant, though this was scant consolation to masses of people who suffered through them. Only in the case of Khalkin Gol did two Great Powers fight each other, and they did so while committing only a small part of their main forces, operating at the end of extremely long lines of communication far from the centers of national power. It therefore required uncommon foresight to realize that, out of the small and fragmented operations of the Freikorps, a new and revolutionary style of military leadership would be born. And whereas the Spanish Civil War provided the Germans in particular with many valuable lessons concerning the conduct of air operations in particular, the importance of Khalkin Gol was overlooked by the rest of the world—which came to judge the Red Army only by its poor performance in the war against Finland—and by the Soviets themselves. When the time to fight the Germans came, they were not ready.

3.5. Uncivilized Wars

Throughout the period in question, armed forces everywhere continued to draw a very clear line between "civilized" warfare, which by definition was waged by the powers of Eurasia, and that which took place in other parts of the world. Employing huge forces of conscripts (in the end, few people accepted the theories of men like Douhet, Fuller, and de Gaulle, who extolled the advent of small numbers of technologically minded elite warriors[54]), Western, and Western-like militaries deployed the most powerful weapons available, which implied the existence of a well-developed infrastructure capable of sustaining a never-ending flow of supplies. By contrast, in Asia, Africa, and Latin America (which, in 1935, witnessed the devastating Chaco War), even where the manpower was available, the organization and ability to raise large forces did not exist. In terms of weaponry, it was taken for granted that they would go to war, if they went to war, with whatever obsolete arms could be scavenged from the Great Powers, as well as such second-rate weapons as they themselves were capable of producing.

By 1918, Europe, and, to a lesser extent, its American offspring, already had several centuries of colonial warfare experience behind them. Distance and the limitations of maritime transport—until 1870 or so even the largest colonial expeditions depended on sailing ships to reach their destinations—dictated that the numbers of personnel involved were small. Having reached their destinations, invariably their first step was to set up fortified bases (originally known as "factories"), before plunging into unknown, often hostile territory. Nowadays it is fashionable to present the members of European colonial expeditions from Hernándo Cortéz down as rapacious adventurers, mass murderers, and plunderers. All of this is true. However, we should also remember that these were men—there were hardly any women among them—of incredible courage, determination, stamina, and resourcefulness. Not an obstacle they did not cross; not an expedition too dangerous for them to undertake. It was these qualities, as much as technological superiority, that enabled them to subdue populations and made possible the creation of the empires over which their countries ruled.

The best-known colonial war of the period under consideration was, of course, the Italian conquest of Ethiopia—at the time, it was usually known as Abyssinia—in 1935–36. Ethiopia was one of the very few African countries that had succeeded in maintaining its independence in the face of European colonialism, its emperor in 1896 having managed to defeat an Italian expeditionary force sent against him. Now Mussolini resumed the conflict.

This, however, looked nothing like the typical nineteenth-century colonial campaign waged by a small group of adventurers or by a regiment or two of redcoats. Where Francisco Pizarro and two hundred men took on the Inca Empire with its estimated population of sixteen million, the Italians used no fewer than a third of a million men, complete with artillery, light tanks, aircraft, and gas. Ethiopian emperor Haile Selassie, to his credit, was able to raise about a hundred thousand men, although in matters of organization, training, and equipment his warriors, many of whom went barefoot, could not compete. Combining offensives from the north and the south, the Italian forces converged in April 1936 at Lake Ashangi, where they inflicted a crushing defeat on the Ethiopian levies. From that point on, it was merely a question of mopping up.

Thus the Italian occupation of Ethiopia is best understood as a conventional campaign that pitted one army against another, albeit it was waged not in Europe but in Africa, against exceptionally light opposition, and at the hand of generals such as Pietro Badoglio and Rodolfo Graziani who, faced with real enemies in World War II, were to prove themselves incompetent and even cowardly. As a colonial exercise the Ethiopian campaign differed from the experience of other European countries, which, having long ago smashed any native armies, focused on the very different task of putting down a rebellion.

By this time, most would-be rebels had learned their lesson. Rarely did they fight in large units or in the open, that being a course of action for which they had neither the organization, nor the training, nor the weapons. Instead, they focused on more or less covert action in the form of ambushes, hit-and-run raids against personnel and property, and what a later generation was to call terrorism. In the years immediately after 1918, both the British in Iraq and the French in Morocco, were facing this peculiar form of warfare.

Of the two, Iraq ultimately proved easier to deal with. Summoned by civilian advisers who knew the area well, British armored cars roamed Mesopotamia shooting up any opposition they came across, a feat made possible by the fact that light, handheld anti-tank weapons in the form of bazookas and RPGs had not yet made their appearance. British military aircraft assisted, dropping bombs and machine-gunning villages suspected of harboring insurgents. As contemporaries realized full well, the main effect of their operations was on the rebels' morale, and in fact the number of casualties was very low.[55] What the oft-repeated air patrols really did was not so much inflict death and destruction as disrupt daily life sufficiently to convince the village elders that opposition had to cease. The outcome enabled advocates of air-power to convince themselves, and their political masters, that they had found a new, cheap, and easy way of policing a country. It would not be the last time such a conclusion was reached.

By contrast, the Riff uprising in Morocco proved a much tougher nut to crack. France's original occupation of the country dated to 1906 when the other Great Powers gave Paris permission to go ahead. In the event, occupying and holding the main towns proved to be one thing; doing the same in the remote, mountainous, practically roadless interior, quite a different matter.

What we today would call counterinsurgency operations began almost immediately and went on practically without interruption until the end of the First World War. Although such operations achieved little—and indeed, from 1920 on much of the country was in a state of open revolt—it was also true that the rebels' greatest victories were won not against the French but in the Spanish-occupied part of the country. At Annual in May 1921 the Riff tribesmen, emerging into the open, actually succeeded in trapping nineteen thousand Spanish troops—out of a total of sixty-three thousand—killing many of them, their commander included. This Spanish Adowa was followed by another rebel victory at Sheshuan, which effectively put an end to Spanish rule there.

The leader behind these successes was a university-educated former Spanish colonial civil servant and writer by the name of Abd el

Krim. In 1923, he proclaimed an independent republic and tried to win international recognition by introducing legal reforms on the one hand and offering mining concessions on the other. Having failed to get what he wanted, he sent his warriors into the northern parts of French-occupied Morocco, where they engaged in hit-and-run guerrilla warfare. In the end it took more than a quarter million Spanish and French troops—the latter commanded by no less a figure than Philippe Pétain, the man who had stopped the Germans at Verdun—four years to finally suppress the uprising. Abd el Krim himself surrendered and was sent into exile.

Even so, it was not until 1934 that the country could really be called pacified. This was not a gentle struggle—as is made sufficiently evident by the fact that a key role was played by their respective foreign legions (the Spanish legion having been created especially for the occasion). Contemporaries felt that the war was "probably the first in history when relatively large numbers of highly mechanized troops succeeded in crushing a strong defense in depth with a few powerful blows."[56] With the benefit of hindsight, it would be more appropriate to say that, for the first time, "relatively larger numbers of highly mechanized troops" had come into contact with guerrillas and, despite their crushing superiority in everything from boots to cannon, aircraft, and radio communications, took many years to defeat them.

The last colonial war that should be discussed in this context was the one waged by the Palestinian Arabs against the British and their Jewish protégés in 1936–39. Unlike Morocco, Palestine is a very small place, and whereas Abd el Krim was able to convince entire populations to join his revolt, in Palestine the number of insurgents was quite small, probably never exceeding more than a few thousand at any one time. Despite all this, the leaderless (the only Palestinian leader with any pretensions to national status, Haj Amin el Husseini, was captured by the British, escaped, and left the country), ill-organized, ill-trained, and ill-equipped bands kept the British at bay for three years. By the end of that period, the number of British troops had gone up from a few hundred to no fewer than twenty thousand; they were armed with many kinds of modern weapons, from armored cars to aircraft. After five thousand Palestinian Arabs had been killed, thousands of homes destroyed, and the Palestinian Arab economy left in ruins, it was still only when the British promised the Palestinian Arabs "evolution towards independence within ten years" (plus an end to Jewish immigration, plus an end to land purchasing by Jews) that the revolt finally died down.

Seen from the point of view of the Great Powers of the time, busy as they were squabbling and preparing for another major war with one another, none of these uprisings was considered terribly important and this was reflected in the quantity of troops, and quality of weapons used to subdue and suppress. Whether by military or political means, every single uprising was brought to an end. Yet a comparison with previous periods shows that the going was getting tougher, and underneath the surface, important shifts were taking place.[57]

3.6. The Unraveling of Peace

By the late 1930s, the twenty years' truce was clearly unraveling. In 1938 the country with the largest "defense" budget was Germany ($7,415 million, in current dollars), followed by the USSR ($5,429 million), Britain ($1,863 million), Japan ($1,740 million), the United States ($1,131 million), and France ($919 million). Italy, for all of Mussolini's ceaseless boasts, only spent $746 million.

Perhaps a truer index of the powers' relative war-making potential is provided by their production of steel, which from the second half of the nineteenth century had been the most important "strategic" raw material of all. Here the figures were 28.8 million tons for the United States; 23.2 for Germany; 18 for the USSR; 10.5 for Britain; 7 for Japan; 6.1 for France; and 2.3 for Italy. Consuming the equivalent of 697 million tons of coal each year, the United States also led the world by a wide margin, and was only distantly followed by Germany (228 million tons), Britain (196), the USSR (177), Japan (96.5), and France (84).[58] With no more than the equivalent of 27.8 million tons Italy, once again, was at the bottom of the list.

Just as in the years before 1914, the most dangerous state of all was again Germany, and not just because it had recovered militarily, but also because it was openly committed to aggression and territorial expansion. Ever since he wrote *Mein Kampf* in 1924, Hitler's ultimate goal had been, in his own words, "to acquire new territories in Europe . . . mainly at Russia's cost."[59] Certainly this was not a goal he could achieve in a single leap, and certainly there were many twists and turns on the way. He probably hoped to do as much as possible without bloodshed, as was proved by his occupation of Czechoslovakia in the spring of 1939, although, he did inform his minions that further bloodless victories were impossible. Indeed, it was with this objective in mind that he rearmed Germany until the ground forces, at least, had become the most powerful war-making machine anywhere. This of course hints that Germany's power was as unbalanced as the man who championed it. And so Germany enjoyed an advantage that was much greater on land than at sea and in the air; was still inexperienced in modern warfare; and, having expanded at breakneck speed, German forces were still somewhat disorganized and needed at least one relatively small campaign (against Poland) before they really hit their stride.[60]

Stalin's foreign policy during those years presents something of a riddle. From the mid-1930s on, the USSR often talked about the need to set up a "collective security front" with the remaining European powers to resist Hitler's growing power. This was clearly not to the liking of at least some Western capitalist circles, who would have much preferred to see the two totalitarian states kill each other. In September 1938, France and Britain did not even invite the USSR to the Munich Conference.

In the spring of 1939, more or less serious talks for establishing an alliance with Britain and France finally got under way, but as the Western powers procrastinated, Stalin performed an about-face and signed a nonaggression pact with Hitler instead. The next two years saw the USSR invade first Poland, then Finland, and finally Romania and the Baltic states, either swallowing them alive or tearing off pieces of them. Yet whether it is true, as has been claimed,[61] that Stalin in 1941 was planning to launch a full-scale military attack on Germany and was only forestalled by Hitler at the last moment remains moot.

By the late 1930s, the Red Army had once again become the largest in the world by far, but in terms of quality it continued to lag behind. In the early 1930s, Soviet ideas concerning armored and airborne operations were as advanced as any, but the country's primitive technical capabilities left many of these ideas stillborn. Worse still, in 1937–38 its officer corps was decapitated by Stalin, with the result that remaining commanders tended to be young and inexperienced.

In both training and general education, Soviet officers (except at the very top) and conscripts could not even remotely compete with their future German opponents. The cultural gap between officers and enlisted personnel that had existed in the tsar's army persisted, and a corps of professional NCOs who might have helped bridge the gap did not exist. As a result, this army of workers and peasants relied on truly draconian methods of discipline. Zhukov dealt with troublesome subordinates by telling them to step down in favor of their deputies and shoot themselves. In 1941–45, the Soviets probably executed a larger number of their own troops than did all other belligerents combined; and considering that one of those belligerents was led by Hitler, that was no small feat. Finally, and perhaps most fatal of all, because the Red Army was totally committed to the offensive, it found itself nearly helpless when it was in fact attacked first. •

On Germany's other side, France was now in full decline. Though its army remained large, neither its population nor its economy kept up with those of the other powers, and in terms of the leading economic indicators it had already fallen behind Japan. As a result, its foreign policy was reduced to trying to cement its alliance with Britain while desperately clinging to its former greatness. This approach was symbolized by the Maginot Line, even though the original idea behind the line had been to use it not simply as a defensive shield but in order to permit the rest of the French army to advance into Belgium.

Along with the British, the French armed forces probably changed least from the World War I era. France held on to the same old generals—in May 1939, General Weygand, who was later to be recalled from retirement to try to prevent defeat, said he could not praise those generals highly enough[62]—the same old doctrine, and, in some cases, the same old weapons. This provided little basis for fighting the most powerful, most innovative, most dynamic, and, in some ways, most highly motivated army in the world. When the time came, even the Germans themselves were surprised by the extent of the victories they had won.[63]

Superficially, the British were in a better position. Like France, Britain had long become a status quo power with a strong pacifist wing. Unlike France, it had the channel between itself and the Germans, and unlike France, when the time came its people stood up and fought. As before, Britain continued to control the world's chief sea-lanes, an inestimable advantage, yet perversely this control proved a weakness as well. Without dominion of the sea, Britain would have to surrender within weeks or months. Yet in 1939 British resources were clearly overstretched; having lost alliances with Italy and Japan, the empire had to defend itself on no fewer than three fronts, the home islands, the Mediterranean, and the Far East. The one power that could have addressed the balance, the United States, remained stubbornly neutral. When the time came, the British wisely decided to concentrate most of their available resources in the first of these theaters. This led to the neglect, and eventual loss, of the Far East during the war, and the Middle East almost immediately after the war had ended.

As the war approached, both the British navy and air force, each in its own way, were probably as efficient as any in the world. This was much less true of the army even though, this time around, conscription had been introduced shortly before hostilities began. US forces apart, only the British army had enough trucks to equip all units and did not have to depend on horses for transport. Nevertheless, as events were to show, especially in point of armored operations, it had much to learn.

In battle, British armored forces never attained the fluidity modern warfare requires—as illustrated, for example, by General Montgomery's failure to destroy Rommel's hopelessly outnumbered, logistically overstretched Panzerarmee after the battle of Alamein. Much was due to the prevailing social system. Strict class distinctions separated officers from everybody else. And for every young, innovative commander there were several Colonel Blimps. After listening to a report on the wreckage left after the escape from Dunkirk, the German chief of the army general staff, General Franz Halder, would say of the British: "Equipment, wonderful; leadership, as bad as bad can be."

On the eve of World War II, Japan was already involved in a bloody conflict with China. The Japanese armed forces were noted for fanatical morale, aggressive behavior, excellent training, and ability to operate in terrain others considered impossible. Their amphibious doctrine led the world, and up until Pearl Harbor much of their equipment, including carriers, fighter aircraft, and torpedoes, was second to none. Yet Japan lacked the industrial infrastructure for taking on a giant such as the United States; nor did it have the necessary research and development facilities to sustain the technical advantages. Many Japanese aircraft in particular were based on foreign designs, whether American or

German, and as hostilities went on and access to foreign technology was lost, the Japanese fell behind both in aviation and, even more critically, electronics, especially radar.

The situation of the United States was exactly the opposite. Having withdrawn into neutrality, in the late 1930s America's main foreign policy concern was to obstruct Japanese expansion wherever possible. Beginning in 1941, Washington also extended badly needed help to Britain. Psychologically, whereas Japan saw itself threatened and hemmed in, the United States felt completely safe against attack. As former president Herbert Hoover once put it: "On this imperfect earth, three thousand miles of the Atlantic and six thousand of the Pacific are as good a defense as any country could hope for."[64] And although the US Navy was now the largest in the world, the army ranked only eighteenth. However, the US war-fighting advantage really was in a gigantic industrial base that would back the forces and expand them quickly if necessary. Technologically, too, the Americans were to prove capable of pulling ahead not only of the Japanese but of all others as well.

Italy remained what it had long been, a small, weak state securely locked in its Mediterranean prison. To break out was Mussolini's greatest wish, but he never had the resources for doing so.[65] Much equipment was antiquated, but far worse was the fighting morale, which was notoriously low. Nor, as hostilities continued, was the country able to keep up in terms of either the quantity or quality of arms produced. As in World War I, Italy was to prove a liability to its allies, who had to provide it with food, fuel, and raw materials.

In 1939, the last year of peace, both Europe and the Far East had once again become armed camps. Only the United States remained aloof, more or less. To be sure, the twenty years' truce also had its fair share of pacifist movements. They were joined by communist parties that were in principle opposed to war (except as waged on behalf of the fatherland of all workers), arms-limitation conferences, and even disarmament conferences. Many of those who participated, were no doubt motivated by the best intentions. One recalls, for example, the Einstein–Freud correspondence of 1931–32. In it, the former asked "why war"; the latter did what he could to give an honest answer that would nevertheless not be so pessimistic as to be altogether useless. Still, in the face of the prevailing international climate and despite the

"International Kiss" presented by the 1928 Kellogg-Briand Pact for avoiding war, the impact of attempts to prevent, or abolish, or limit, war was probably even smaller than ever before. When the conflict everybody had expected did break out, it was received with resignation, no joyful demonstrations held in the streets this time.

World War II, 1939–45

4.1. The Blitzkrieg Era

Looking back, the German victories in World War II probably peaked on October 16, 1941, the day on which the Wehrmacht seemed poised to enter Moscow. The city was seized by panic. According to official figures, two million people had been evacuated or had fled. Soviet officials and foreign embassies destroyed documents as they prepared to leave. As discipline broke down and looting got under way, the British embassy was pillaged.[1] On this day, field-gray German troops stood guard in places as far apart as southwestern France, Norway, and Egypt, where Erwin Rommel's Afrika Korps had reached Sollum a few months earlier. With the exception of Sweden, Switzerland, Spain, Portugal, and Ireland, the whole of Europe was either under the German boot or else had allied itself with Berlin more or less of its own accord.

Looking back, the really surprising thing is how easy it had all been. In the 1930s, during the period of rearmament, many of Germany's top military commanders had been afraid of war. Having neglected to take economic considerations into account before 1914, they now regarded their country as insufficiently prepared, and believed the experience of World War I might repeat itself. But by the spring of 1938 the Fuehrer had rid himself of the most influential naysayer, Chief of the Army General Staff General Ludwig Beck, and, by inserting another command echelon, the Oberkommando der Wehrmacht (OKW), between Beck's successor and himself, he ensured that the army's power to influence policy would be diminished. Still, the Anglo-French declaration of war on September 3, 1939, rattled Hitler and for a time left him speechless and unsure as to what he might do next.

Once it became clear that France and England would not attack in the west but stay on the defensive, Poland's fate was sealed. Geographically, Poland was surrounded by Germany on three sides—west, north, and south—and only a few days after the German offensive began the USSR attacked from the east, the result of the German-Soviet nonaggression pact signed just a week before the war began. Beaten in the air—most Polish aircraft were destroyed on the ground, and the rest did not prove a match for the Luftwaffe—and outnumbered and outqualified on the ground, Poles saw the end come after a mere seventeen days. The next eight months proved an anticlimax. Having started the war only a few years after the beginning of rearmament, the Germans were not satisfied with their forces' performance and spent the time reorganizing and retraining.

By contrast, the British and the French did absolutely nothing. The outbreak of war caught the British army in turmoil as conscription was reintroduced. As in 1914, a small expeditionary force was sent to the channel ports and took up positions on the French left flank. As in 1915, plans were created to carry out wide-ranging strategic sweeps so as to avoid the need to meet the full power of the German army in its fortified positions. One plan was to attack Romania, from which the Germans derived most of their oil, but since the necessary air bases were unavailable nothing came of it. Another was to assist Finland, which was fighting for its life against the Soviet Union, and cut off the supply of German nickel in the process. In the end, the Allied plan that came closest to realization was an invasion of Norway aimed at the same objective: cutting off the supply of Finnish nickel that reached Germany by way of Narvik.

German planning in some ways was a mirror image of these schemes, and plans for an invasion of Norway, with the objective of securing the supply of nickel as well as providing the navy with additional submarine bases for operations in the North Atlantic, began to be hatched as early as October 1939. Given the geographic background, as well as the balance of forces, the occupation of Denmark, which began and ended on the same day, April 9, 1940, presented few difficulties. Taking Norway was a different matter, involving the transport of forces across the sea in the face of the much more powerful British navy. Norway's capital city, Oslo, was relatively close at hand, so that the ships destined for it could be given air cover. However, the remaining objectives were not only much farther away, but actually nearer the British bases in Scotland and the Orkneys than to German bases in the North Sea. Finally, in order to preserve surprise, all had to be captured at once, which in turn meant that the German naval forces, weak to begin with, would have to be dispersed.

After much argument it was decided to load the troops aboard warships—which did not thereby gain in efficiency—and make landings in approximately regimental strength at Oslo, Kristiansand, Bergen, Trondheim, and Narvik. Smaller forces went ashore at Egersund and Arendal, where they seized the cable cars. Stavanger was to be taken by airborne troops. So unprepared were the Germans for mounting the invasion that the initial planning was based on Norwegian tourist guides.

In the event, the hair-raising plan worked. At the cost of 1,317 dead, 1,604 wounded and 2,275 lost at sea, the Germans achieved all their objectives, although these figures reflected the considerable resistance they met. The Norwegian defenders in the entrance to Oslo harbor launched a torpedo that took down a heavy cruiser, the *Bluecher*. More German troops were lost near Narvik, where no fewer than ten German destroyers were sunk. So costly was the operation to the Kriegsmarine that by the end of June 1940, Germany only had one heavy cruiser, two light cruisers, and four destroyers fit for action. Resistance on land proved much lighter mainly because the Norwegian chief of staff resigned his post on the day the invasion started. Oslo itself was occupied by a battalion of airborne troops that had landed in the airport and marched into the town while accompanied by a band. The only really serious fighting occurred at Narvik in the far north, where the Allies were able to carry out an amphibious landing, and where the German troops at one point thought they might have to retreat into Sweden and be interned. In the end, the Germans were able to hold out until help arrived from the south.

Despite the losses, Norway was merely a sideshow. Some German commanders even thought the campaign should have been postponed until victory over France had consolidated Germany's hold on the Continent.[2] Even as events were unfolding in the north, 135 German divisions, now freed from their commitment in Poland, were directed toward the west. The corresponding figure on the Allied side (combining Dutch, Belgian, French, and British forces) was 151 divisions. Thus, qualitatively the Allied ground forces were roughly equal to their German counterparts, and in terms of numbers they were certainly a match. Why the Allied forces were not able to counter the German onslaught has become one of the great mysteries of military history, and one about which vast amounts of ink have been spilled.

The original German plan was essentially a repetition of the 1914 Schlieffen Plan, although this time around the Netherlands would be included in the invasion so as to reach the North Sea and acquire bases from which the Luftwaffe could fight Britain. The original Allied plan was to advance into Belgium from the southwest, meeting the Germans head-on, thus denying the Wehrmacht the opportunity of outflanking them as it had tried to do in 1914. However, in the winter of 1939–40, after a complicated series of debates among the most important German commanders, including Hitler himself, the decision was made to move the *Schwerpunkt,* center of gravity, from the right flank of the front to its center. Rushing into Belgium, the Allies would be taken in the flank and rear by German forces coming from the Ardennes, long considered impassable for large motorized formations. As Schlieffen himself had once written, for a great victory (what he called a "Cannae") to take place, it was necessary for the commanders on both sides to cooperate, each in his own way. In the event, that was just what happened.

The sector of the front that the Germans attacked on May 10, 1940, was weakly held by second-rate troops whose nerves shattered under the impact of screaming German dive-bombers. The French high command, saddled by a completely inadequate communications network, was unable to react to the German movements in time. So bad were things in this respect that, later in the campaign, the freshly appointed commander in chief, General Maxime Weygand (the same who had praised French generalship to a British audience a year earlier), had only a single telephone apparatus to transmit his orders, and the female secretary responsible for it insisted on going out for lunch every day between 1200 and 1400.[3]

Worst of all was the performance of the French air force, which not only deployed its aircraft well to the rear, but got off only a quarter as many sorties per day as its German opponent. Nothing is more characteristic of its operations than the fact that, when the campaign ended, the Armée de l'Air actually had more serviceable aircraft than at the beginning of hostilities.

As brilliantly as all this was progressing, and despite his boast—in a letter to Mussolini describing the Norwegian campaign⁴—that fortune always favors the bold, Hitler rebuked his generals for their reckless daring and insisted that the armored divisions stay in place for days on end until the infantry could catch up and secure their communications. Therefore, whatever setbacks the Germans suffered were self-inflicted. Indeed, Hitler's "halt" order made the evacuation of the British expeditionary force from Dunkirk possible, which people spoke of as a "miracle."

The German victory over France set the stage for invading the USSR, Hitler's ultimate goal. At one point, the Fuehrer considered launching the operation in the autumn of the same year as the invasion of France, but saner counsels prevailed. Meanwhile, since Britain still refused to come to terms, the Germans were forced to prepare for a sea and air campaign in the hope of defeating it by these means.

It wasn't until February 1941 that German ground forces went into action again. Two divisions under the leadership of Erwin Rommel were sent to help the Italians shore up their defenses against the British in Libya. A month after his arrival, Rommel defied his orders, rushing forward across Cyrenaica and into Egypt. It was only when his supply columns could no longer keep up that he was forced to halt. He was still there in November 1941, when the British counterattacked and forced him to retreat.

While these events were taking place, the Germans were also preparing to invade Greece, which the Italians had tried to do in October 1940. When that campaign began going wrong, which it did within a few days, Hitler was forced to intervene lest the British, who were already assisting Greece, gain air bases in the country to be used to bomb the Romanian oil fields on which Germany depended.

Throughout the winter and early spring of 1941, German forces moved across Hungary into Romania and from there into Bulgaria. They were just about ready to start operations when, on March 27, a coup took over in Belgrade, bringing to power a government that was unfriendly to Germany and threatening Germany's Balkan right flank. Only a masterpiece of improvisation enabled the Germans to react rapidly, redeploying their forces and bringing up eleven divisions in addition to the eighteen already in the theater of operations. In just three weeks, German troops had occupied Yugoslavia and the swastika flag was raised at the southern tip of the Peloponnesus. This, in turn, was soon followed by the successful, if costly, airborne assault against Crete. No wonder that Hitler, speaking to the Reichstag on May 4, 1941 and looking back on a year of unprecedented victories, told his listeners that to the German soldier, nothing was impossible.[5]

The greatest challenge of all, though, was still to come. Until November 1940, Hitler, and even more so his foreign minister Joachim von Ribbentrop, had hesitated as to whether Germany should attack the USSR or try to form an alliance. After talks with Soviet foreign minister Vyacheslav Molotov failed, the decision to launch the offensive was made in December. Preparations, such as preparing bases and bringing up forces, went on throughout the following winter and spring; the number of trains used, seventeen thousand in all, speaks for itself. The German offensive would safely be the largest ever. No less than 144 divisions (out of a total of 200 or so) divided among three separate army groups—one for Leningrad, one for Moscow, and one for the Ukraine—stood ready. Three and a half million troops, thirty-five hundred tanks, and six hundred thousand vehicles (most of which were horse-drawn) would ride or march into the history books.

On June 22, 1941, Operation Barbarossa opened with a devastating attack against Soviet airfields, destroying some eight thousand aircraft. In a matter of hours, the Germans had command of the air. Faithful to its now well-developed Blitzkrieg doctrine, the Luftwaffe pressed on, interdicting Red Army communications and providing close support for the Wehrmacht's ground troops. "Strategic" attacks were made on armaments factories in Moscow and warships in Kronstadt and Leningrad. Russian frontier defenses, having been breached by infantry and artillery, were now open to the armored divisions.

Initially, progress was even more rapid than it had been against France, what with Army Group North reaching the outskirts of Leningrad by July 10. Its neighbor to the right, Army Group Center, entered Smolensk, four hundred miles away from the starting line on the River Bug, only three weeks after the beginning of the campaign, setting a record that not even the Americans advancing to Baghdad in 2003 could match. As in France, a deadly combination of surprise, mediocre organization and training, and technical backwardness contributed to Russia's dire situation.

And yet, again compared with France in the previous year, there were also important differences. Although the size of the Soviet Union dictated heavy reliance on the railways, those that were captured were broad-gauged and had to be converted in order to be compatible with German rolling stock. Also, since there were hardly any paved roads, progress was often slowed or stopped by the weather, and consumption of fuel and spare parts far exceeded expectations. It is true that the skill of Soviet commanders could not match their German counterparts at this stage. Still, their men fought stubbornly, especially on the defense and especially when provided with suitable terrain such as swamps and forests which favored the defenders. All translated into very heavy German casualties, which by the end of 1941 had amounted to eight hundred thousand, far more than in all previous German campaigns combined.

By the middle of August 1941, the Germans, finding their forces dispersed in an ever-expanding Russian countryside, were unsure what to do next. Hitler's decision to besiege Leningrad rather than try to capture it did not, apparently, lead to much argument. Things were different at the center of the front. There, Hitler had his eye on the Ukraine, where he hoped to obtain wheat, coal, and, at a later stage, oil—without which, he said, he could not continue the war. By contrast, the army general staff would have preferred a direct advance on Russia's capital, Moscow. The city was an important manufacturing and transportation center; besides, it was the only objective the Soviets could not abandon and where they could therefore be brought to battle and defeated.[6] However, Army Group Center was suffering from severe supply difficulties,[7] and, adopting such a plan would have meant missing a magnificent opportunity to trap the Soviet forces in the Ukraine. Hitler's will having prevailed, the German advance into the Ukraine proved a huge success, and no fewer than 650,000 Red Army troops were captured.

Twenty German armored and motorized divisions, plus about forty infantry divisions with their horse-drawn equipment, now converged on Moscow from the north, west, and south, although many of the units had been attrited to the point that they were divisions in name only. Lines of communication were lengthening, and the autumn rains were turning the roads into seas of mud, leaving small parties of men—their vehicles stuck miles behind—desperately trying to make their way on foot.

The onset of winter and frost witnessed a stiffening of Soviet resistance, whereas bad weather prevented the Luftwaffe from making its impact felt. At Bryansk and Vyazma, the Germans were still able to register a final triumph, fighting twin encirclement battles, capturing almost as many prisoners as in the Ukraine, and coming almost within sight of the Kremlin. There they were met by the victor of Khalkin Gol, Zhukov, who was now in charge of the Western Front. Armed with intelligence that Japan had no plans for attacking, Zhukov was able to amass fresh forces from Siberia and counterattack. On December 8, Hitler declared the offensive suspended.

With the setback in front of Moscow, the Blitzkrieg era ended. For two years, the "Lightning War" was the foundation of a series of brilliant campaigns, leading to numerous spectacular victories and leaving an almost legendary reputation. Still, most of its achievements were due as much to the weakness and incompetence of Germany's enemies as to the Wehrmacht's own prowess. Given their quantitative and qualitative superiority, the fact that German troops were able to overrun Poland, Denmark, Norway, the Netherlands, Belgium, and Luxembourg is not surprising—although, had the British been more enterprising, the occupation of Norway at any rate might have been prevented. In Greece and Yugoslavia, both very weak militarily, the same was also true; in both cases the terrain did as much to obstruct the German advance as the defenders. France was the real surprise, and given the balance of forces, its collapse can only be seen as astonishing.

4.2. Global War

As in the First World War, the German bid to win by means of a mighty land offensive against neighboring countries had failed, causing operations to expand until they, even more than in 1914–18, assumed truly global dimensions.

Though the Anglo-German agreement of 1936 had all but ended the limits imposed by the Treaty of Versailles, the remaining three years before Germany's first offensive did not provide enough time for that country to create a strong navy, which would only be truly ready by 1943–45. Compared with the British, the outbreak of war saw the German navy much weaker than it had been twenty-five years previously, with, the early, heavy losses suffered during the Norwegian campaign further clipping its wings. Apart from the fact that resources were limited, the state of the Kriegsmarine may have had something to do with Hitler's own tastes; as he once put it, "On land I am a hero, at sea, a coward."[8]

Because the Royal Navy presented a formidable obstacle to any German attempt to wage surface naval warfare, and indeed almost all attempts to do so—whether by warship or by commerce raiders—ended in failure, Germany's only hope of gaining some influence over the seas was through its submarines. The construction of U-boat bases in the Netherlands, Belgium, and France now placed Germany in a much better position to break into the Atlantic and blockade Britain. This was all the more so because the Irish Free State remained neutral, depriving the British of useful bases there. Still, the German submarine arm was much too small to exploit its new bases to the full; it also needed time to set up the necessary material and organizational infrastructure. Hence, during the next few months, the fate of the war would be played out in a great air battle, the battle of Britain.

In July 1940, the Luftwaffe in the West had some twenty-eight hundred aircraft, the opposing Royal Air Force about half as many. Technically, the two sides were very closely matched; there were, however, important differences in emphasis. Having been organized for attacks against civilian centers deep in enemy territory, the RAF had relatively few fighters, though those it did have were excellent. Having been organized for close support and interdiction, the Luftwaffe had relatively more of them. In August, as the Germans went on the offensive and the British tried to defend themselves, each side found that the majority of its aircraft were not really suitable for the task at hand. However, single-engined fighters were easier and cheaper to produce and man than twin-engined bombers with their normal crews of three; as time went on, this was an important factor in causing the numerical balance to shift. Planning to attack, Luftwaffe technical development had focused on navigation aids so as to help its pilots locate their targets in bad weather and at night. Planning to defend, the RAF had focused on radar as a means to identifying approaching aircraft, tracking them, and guiding its own fighters to intercept.

The Germans' initial objective was to gain air superiority, which implied that their attacks should be directed primarily against radar stations and airfields. Had they persisted, they might very well have broken the RAF's backbone, which in turn might have opened the way to a seaborne invasion they were planning. In the event, the Germans, in response to a British attack on Berlin, changed targets and mounted a massive raid on London on September 7. Apparently, the Berlin attack had been ordered by Churchill with just that purpose in mind.[9]

With the pressure now off of Fighter Command, and industry now turning out fighters like matchsticks, Britain began to recover and strengthen. By contrast, the German fighters were operating at the limit of their range and had difficulty protecting their bombers. The result was that losses mounted to the point where they could no longer be replaced. Though Britain's cities suffered terribly—by the spring of 1941, thirty thousand people had been killed—in the end, the Luftwaffe simply did not have the weight of sustained firepower needed to break Britain's economy, let alone break its morale. In May, with preparations for the invasion of the Soviet Union entering their final stages, the Germans were forced to end their blitz.

Once again, the German submarine arm was left as the sole means that might have brought the war to an end. Once again, the most important task facing the British was to protect transatlantic trade by preventing German submarines from reaching them, a task made much harder by Germany's control of much of the Continent. Once again, merchantmen were grouped into convoys—this time it did not take the admiralty long to order the necessary measures into effect—that were escorted by light warships and covered from the air by aircraft (ultimately, they came under a command especially established for the purpose) based either on land or at sea. Sonar was now fully developed and played a key role. So did depth charges.

On the other side, German tactics had evolved from those used in the previous conflict.[10] Individual U-boats were spread across the most likely trade routes, waiting for prey. When they encountered a convoy, instead of attacking immediately, they used radio to report its position, course, and speed to central headquarters, which would direct additional U-boats to the target area. Only when sufficient forces were in place would Admiral Doenitz and his staff relinquish control, permitting individual commanders to attack as they thought best. In this way, centralized control arid flexible, "swarming" tactics were combined. Torpedoes, launched in far greater number than individual submarines could carry, did the rest.

As in the last war, however, the Germans began with so few submarines that, throughout 1940, they could never maintain more than twelve to fifteen on station at any given time. Also, another great weakness that reappeared was the virtual absence of air reconnaissance to locate targets. In large part, this was because Hermann Goering did not permit a separate naval air arm to be established, so although German submariners had worked out a relationship between their own arm and airpower from the 1920s on, by the time hostilities began Germany possessed not a single operational aircraft carrier. The handful of aircraft, using French and Norwegian bases, had the range to fly all around the British islands. The outcome was that, over most of the Atlantic and aside from the interception and decryption of radio messages, almost the only way to locate a target was by means of visual identification by the submariners themselves.

These problems were compounded by the fact that submarine operations depended on radio transmissions that, even if they could not be decrypted, could be tracked back to their place of origin by means of HF/DF (high-frequency direction finding). Some naval historians consider this factor the most important in deciding the outcome of the entire naval campaign;[11] yet as time passed the Germans, by compressing their transmissions into very brief bursts, found a means to counter or at least mitigate its effects.

Finally, and again as in 1914–18, submarine warfare played a major role in bringing the United States into the conflict as President Franklin D. Roosevelt, starting in the summer of 1941, increasingly used his country's navy to escort convoys and defend them.

As the number of operational submarines increased, the periods of the greatest German successes were the spring of 1942 and that of 1943; then, however, things changed. Submarines had to spend much of their time on the surface in order to recharge their batteries, and also because surface sailing was faster. The introduction of centimetric radar (apparatus operating at wavelengths of less than ten centimeters) enabled escorting ships and aircraft to spot surfaced submarines from afar, even at night and in bad weather. The Germans reacted by developing paint that absorbed some of the radar waves as well as apparatus that warned submarines they were being targeted; when these measures proved insufficient, Doenitz provided his submarines with anti-aircraft guns and ordered them to fight it out on the surface. By the summer of 1943, as a result of these technological advances, the submarine menace, which just a few months earlier had threatened to bring Britain to its knees, had been reduced to a mere nuisance, though it never came to a complete end.

And what of surface warfare? Both in the Mediterranean and the Atlantic, aircraft, whether land- or sea-based, played a considerable role in most engagements, providing the side that had them and employed them better with a critical advantage. Thus the Italians tried their hand at high-altitude bombing at sea; however, compared with the British torpedo bombers and the German dive-bombers that joined the struggle in the winter of 1941–42, their efforts were insignificant.

In the end, perhaps nothing symbolized the fate of big-gun vessels better than one of the largest battleships of all, the German *Tirpitz*. Commissioned in February 1941, a year later she was sent to Norway. Fear of what she might do forced the Allies to devote considerable forces to cover the supply convoys going to Murmansk. The mere rumor that she had gone to sea caused the escorts of convoy PQ-17 to disperse, thus leaving the merchantmen without protection and ravaged by German aircraft and submarines.[12]

In fact the German admiralty, afraid the *Tirpitz* might share the fate of her sister ship the *Bismarck* (which had been sunk in the Atlantic in May 1941), never permitted her to sail. Instead, the *Tirpitz* spent two and a half years hiding in a fjord near Trondheim, protected by batteries of anti-aircraft guns, anti-submarine nets, and smoke generators. This tempting, sitting target was ultimately attacked from the air and sunk.

Since neither the Germans nor the Italians possessed carriers, most of the really large surface battles that did take place were located on the other side of the world in the Pacific. On December 7, 1941, the Japanese attacked Pearl Harbor, thus bringing the United States into the war and turning it into a truly global struggle. The immediate cause behind the attack was the imposition of an American embargo on fuel and scrap metal, which—had the Japanese accepted the conditions attached to it—would have forced them to relinquish all their gains since 1937. By this time, those gains included not just most of China's coastal region but Indochina as well.

With the war in Europe demanding most of Britain's forces, and the Wehrmacht standing at Moscow's gates and thus removing any threat from that direction, it appeared to Japan's prime minister, Prince Konoye, and to the minister of war, General Hideki Tojo, that the time had come.

Tactically speaking, Pearl Harbor was a near-perfect demonstration of combined aero-naval techniques only recently developed. Maintaining radio silence, a Japanese task force made up of six aircraft carriers and numerous supporting vessels approached Hawaii from the north. At the time, the US Navy and War Department were using every existing form of intelligence, from air reconnaissance to radar to signal interception and decryption. Yet an immensely complicated chain of errors prevented them from discovering what was afoot until the first wave of Japanese aircraft were on top of them; later, generations of experts were to exercise their minds trying to figure out what went wrong and how to prevent a repetition.[13]

The attack damaged six battleships; sank two, the *Oklahoma* and the *Arizona;* destroyed some 150 aircraft; and was responsible for 4,575 casualties. Japanese losses amounted to twenty-nine aircraft, most of them shot down by ground fire during the second wave of attack. Still, the United States could take consolation in the fact that its aircraft carriers, as the most important targets of all, were out at sea and escaped. The base, with its repair facilities and stores of fuel, also continued to function.

The next six months saw a vast offensive, extending over millions of square miles. Attacked on land and from the air, the first Western possession to fall was Hong Kong, which surrendered on December 25. Fifteen days earlier, Japanese aircraft had sunk two British battleships—the *Repulse* and the *Prince of Wales*—thus securing command of the sea throughout East Asia. This in turn opened the way for the occupation of Singapore, Borneo, Dutch Indonesia, and part of New Guinea. When the Dutch East India naval squadrons tried to interfere with the transports, they were destroyed by Japanese ships. Japanese expansion in Asia continued after Thailand was forced to admit Japanese troops, which in turn led to the occupation of Burma. Only when they reached the borders of India did Tojo's troops come to a halt.

As the fate of the British and Dutch naval forces proved, by this time naval power was almost useless without aircraft to cover it. Of all forms of warfare, that waged by a combination of air and naval forces is probably the most capital-expensive. This explains why, in terms of numbers of men, the forces engaged could not compare to the millions seeking to kill one another in Europe. The largest single operation of all was the capture of Singapore, for which the Japanese employed four divisions. The largest landing the Japanese attempted took place in the Philippines, where they used forty-three thousand men. Other attacks on Guam, Wake Island, and the Gilberts used forces that were much smaller. For amphibious operations, the Japanese rarely used formations larger than division size, which were rarely armed with anything more powerful than light artillery and tanks.

Like its Axis partners Germany and Italy, moreover, Japan never developed heavy, four-engined bombers. Hence whatever "strategic" bombardments it tried to deliver amounted only to pinpricks. From beginning to end, all it could do to threaten the US mainland was to send over some bomb-laden balloons in the hope of setting fire to the forests of California.[14]

Whereas, in Europe and North Africa, the Wehrmacht in the summer of 1942 had resumed the offensive in a last, desperate bid to win the war before their much more powerful opponents closed the ring on them, developments in the Pacific were also about to climax. The Japanese suffered their first setback in the battle of Coral Sea early in May 1942 when, for the loss of one carrier, they sank an American one and badly damaged another. This was the first naval battle in history during which the ships of the opposing forces never even saw each other, a portent of things to come. The immediate strategic result: The Japanese had to give up on their attempt to capture Port Moresby, which in turn meant that Australia would never be invaded.

Much worse for Japan was its defeat at Midway in June. The Japanese objective was to capture the island as a stepping stone to an ultimate landing on Hawaii, a thousand miles away. By way of a feint, a small task force went off to capture some of the Aleutians. Meanwhile, the main force, consisting of four carriers, the battleship *Yamato* (which was serving as Admiral Yamamoto's flagship), and an entire armada of smaller warships and troop transports, set course for the island.

As at the Coral Sea, the Japanese fleet was discovered with the aid of radio interception and decoding, causing the American commander of the Pacific Fleet, Admiral Chester W. Nimitz, to order his own two carriers (which Yamamoto believed had been sunk in a previous battle) to sail. Taking their opponents by surprise, the Americans, using land- and sea-based torpedo-carrying aircraft, were the first to attack. They inflicted little damage, but their attacks forced the Japanese fighters to go into action. When the fighters landed to refuel, a second wave of planes, this time American dive-bombers, arrived, sinking three carriers and badly damaging a fourth. Many experienced naval pilots were also lost. It was a blow from which the Imperial Japanese Navy never recovered.

Both in the European theater of war and in the Far East, the aggressors hoped to either crush their opponents quickly or make them realize that a reconquest of lost territory would be so expensive that they would desist. Still, the numerous spectacular Axis victories did not, in the end, disprove Napoléon's dictum that God favors the side with larger battalions.

4.3. Total War

As we saw, the most important factor that shaped World War I was the superiority of the defense, and with it the inevitability of war by attrition. So ingrained had this idea become that, even after it had been finally overcome on the tactical level, it continued to prevail on the operational and strategic levels. To a very large extent, military theory during the twenty years' truce that followed was an attempt to restore the power of the offense by various means. Out of the four major military thinkers discussed in the previous chapter, three saw this as their most important task; so did figures such as General Heinz Guderian and Colonel Walther Wever (the man primarily responsible for developing German air doctrine in the 1930s).[15] Only one, Ludendorff, fully accepted that total war was inevitable and sought to work out the implications of this development.

In the end, the attempt to use armor to restore the power of the offense and thus prevent the war from degenerating into attrition failed. The failure was due to a number of factors, all of which were linked and interacted in complex ways that reflected the character of specific campaigns on land, in the air, and at sea.

Starting at the tactical level, it turned out that armored divisions, provided they were correctly employed, were no less useful on the defense as well. "Correctly" employing armored divisions for this task did not simply mean that the tanks should take up stationary positions, as the French did in 1940. Rather, better results could be obtained using a combination of efforts: obstacles in the form of ditches and minefields so as to draw the enemy into a predesignated killing ground, covered by well-positioned, concealed batteries of anti-tank guns and artillery. Tanks, followed by mechanized infantry, then were deployed as a counterattack at the appropriate moment.

The first time these measures may have been used was during the battle of Kursk, enabling the Soviets to defeat the last major German offensive on the Eastern Front.[16] From then on, such tactics became standard even though the Germans, who had more occasion to use them than did their enemies, were often handicapped by Hitler's "not a step back" orders.

What was true in respect to ground operations was equally valid in the air. Leaving aside the question of "strategic" bombardment, on which more later, many of the initial achievements of the Luftwaffe were due to surprise. The same also applied to Pearl Harbor, where three times as many Japanese aircraft were shot down during the second attack as during the first. As radar became more developed and commonly used, opportunities for surprise and, therefore, a successful offense became rarer.

Both armies and air forces march, or fly, on their stomach. A World War II German infantry division needed about 200 tons of supplies per day to remain operational. Its armored equivalent needed 300, whereas in 1944–45 an Anglo-American division, being much more lavishly equipped with vehicles and artillery, needed no less than 650.

In most of the European theaters of war, at least some railways were available and could carry part of the burden. However, railways were not completely suitable for supplying fast-moving mobile operations, and though tracks were hard to hit and easy to repair, railway stations and marshaling yards made excellent targets for bombers, and rolling stock attracted fighter-bombers as flowers attract bees. In the spring of 1944, while preparing to meet the Normandy invasion, the Germans in particular were to learn that operating railways in the face of enemy air superiority was tantamount to suicide.

From 1941–42 on, these problems affected the belligerents in different ways. On the German side, the only part of the Wehrmacht that was fully motorized was Rommel's small "hunting expedition" (the phrase used by Hermann Goering at Nuremberg)[17] in North Africa. Elsewhere, a growing imbalance between the size of the forces and the productive capacity of German industry, as well as fuel shortages, forced the high command to demotorize its forces. By 1944, the number of horses stood at one and a quarter million, an increase over the 1941 figure.[18]

The British and the Americans because they had the necessary industrial infrastructure, and the Soviets because they received several hundred thousand trucks from their allies, were at an advantage. Even so, measured in terms of personnel, fuel, spare parts, and maintenance work per ton/mile transported, trucks were much more expensive than railways.

Air transport helped, but not much. Cargo aircraft could quickly lift supplies to the places they were needed at the times they were needed. However, they were usually too vulnerable to land close to the front, and the loads they carried were too small.[19] In Russia, in North Africa, and finally in northwestern Europe, experience was to show that each time a large ground force moved more than two hundred or so miles from its railheads or ports, logistical difficulties would set in and bring an advance to a halt. Only after proper bases, including air bases for the fighters providing air cover, had been built, the supporting echelons moved forward, and the depots filled, could operations resume.

While intelligence and surprise aided the Americans dramatically in the great naval battle of Midway, neither factor played much of a role in amphibious landings. Uncooperative weather, wind, waves, and tides apart, one reason for this was because the defender could construct fortifications. A second was because it was easier for him to conceal his weapons, including, above all, his artillery; a third, because land-based aircraft, not being limited to short runways and not requiring folding wings, usually had a slight edge over their sea-based equivalents (which they to the present retain). For an amphibious offensive to succeed in overcoming a forwarned, well-prepared defense, it had to enjoy crushing superiority.

In this way, a combination of tactical, operational, and logistical factors, albeit working in different ways in different environments for different belligerents, ensured that the struggle should be one of attrition. A few figures will illustrate what happened next. Whereas, in 1914–18, 13 million, 15 million, and 4 million men went through the German, Russian, and American armed forces respectively, in 1939–45 the figures were 18 million, 33 million, and 15 million. Production figures were even more impressive. Combining the five main belligerents—Britain, the United States, the USSR, Germany, and Japan—the production of aircraft rose from 53,433 in 1940 to 231,066 in 1944 (at peak, one aircraft was coming off the American assembly lines every five minutes and forty-five seconds). The construction of major warships by the same five powers went up from just 251 to 2,895, an elevenfold increase. Excluding Japan, the corresponding figures for tanks were 7,816 and 74,029; for artillery pieces, 24,000 and 209,358.[20] By 1944, American production of tanks and artillery was already declining, given that the depots were bursting at the seams and more weapons were available than could be shipped to the theaters of war or deployed. Nothing like it had ever been seen before, or likely ever will again.

The prize for the most efficient mobilization of resources probably goes to Britain. With a democratically elected, highly centralized system of government that had cut its teeth in 1914–18, the national commitment was exceptionally strong. Britain was the only Allied country that fought Hitler and Tojo from the beginning and went on fighting them to the very end. Of course, being an island helped. Unlike some other belligerents, Britain never suffered an invasion, and although it is true that some industrial areas, particularly in Oxford, Coventry, and Birmingham, were heavily hit from the air, even at the height of the Blitz, only 1.7 percent of its stock of machine tools was damaged.[21]

The principal constraints on production were a relatively small labor force, a somewhat antiquated production system with too many small factories, and the need to import food, weapons, raw materials, and oil from abroad. In fact, had it not been for the Lend-Lease program, proclaimed in March 1941, Britain would have gone under. American munitions contributed to 11.5 percent of the British total in 1941 and climbed to 28.7 percent by 1944. Even so, Britain emerged from the war bankrupt, which in turn played a role in the breakup of its empire.

Having conquered most of Europe, in the first two years of the war Germany was able to expand its economic base until, in 1941, it produced twice as much steel as Britain and the USSR combined. Thanks to ruthless exploitation of the occupied territories, some of which were reduced to starvation, its population did not suffer from hunger as much as it had in 1914–18. Millions of prisoners of war, as well as foreign labor, were impressed to support Germany's war economy. Germany's main weaknesses were a shortage of oil—in essence limited to the Romanian fields, a few native wells, and expensive synthetic production.

As in 1914–18, the military did not prove very understanding of the needs of industry, repeatedly calling up vital workers who had to be released, if they could be released at all, only after fierce bureaucratic infighting. Partly as a result, during the first two years of the war production stagnated; it was only from the spring of 1942 on, probably already too late, that it really began to rise.[22]

Technically the Germans were very inventive. Indeed, it has been argued that almost every weapons system deployed from 1945 to 1991, including, in particular, certain kinds of submarines and many kinds of missiles, was already on the German drawing boards in 1944–45. However, in some ways this very inventiveness worked against them. It resulted in a very large number of different types, models, and versions of weapons, which in turn led to frequent changes, disrupted production schedules, and endless maintenance problems; at the end of 1941, Army Group Center, fighting in front of Moscow, needed a million different spare parts.

Whereas the Nazis were able to squeeze resources out of Western Europe, France in particular, the economic contribution of the occupied Russian territories never met expectations owing to Stalin's scorched-earth policy. The appointment of Albert Speer as armaments minister in early 1942 did lead to a considerable increase in production, but not to the point that Allied superiority was ever threatened. Having risen until July 1944, from that point on production declined as Allied strategic bombardment started showing results and many of the occupied countries were liberated or switched sides. Germany also started suffering from a shortage of certain strategic materials, such as chromium, without which the production of high-quality weapons was impossible.[23]

The fact that Russia even survived the war, much less serving as one of the major contributors to the defeat of Germany, is astonishing given the losses it suffered from July to December 1941—half of its wheat production, more than half of its meat production, and a third of the Soviet rail network. Lost, too, was 40 percent of the electrical-generation capacity; two-thirds of the supply of such vital raw materials as aluminum, manganese, and copper; and at least three-quarters of iron ore, steel, and coal production.[24]

Things were made worse by the fact that, whereas in the West, the Germans for the most part stuck to the international rules of war, on the Eastern Front they waged a campaign of extermination that condemned tens of millions to die of hunger. The situation was saved by the evacuation of entire industries from the west (the Ukraine in particular) to the east of the Urals. Other factors were a drastic reduction in living standards, which for Soviet citizens were already the lowest of any of the belligerents. Workers in armaments factories could be shot for tardiness or absenteeism. The result was that in terms of production, the Soviets produced weapons with an efficiency that was unparalleled. Thus, in 1943 the Soviets turned 8 million tons of steel and 90 million tons of coal into 48,000 heavy cannon and 24,000 tanks. The Germans—using more than three times as much steel and almost four times as much coal—could only make 27,000 heavy cannon and 17,000 tanks.[25] And these weapons, rather than being concentrated on a single front, had to be distributed among several.

Of all the major belligerents, the only one that escaped all enemy attempts to disrupt production was the United States. Though not entirely self-sufficient, the United States possessed vast domestic resources of food, coal, and iron ore. Until 1948, it was even a net exporter of oil, extracted from the fields in Texas, Pennsylvania, and elsewhere.

In 1941, it produced more steel, aluminum, oil, and motor vehicles than all the other major powers combined. The enviable "problem" was how to translate this capacity into military power. In terms of workers, even as 15 million people (of whom about 350,000 were women) served in the military, the labor force was still able to grow by 7.3 million workers between 1939 and 1944, an increase of 14 percent.[26]

Once mobilization hit its stride in 1942–43, American factories poured forth a flood of munitions such as the world had never seen. In the eyes of friends as well as enemies, what the GIs had in terms of money, food, uniforms, fuel, weapons, trucks, jeeps, weapons, and equipment of every kind, from movie projectors to condoms, appeared incredible. And no other country attained excess production like the United States: Between 5 and 11 percent of all production went to the Allies under the terms of Lend-Lease.[27]

On the eve of the war, the best available calculations showed that Japan's war potential amounted to rather less than one-tenth of that of its principal enemy.[28] Even this figure concealed a whole series of other weaknesses. The most important was Tokyo's utter dependence on imported food, iron ore, coal and oil; ironically, had it not been for this factor, Japan might not have gone to war in the first place.

In theory, Japan's occupation of much of the French, Dutch, and British colonial possessions in Southeast Asia should have enabled it to solve most of these problems. In practice, American submarines, based mainly on Midway and Australia and operating in a highly decentralized manner, proved extremely effective in cutting Japan's supply lines. By the spring of 1945, almost 90 percent of the empire's merchant fleet had been sent to the bottom. Coal imports had been reduced to a trickle, and the flow of oil had come to a complete halt. Even maritime transport among the main home islands was no longer secure. By the end of hostilities, Japan was teetering on the edge of starvation.

Given the amount of attention the issue has received in the literature, one might think that the role of women in the mobilization process was critical. In fact this was only true in the Soviet Union, where, at the peak of the war, women actually outnumbered men in the labor force. They formed a majority even in the mines, the only time in history this has happened anywhere.[29] In dramatic contrast, in 1941 almost one-third of all British women flatly refused to do any war work at all. Even at the peak of the war in 1943, there remained ten million unemployed British women with, on the average, less than one child to care for. At no time did women form more than 38.8 percent of the labor force, which means that, after five million men had been put into uniform, working men still outnumbered women by almost two to one. Only toward the end of 1943 did the authorities finally start "directing" women without children under fourteen to war work. Even so, fear of social unrest caused the policy to be applied quite cautiously. The higher the class to which a woman belonged, the less likely she was to hold a job of any kind. Some even got an exemption because they had large houses to look after.[30]

Even in 1945, out of fifty-two million American adult women, only nineteen and a half million held jobs; among married women, only a quarter did. Though the image of Rosie the Riveter dominated propaganda, its link to reality was tenuous. In metalworking plants male workers outnumbered females more than three to one.[31]

In some ways, the countries that treated women best were Japan and Germany. In the former, the government did what it could to protect women from the rigors of war, work-related rigors included.[32] In the latter, Hitler personally was determined to make sure German women would not again be subjected to the hardships experienced in 1914–18. As a result, from May 1939 to May 1944 the total number of German working women only rose by 180,000. Since the number of those in public administration increased from 954,000 to 1,746,000,[33] clearly the number of women doing hard work in agriculture and industry actually fell, their places taken by foreign workers, 2 million of whom were themselves females forcibly imported from the east. German provisions for soldiers' wives' pay, public kindergartens, and the like were also exceptionally generous.

In the world's armed forces between the wars, women accounted for a small number of nurses, telephone operators, and the like. After 1939 this changed; 9 percent of the British armed forces were female at peak strength. American and Soviet forces were 2 to 3 percent female.[34] Military women differed from the camp followers of previous periods in that they wore uniforms and had their own chain of command, yet they resembled them in that they filled a very large number of service duties, from food preparation to communications and from administration, to driving cars and trucks behind the front. Like camp followers, too, they were only semi-soldiers in the sense that they were volunteers (at a time when men were conscripted by the millions), could not be sent overseas against their will (in Britain and the United States), and, in case they had violated military law, were not punished nearly as severely as men. Though some British women helped "man" anti-aircraft defenses in the homeland, only Soviet women saw combat, both on the ground and in the air, but their numbers were very limited.

As has been emphasized elsewhere,[35] the size of the Allies' economies and their ability to translate resources into military power was not the only factor behind their victory, although it clearly was important. Whereas, in 1944, the Allies had some twenty-seven million men (including about a million and a half women) under arms, the figure on the other side was around thirteen million; throughout the war, indeed, Japan never had what it took to arm all the manpower it could have mobilized. Between 1941 and 1944, the number of aircraft produced by Britain, the United States, and the USSR outpaced Germany and Japan by a ratio of 3.6 to 1. In terms of major naval vessels, the corresponding figure was 6.1; in terms of tanks, 3.2. All this explains why, late in September 1944, one German document estimated that, in the west, the Wehrmacht was outnumbered "to an almost unlimited extent" in the air, ten to one in tanks, and three to one in artillery. The last-named mismatch was regarded as "not too serious"—except that the Germans did not have ammunition, either.[36]

The farther mobilization proceeded and the more total the war effort, the greater the tendency of mobilization to swallow the arm that should have directed it: civilian politics. The process is well illustrated by the career of Albert Speer, the architect-turned-manager who headed the German armaments ministry, a post that did not even exist before 1939. By 1943, Speer had reached the point where he was second only to Hitler in power. Theoretically, and to a large extent in practice as well, he possessed absolute authority to decide who would produce what, in what factories, by what means, on the basis of what raw materials, and at what prices. In terms of the funds he commanded as well as the manpower working for him—some twenty million people, half of them foreigners—Speer totally eclipsed any other minister as well as the commanders of the armed forces.

Nor were things very different on the Allied side. Stalin's mobilization was, of course, just as ruthless as Hitler's—and to the extent that it did not spare women, much more so. And though Britain and the United States did not go so far, both put substantial constraints on personal freedom. In America, the number of those who, working for the

FBI or other internal surveillance organizations, spied on their fellow plant workers reached the hundreds of thousands.

Thus, inside each country, any attempt to play internal politics was at once branded as treason. War, of course, also had a truncating effect on foreign policy. After Germany invaded Russia, all it could still do was attempt to enlist the aid of minor neutrals and, later on, try to dissuade them from joining the Allies. Similarly, when Churchill and Roosevelt in 1943 announced that they were aiming at unconditional surrender, foreign policy, in the ordinary meaning of the word, had ceased to exist. The objective was now to crush the enemy without regard either to internal hardship or the suffering inflicted on the other side. In this way, Ludendorff's prediction that war would, and should, emancipate itself from political control and take charge was fulfilled.

4.4. Esoteric War

During most of history, war had been a relatively simple activity as men discarded the refinements of civilization, took up the sword, and marched to slaughter one another. Even as late as the American Civil War, 90 percent of the troops on either side walked on foot and carried fire to the enemy. Even as late as World War I, outside certain services such as the railway section, the artillery, and the navy, very few officers thought that a specialized technical training was necessary. As to the idea that a university education might be useful, it was so preposterous as to never surface at all.

World War II changed all this. Already during the twenty years' truce, the winds of change could be felt as the US Industrial College of the Armed Forces opened its doors. Its purpose was to facilitate the interaction between officers and the economy—on which, in case another conflict broke out, those forces would have to rely for everything they needed.[37] Other countries followed, more or less. By 1939, Berlin even boasted something known as the Wehrtechnische Universitaet, a technical-military university.

In particular, four fields had developed to the point that even prime ministers, the ministers responsible for waging war on land and at sea, and commanders in chief often could no longer understand them on their own but had to call on experts, many of them civilians, for advice. They were, first, the process of research and development proper; second, the ever-changing, ever-evolving weapons and weapons systems to which it led; third, operations research, designed to find the best way to use those weapons and weapons systems; and fourth, intelligence.

As Trotsky once said, war has always acted as the locomotive of history, forcing men to come up with better and better weapons if they wanted to survive. Traditionally, inventions had come from individuals, which even as late as the last years of the nineteenth century led to devices with names such as the Chassepot rifle and the Gatling and Maxim machine guns. During World War I, the process of research and development began to be institutionalized. Teams of scientists and engineers were assembled, subordinated to a central directing hand, and put to work. Their task was to experiment, draw up proposals, submit them to the appropriate committees—themselves consisting of scientists, engineers, military men, and officials—and seek approval as well as money in order to put them into effect.

During World War II, many senior policy makers and commanders surrounded themselves with scientific advisers. Their job was to judge, as best they could, which of the numerous proposals being made were feasible; which would be useful and which could be ready in time for service.

Under such a stimulus, technology advanced in leaps and bounds, and one of the most critical fields was radar. The British, who throughout the 1930s had been obsessed with air defense, pioneered the use of radar for such a purpose, as well as the complex communications infrastrucure needed to coordinate it with its fighter command. The Germans were the first to put radar to sea. Later, both sides developed sets sufficiently small to be put aboard aircraft, the British to enable bomber pilots to find their targets by night and the Germans so they could locate the bombers and shoot them down. The Germans were also the first to use electronic navigation aids, sending out electronic beams that aircraft could receive and use to orient themselves. The British countered by generating their own beams intended to mislead the Germans, and so on in an endless series of moves and countermoves that Churchill, in his memoirs, was to dub "the wizzards' war."[38]

Radar and navigation aids, though, were only a very small part of the technological battle. Other devices that owed their existence, or at least their forced development, to the war included jet engines, rocket engines, ballistic missiles, and computers, all of which had great careers ahead of them. Jet engines were pioneered in Germany and Britain during the last years before 1939. The first fighter aircraft powered by jets came in time to participate in the war; there is, however, no record of the German Me 262 and the British Meteor meeting in combat.

Rocket engines and ballistic missiles, as well as crude cruise missiles, were pioneered by the Germans. The V1 was cheap and easy to produce but, owing to its relatively low speed, not too hard to counter. Against the V2 ballistic missile no defense was possible, but in terms of labor, raw materials, and engineering talent its cost was enormous. The V1 could deliver half a ton of explosives, the V2 twice as much. Given that both were too inaccurate to be used against any target smaller than a city, it is doubtful whether either was worth the resources invested in it.[39]

Computers were developed in Britain, where they played a key role in secret intelligence, as well as in Germany and the United States where the earliest mechanical examples were used to calculate the trajectories of anti-aircraft artillery rounds and assist in aiming the guns. The Americans also built the first electronic computer, but it came too late to play a role in the war.

If only because the opponents watched and imitated one another very closely, a swing effect set in. Few technological advantages lasted for long; some inventions, such as proximity fuses, were even held back out of fear that the enemy would copy them. Early in the war, the German and Japanese forces were able to hold their own, technologically speaking, but Japanese research and development efforts in particular had always been rather narrowly based, and from 1942 on they were no longer able to keep up with their enemies. The Germans were better placed, countering most Allied developments in the field of electronics until the end of the war and pioneering in some of the abovementioned fields. It is true that, from 1942 on, German aircraft became less competitive with Allied examples—a fact that drove the head of the Luftwaffe's Technical Branch, General Ernst Udet, to commit suicide—but this was due less to lack of capability than to the fact that the Germans focused on developing jet engines, neglecting the rest. In the event, their jet-powered aircraft came too late in the war, and in insufficient numbers, to change the outcome.

On land and at sea, the situation was very different. German ground weapons, tanks and artillery in particular, were as good as anything the Allies or Soviets could produce. Some of them were clearly superior; a few, indeed, remained in the service of the Bundeswehr for decades after 1945. Though no further surface vessels were built after 1942, had the war not ended when it did, Doenitz would have been able to confront the Allies with an entirely new generation of submarines capable of underwater speeds beyond anything previously available. Perhaps the best comment on this entire question is offered by the fact that, in 1945–47, the Americans, the Soviets, the British, and even the French all hunted for German scientists to interrogate and employ.[40]

How best to use the new weapons and technologies, was a problem in itself. In the past, such matters had normally been dealt with with the aid of experience and rules of the thumb; now they became proper subjects for scientists to study. Some of the earliest experiments in operations research had been made during World War I by mathematicians such as Frederick W. Lanchester, who tried to apply it to air combat.[41] From 1939 on, other scientists—some of them, like the Englishman Solly Zuckerman, coming from unexpected directions such as zoology—were asked to answer questions such as: How should a command and control system for fighters, intended to intercept incoming bombers, be organized? How to best configure a convoy crossing the Atlantic so as to minimize the chances of the U-boats preparing to attack it? In what pattern should destroyers, chasing those U-boats, drop their depth charges? How to best combine squadrons of aircraft carrying high explosive and firebombs to demolish a city?

People who were not themselves scientists had trouble making sense of the endless, often very complex new devices and techniques. They would, however, be even more nonplussed by the esoteric world of intelligence and counterintelligence. Of course, there is a sense in which none of the methods used by the belligerents was entirely new; from spies (and spies who were turned around) through prisoner interrogation to encryption and decryption, all had been commonplace at least since the time of Julius Caesar.

Nevertheless, the conduct of far-reaching mobile operations, the hallmark of twentieth-century warfare, would have been impossible without radio. Radio transmissions, though, could be readily intercepted, which made the discovery of fast, easy-to-use, and reliable methods for encrypting messages and decrypting them imperative. Accordingly, the 1920s saw the first attempts at devising electromechanical devices that would make transmissions secure. Originating in commercial firms, later the relevant patents were bought by the military, which continued to develop them.

The encryption device that acquired the greatest fame, albeit because of its failure to keep secrets secret, was the German Enigma, a typewriter-like machine that, using complicated mechanical and electronic gear, automatically translated clear text into gibberish that could then be decrypted by a recipient using a similar machine. The organization that acquired the greatest fame, this time because it succeeded in its task of cracking the Enigma code, was the British Ultra. In some ways, both the bad reputation of the Enigma and the sky-high one of Ultra are exaggerated.[42] This is not because the latter did not play a role in winning the war—by helping convoys avoid submarines deployed in their way and revealing the sailing details of Axis convoys in the Mediterranean, it certainly did—but because it was only one of many. By 1939, all the main belligerents had in place proper devices for encrypting their radio messages, though some were clearly better than others. At the same time, all the main belligerents had in place organizations, many of them going back all the way to the "black cabinets" of eighteenth-century fame, that specialized in intercepting messages, decrypting them, and turning them into the kind of information decision makers could use. All read their enemies' (and, often just as importantly, their allies'!) messages. For example, even as the British were breaking the code of the German navy, that navy's so-called B Dienst was doing the same to its opponents.[43]

On the other hand, much of the most important traffic went by wire and could not be intercepted at all. So, for instance, the Churchill–Roosevelt correspondence, Stalin's orders, and Hitler's war directives; apparently none of these documents ever fell into enemy hands. At a lower level, the availability of a cable between Hawaii and Midway was a key factor that helped the United States win the Midway battle, and this is certainly not the only case that could be cited. Even where transmissions went by wireless and were intercepted, the results were not always of earthshaking importance, and a great many were of no importance at all. The problems were compounded by the fact that each belligerent used many different codes at any one time: one for the high command, say, along with one for each service, and often one for each arm and theater of war as well. All changed their codes quite frequently. The fact that, at any one time, there were many different codes meant that the emerging intelligence picture was seldom even nearly complete. The frequent changes often caused days, weeks, or even months to pass before the flow of information could be resumed, and sometimes caused it to cease flowing at all. Even during periods when the traffic could be read there were often delays, causing at least some of the decrypted material to lose at least some of its value. On other occasions, when everything was working smoothly, those whose job it was to make sense of it simply did not succeed in their task.

All this formed an emormously complicated, kaleidoscopic world. Surrounded by miles of barbed wire, mathematicians, high-level chess players, linguists, and cultural experts, all controlled by the inevitable security personnel, matched their wits against the enemy. By devising better encryption methods, they sought to prevent their own secrets from leaking, while attempting to ferret out those of the enemy and doing their best to present him with a false picture of their own side's resources, deployment, and intentions. For example, preparing to land in Normandy in the spring of 1944, the British and the Americans used various means to succesfully fake an entire army preparing for a landing at the Pas de Calais. Even so, it was only one part of a secret planet where information rather than bullets counted; one that, on this occasion, succeeded in leading Hitler by the nose for weeks.

Wars are decided by a combination of quality and quantity, intelligence and brute force. It is doubtful that any mathematical model currently available, or likely to become available, will be able to embrace all the various factors, relate them to one another, and assign them their proper relative weight. As I have argued elsewhere, should such a model become available then it is quite likely that war itself will come to an end; after all, there is no point in a contest, least of all a deadly contest such as war, if the outcome is assured in advance.[44] Hence it is impossible to say just how large are the roles played by the esoteric new technologies, new methods, and new intelligence sources. To the belligerents of World War II, these factors were absolutely critical to success, and their war effort reflected this belief. Particularly in the early stages of the war, superior intelligence, superior doctrine, superior training, and superior leadership could and did make a difference.

Later, things changed. From 1943 on, American superiority over Japan, both quantitative and qualitative, was clearly overwhelming. During the battle for the Philippines, for instance, fifteen times as many Japanese troops died as Americans.[45] By contrast, the Germans were in a much better position to hold their own, qualitatively speaking. The most important single factor that led to their defeat was the Soviet steamroller; out of every four Wehrmacht soldiers who lost their lives, three met their fate on the Eastern Front. Either way, counting from the high tide of Axis expansion three years of fighting on an unprecedented scale were needed to bring the war to an end. Ultimately it was attrition that decided the Second World War, just as it had the first.

4.5. Closing the Ring

In any form of coalition warfare, the essential condition for victory is political unity and a combined command system. In 1939–45, the Allies did much better in meeting this condition than the Axis countries did. Given the geographic distance that separated them, cooperation between Japan and its European allies was bound to be loose indeed. This problem was compounded by the fact that, instead of striking the USSR in the rear, Tokyo went its own way; by so doing it probably hastened, if it did not cause, America's entry into the war.

In 1942, the Axis partners talked about mounting a combined campaign against India. However, neither Germany (the Italians hardly counted) nor Japan had the logistic resources such a gigantic pincer operation would have required, and it never even reached the planning stage.

Meanwhile, in Europe, Germans and Italians never set up a combined command system. Instead, they relied on liaison officers. The most important of them was the German military attaché in Rome; only in the North African theater was there something approaching a joint

Italian-German chain of command. Hitler himself saw Mussolini, the only Roman among mere Italians as he once put it, as a personal "friend." Like some mythological hero, he vowed to stand with him to the end, and, in a sense, he kept his word. However, farther down there was as much friction as there was cooperation. In time, many high-ranking Germans came to see Italy as a drain on their own war effort—at one point they even suspected their allies, the Royal House specifically included, of leaking secrets to the British. On the Italian side, many blamed Mussolini, first for entering the war and then for doing so on the wrong side.

Churchill and Roosevelt succeeded in establishing a good personal relationship that started even before the United States entered the war and lasted until its final months. In preparation for the landings in North Africa, a combined command, SHAEF, was established, and on the whole it functioned well. To be sure, the British found their American cousins arrogant and overbearing—"overpaid, oversexed, and over here," as the saying went—whereas the Americans often suspected their wily allies of trying to lead them by the nose. On the other hand it was General Eisenhower, as SHAEF commander, who at one point issued a directive to the effect that while he did not mind his subordinates calling one another "sons of bitches," he would mind if anyone spoke of Americans or British in general as members of such a group.

Relations with Stalin were more difficult, and cooperation with him was never close. At times it seemed as if the Soviets were playing a deliberate game of hard-to-get, now showing a friendly face, now refusing to cooperate. Many of the problems were due to the fact that the Second Front was so late in coming. Furthermore, the need to work with the USSR itself gave rise to differences within the Western alliance, Churchill being much more suspicious of Stalin than Roosevelt was. Still, as long as the war lasted, these differences were never allowed to disrupt the alliance. Instead, there was some actual cooperation (as, for example, when the Soviets coordinated their 1944 summer offensive with the Normandy landings), and when critical Allied supplies reached the Soviets.

The summer of 1942 opened with another German offensive in Russia, complete with a gigantic battle of encirclement in the Ukraine. Next came a rapid, almost bloodless, pursuit that brought the Wehrmacht all the way to Stalingrad. Operationally speaking, it was a very great achievement. Strategically, as the small number of Soviet prisoners showed, it led nowhere. Having suffered heavy losses during the winter, the Wehrmacht at this time simply no longer had what it took to defeat a mobilized Soviet Union. After the failure of its offensive at Kursk in July 1943, it no longer even had the wherewithal to launch a large-scale offensive, the more so because Allied landings first in North Africa, then in Sicily and in Italy, forced Hitler to redirect forces away from the Eastern Front to assist his ally. By the end of 1943, the Soviets, relying on a crushing superiority in everything from infantry to tanks and artillery, had recaptured two-thirds of the territory lost in 1941.

If ever there was a savage war, this was it. Hitler, of course, intended it to be a war of conquest aimed at the extirpation of Bolshevism, the permanent occupation of much of Russia as far as the Urals, and the extermination of anyone who stood in the way. To carry out these aims, he had engaged in years of race-hatred propaganda. On the eve of the invasion, he explicitly told his generals that the Geneva Convention, as well as any other "chivalrous" ideas they might have, would not apply.[46] The USSR on its part had never signed the convention, and Stalin's offer to respect it soon after hostilities broke out was left unanswered. The results were there for everybody to see.

Both sides fought with enormous ferocity, sometimes, as at Stalingrad, to the point of literally using hands and teeth. Entire formations were wiped out not once but time after time.[47] Both sides murdered certain categories of prisoners, such as commissars or SS men, out of hand. Each, in turn, also herded millions of captives into camps where they were either left to freeze and starve—among Soviet POWs there were outbreaks of cannibalism—or put to work under such terrible conditions that few survived. Individual war crimes, whether committed in quest of information or out of sheer hatred, abounded.

All these horrors were compounded by atrocities against the civilian population. The Germans shot and gassed Jews, obliterated entire villages suspected of assisting "partisans," and deliberately set out to starve the population of European Russia. In their turn, from entering Germany, the Soviets retaliated by raping practically every woman aged ten to sixty.[48] By comparison, the toll taken by special units such as the NKVD and the Gestapo of members of their own armed forces and civilian populations accused of crimes or suspected of disloyalty was minor. Still, it certainly ran into the tens, and possibly hundreds, of thousands killed.

In 1943, as in 1944–45, major Soviet offensives usually opened with some of the more massive artillery bombardments and air strikes the world has ever seen. It is true that the Red Air Force had no heavy bombers and never became very good at interdiction, either. However, it did provide the ground forces with effective close support, the more so because the Luftwaffe's best fighter pilots were kept busy defending the skies of the Reich. The bombardments and air strikes were followed by equally massive waves of infantry shouting "hurrah" and, if the German generals' postwar memoirs may be believed, often roaring drunk. A sector of the front having been torn open, the armored divisions, their backbone formed by the cheap, badly finished, but reliable and effective T-34 tanks, would pass into the breach on their way to the rear. In the summer of 1944, it was by these methods that the Soviets brought about the collapse of Army Group Center, the largest single German formation of all.

As in 1917–18, the Germans dug in and formed deep defensive lines, often taking over entire villages where positions were heavily fortified and well camouflaged. These fortifications not only permitted a stationary defense, but also served as a starting point for counterattacks—a form of war in which the Germans, thanks to generally superb training, great flexibility, and good coordination, excelled. They used large numbers of tank destroyers, a weapons system that had the advantage of being cheaper to build than a tank, and could carry a heavier gun. Originally, tank destroyers—known to the Germans as *Sturmartillerie*, storm artillery—were developed to provide fire support for attacking infantry. Their low profile, though, made them equally useful on the defense, given that they could be easily hidden and that they could be moved from one position to the next much more readily than towed anti-tank guns could. Right to the last months of the war, the Wehrmacht's tactics were superior, often inflicting far more casualties than it took. Ultimately, though, the Germans were being forced back, it was only logistical constraints that really compelled the Red Army to halt, and then only temporarily.

In November 1942, the Allies invaded Northwest Africa. The decision was dictated as much by Roosevelt's need to show the US electorate that something was being done as by strategic considerations. At the time American, and even more so British, commanders felt a long time would pass before they would be ready to tackle the Wehrmacht's main forces in France.

Despite initial resistance, defeating the French Vichy forces in Morocco and Algeria didn't prove too difficult. Doing the same to the quarter million German troops in Tunisia was a different matter, and several months of very hard fighting had to pass before the job was completed. Still, from beginning to end the Germans, whose rear was also being threatened by Montgomery's Eighth Army coming up from Libya and whose supplies were being sunk as they tried to cross the Mediterranean, did not stand a chance. If, during all the years that World War II lasted, there was one occasion when quantity prevailed over quality, surely this was it.

What was true of the Tunisian campaign was equally true of those that followed in Sicily and Italy.[49] In Sicily, the Germans put up a stubborn resistance and were only forced to give up after the American general George Patton outflanked them by land and by sea. Even so, they succeeded in extricating most of their troops as well as much of their equipment. Churchill's original idea in pressing for these invasions was that they would draw German forces away from northwestern France, where he and the Americans hoped to land eventually. In the event, the opposite happened: The campaign demanded more Anglo-American troops than expected. The mountainous Italian terrain provided the defenders with countless strong positions, including many rivers that wound so much that they had to be crossed several times. On the other hand, it seldom allowed large armored forces to be used in exploitation and pursuit. It also helped nullify, or at least reduce, the effects of Allied air superiority—which, had the country been flat, would have been devastating. These facts of life neither Italy's decision to change sides in September 1943, nor two Allied attempts to outflank the Germans by landing in their rear at Salerno and Anzio, could change.

Though the fighting was very tough, by and large these campaigns did not witness the large-scale atrocities so characteristic of the Russo-German War. The "strategic" bombing campaign against Germany's cities, which got into gear during the same period, was a different matter. Even if it is true, as has been claimed,[50] that Churchill was the first to give the order to deliberately bomb civilians as part of a plan to ease the pressure on the fighter command, then one should by no means overlook the fate that Warsaw and Rotterdam had already suffered at the hands of the Luftwaffe.

During the first two and a half years of the war, the attacks on Germany's cities, mounted first by the RAF and then by the RAF and the US Army Air Force together, were insignificant. In 1941, losses among British pilots actually exceeded the number of Germans killed. Thereafter, better aircraft, better auxilliary technologies such as airborne radar, better methods, and the sheer number of heavy, four-engined bombers, bombing Germany by night and by day, started making their impact felt. Tens of thousands of civilians, some of them indeed working in arms factories (the British chief of bomber command, Air Marshal Arthur Harris, justified his campaign by claiming it "dehoused" workers, lowering their morale and disrupting production) but most not, were blown to pieces, asphyxiated, cremated, or buried. Hundreds of thousands more were wounded, and millions lost their homes. When US troops entered Aachen in October 1944, they found it deserted even by the birds.

This, then, was total war with a vengeance. It did not content itself by killing enemy soldiers at the front. Instead, it did what it could to slaughter and destroy whatever supported them in whatever way, however indirect. Men, women, old people, young people, all suffered together and perished together, often in the most horrible ways as the places in which they tried to shelter were transformed into red-hot ovens.

But what impact did strategic bombing have on the German war effort? Allied commissions that looked into the question soon after the war distinguished between civilian "morale" and "behavior," claiming that, while the former had suffered, the latter remained more or less intact and enabled production to go on, even expand. Subsequent commentators were less sure. It is true that, taken as a whole, German armament production continued to rise until the summer of 1944, when it fell for the first time. By that time, though, Germany's own synthetic oil plants had been destroyed (and Romania had changed sides), causing the war effort to literally grind to a halt. In 1944, bombing cost

Germany 14 percent of its armament production, including 20 percent of its tanks, 35 percent of armored vehicles, 31 percent of aircraft, and 45 percent of trucks. By 1945, production of all armaments was down 48 percent.[51]

These direct losses apart, the bombing campaign forced the Germans to disperse and bury what remained of their industry, at what cost in labor, transportation, and raw materials can easily be imagined. Fighting back also required massive resources. As a result, a third of all guns produced were used in anti-aircraft defense. Meanwhile the Luftwaffe, forced onto the defense, all but disappeared from the skies above the fighting fronts. On the Allied side, the losses suffered by the aircrews were very heavy relative to their own numbers, but compared with the gigantic number of men killed at the front they were trifling.

On June 6, 1944, after having mounted a massive deception campaign, the Americans and the British landed in Normandy. At that time the Third Reich, though faced with the Soviet steamroller on the Eastern Front and suffering badly under air attack, was still intact. Because of the vagaries of the weather, and stiff German resistance, the invasion itself was a close-run thing. Though they were grievously short of air support, the German forces in France were much stronger than they had been in the previous year. Only a series of errors on Hitler's part prevented additional armored divisions from being sent to seal off the beachhead and counterattack. Conversely, not for nothing did General Eisenhower prepare a note that he intended to publish in case of failure and in which he took the blame upon himself. Had Operation Overlord failed, the German high command could have moved as many as a million troops, including some of its very best, to the Eastern Front. At the very least, the war would have been prolonged and the subsequent peace, if there had been a peace, assumed a different form. There is, of course, another possibility. Instead of Hiroshima, some German city such as Heidelberg or Goettingen might have become the first victim of the atomic bomb. Both were still intact, and so would have been suitable targets.

The landings themselves combined airborne operations—both by paratroopers and by gliders—with seaborne assault. On the first day alone seven divisions, the minimum figure considered acceptable by the invasion commander General Montgomery, were put ashore. By the end of July, the figure had grown to thirty-six divisions, nineteen American and seventeen British. The Americans alone needed an average of twenty-two thousand tons of supplies per *day*. Still, the Western Allies never quite succeeded in imitating the Blitzkrieg methods pioneered by their opponents. Perhaps this was because they enjoyed an overwhelming advantage in numbers, which slowed them down and paradoxically caused them to proceed cautiously in the hope of saving lives. Perhaps it was because many of their generals were inclined toward attrition and not very good at orchestrating the cooperation of all forces available; that, at any rate, was how it was interpreted by the Wehrmacht's senior commanders both at the time and later on. Perhaps, too, it was because they met an enemy "as hard as steel" who did not yield an inch.

In any case, operations tended to be heavy-handed and slow. Offensives such as Operation Goodwood, July 1944,[52] were preceeded by massive air and artillery bombardments, by which the commander of the U.S. Army Service Forces, General Lesley McNair, who was visiting the front, was killed. The advance went according to an elaborate timetable, leaving little room for junior commanders to seize fleeting opportunities. As had already happened in Sicily in the previous year, even when the Allies engaged in maneuvers, as at Falaise, they were hesitant to close the ring and thus enabled the Germans to extricate many of their fighting men. For these reasons, and because of logistical difficulties of the kind described above, the front froze. From mid-September 1944 to late January 1945, almost the only important move that took place was the German counteroffensive in the Ardennes.

A blow-by-blow account of the final agony is not required in the present context. Suffice it to say that the Germans did not surrender with their forces largely intact as they had in 1918. Instead their troops, out of fear for the enemy and for the SS, who executed anyone they considered a deserter, continued to fight to the end.

Faced with such tenacious resistance, both in the west and in the east the Allied operations proceeded on an enormous scale. During the battle of Berlin alone, the attacking Soviet armies are said to have numbered two and a half million men, forty-one thousand artillery pieces and mortars, and sixty-two hundred tanks.[53] The two and a half months' fierce fighting that took them from the Oder to the German capital cost them no fewer than a thousand tanks—amazingly without that loss making the slightest difference to the outcome or, indeed, reducing the Soviet order of battle to any appreciable extent. On the Anglo-American side, such was the surplus of matériel that factories were being switched back to civilian production months before the war ended.

Such massive armaments could only have been made available by the methods of mass production as first developed by Detroit and then imitated by the Soviets in particular. Yet on the whole, quality was not sacrificed. It is true that different countries approached things in somewhat different ways; the Soviet preference for quantity, for example, differed from the German emphasis on quality. Yet in these countries, as well as all the rest, each new tank, combat aircraft, aircraft carrier, and submarine represented the latest available technology and incorporated the latest available inventions. Compared with what had existed only a few years earlier, practically every new weapon fielded was much more advanced and powerful. The British Spitfire, the most famous fighter of all, went through eight different versions—an average of more than one per year—that caused the power of its engine to more than double; yet before the war ended it was already being replaced by the even more advanced Tempest. To adduce but one more, rather trivial example, when the Germans in 1944 came to man the Westwall, the construction of which dated back to 1938–39, they found that the bunkers were too small to take the latest anti-tank guns; yet it was only those guns, rather than the door-knockers available in 1939, that stood any chance of penetrating the other side's armor.

Thus, the most intensive research and development did not proceed at the cost of mass production but simultaneously with it; as a result, obsolescence was extremely rapid. This became even more evident after the war when the Soviets, perhaps because their economy was smaller, made an effort to gather their weapons and store them in huge depots. There they helped augment the order of battle, at any rate, on paper; over the coming decades, they were often sold at rock-bottom prices to clients all over the third world who thus acquired the capability to fight one another on the cheap. The Americans also sold many of their surplus weapons to their Western European Allies (West Germany, once it joined NATO, included). Unlike the Soviets, though, often they did not even bother to evacuate the rest, leaving them to rust instead.

Nothing is more indicative of the speed of technological development than the fact that the atomic bomb, the largest and most expensive R&D project in history by far, took only three years from the moment the green light was given in 1942 to the moment it produced the first mushroom cloud. Before we can tell that story, though, it is necessary first to see how the war in the Far East proceeded.

4.6. The Road to Hiroshima

The war in the Far East was very different from the one that took place in Europe. This, after all, is a world of islands; hence, except in Burma, China, and for a few days Manchuria, the role played by ground forces was smaller. Even when they operated on the mainland, both sides had to bring in their supplies from overseas. For example, an American infantry division took up no less than 144,000 tons of shipping; the figure for an armored division was almost double that.[54]

Once the troops had been deployed in the theater, they often found the climate to be brutally hot, the roads few and far between, and a terrain full of formidable obstacles. All these factors prevented ground warfare from reaching anything like the size and sophistication of its European equivalent. In particular, large-scale, deep-ranging armored operations were largely absent. Instead it was a question of relatively small units clawing their way through jungles, or else of laboriously climbing mountains.

By contrast, the role played by air and sea forces was much greater. This elementary fact was reflected by the kind of weapons the forces fielded, the supplies they needed, the methods they used, and the casualties they suffered. Both of the main protagonists, Japan and the United States, had realized the role airpower could play at sea right from the beginning and constructed their forces accordingly. Land-based and carrier-based aviation, amphibious units, and submarines proved to be the most effective means by which war was waged. American submarines in particular had to be capable of crossing the Pacific before they could go into action. To carry the necessary fuel, they tended to be larger than their German equivalents.[55]

The vast number of ocean islands and atolls, even such as were too small and too barren to carry human settlement in times of peace, formed indispensable bases for ships, submarines, amphibious forces, and, even more so, aircraft whose range, as well as endurance, was much more limited. The war, therefore, was very much about defending these islands and trying to capture them.

Originally Roosevelt and Churchill, considering their enemies' relative strength, had decided on a "Germany first" strategy. However, as the United States mobilized and more resources became available, it became possible to proceed in both theaters at the same time, and as so often occurs, one factor that dictated American strategy was the age-old rivalry between the country's army and its navy.

US operations were divided into two gigantic arms. One was a ground force commanded by army general Douglas MacArthur; the other was composed of a huge naval force headed by Admiral Nimitz. MacArthur's forces fought their way through New Guinea and the Solomons to the Philippines—where the Japanese had ejected him back in 1941—and Borneo. Nimitz's did the same by way of the Gilberts, the Marianas, Paulas, the Philippines, Iwo Jima, and Okinawa. Centering on the indispensable landing craft—it was the availability of these relatively small, relatively simple vessels that often determined whether or not an operation was possible—American amphibious technique gradually improved.

The first stage was often to isolate the target by what became known as island-hopping. As the landing began, enormous firepower from battleships and carriers was brought to bear, forcing the defenders to keep their heads down. Next, the marines, from their landing craft, stormed the beaches, bringing with them heavy weapons, vehicles, and supplies. The defenders, having constructed well-camouflaged cannon and machine gun emplacements, put up tremendous resistance. Clearing them often required weeks, and culminated in ferocious hand-to-hand fighting.

The naval battles that ensued, which in the Pacific were the last large-scale fleet actions the world has seen, had little in common with any of their historical predecessors. With the aircraft carrier acquiring preeminence as a naval weapon, battles were now fought at such long ranges that the only combatants to see the other were the carrier-borne pilots. Conversely, any surface forces that did not have carriers to defend them were sitting ducks. Because, without ships, men at sea cannot survive, let alone fight, naval warfare is heavily dependent on technology. As the years of fighting went by, the more pronounced grew the American advantage in advanced aircraft, sophisticated electronics (radar in particular), and powerful naval vessels. The Japanese took an anachronistic step to compensate by building a couple of giant battleships more powerful than anything the United States had, but this proved a costly error: They were quickly sunk by carrier aircraft. Overall Japanese weaponry became less sophisticated as the war dragged on. Perhaps nothing demonstrated this trend more so than the rise of suicide attacks, whether they be aerial (kamikaze), at sea (human-guided torpedoes), or on land (suicidal attacks against Allied armor).

This, too, was a war without mercy. At Kwajalein in January and February 1944, the Americans used 41,000 men and lost 400 killed. For the Japanese, the respective figures were 8,000 and 7,870—probably a record for a force that size. Japanese atrocities in China, first meant to intimidate the population, then to combat incipient guerrilla warfare, and finally to perfect methods for waging biological warfare, have become deservedly infamous. Waged as it was against the background of racism that had taken decades, if not centuries, to form, the war against the Western powers was also marked by intense hatred. Allied prisoners who had surrendered to the Japanese were considered by their captors to have forfeited their honor and were often deliberately humiliated, maltreated, starved, and worked to death.

The Allies in their turn often refused to take Japanese prisoners at all. Sometimes they used flamethrowers to exterminate the garrisons of occupied islands almost one by one, as if they were rats; there were also instances when body parts, such as fingers and ears, were severed and taken as souvenirs, and enemy dead subjected to sexual abuse.[56] Cut off from the world, unable to receive reinforcements, and ordered to fight to the end, the Japanese troops' fear of what might await them reinforced their determination and sometimes led to actions of mass suicide. And so on in a vicious cycle of violence and cruelty that, if anything, became worse as the war went on.

During their period of expansion from 1937 to 1942, the Japanese bombed numerous Chinese cities, Port Moresby in New Guinea, and the Australian town of Darwin, but since they simply did not have the resources to build fleets of long-range heavy bombers they were never able to engage in systematic strategic bombing that alone did any decisive damage. During much of the war in the Pacific, the same was true of the Americans. They, too, were forced to rely primarily on light to medium, carrier-borne, single- or twin-engined aircraft. They, too, did not possess the long-range bombers needed to cross the immense expanses of ocean and reach the Japanese home islands. Such bombers, in the form of the B-29, plus the necessary bases, first in China, then in the Mariana Islands, were not available until late in 1944.

The man in charge of America's strategic bombing effort was General Curtis LeMay, a colorful, cigar-chomping character, then only in the middle of a long career that would see him rise to become one of the most influential American commanders of the entire postwar period. His idea was to do something very different from what the bomber fleets in Europe were doing: Strip the B-29s of their defensive armament; make them carry nothing but incendiaries; and, to evade antiaircraft fire as well as improve aiming, force the crews to fly low instead of high. The method, assisted by the fact that Japanese cities were built largely of wood, worked. The attack, by 325 aircraft, on Tokyo in March 1945 incinerated as many as one hundred thousand people. This was more than any other single bombardment in history before or since; touring the city in 2002, I was told that, aside from the Imperial Palace, there was only a single pre-1945 building remaining. Yet even this was only the opening move in a sustained campaign, leading to the total or partial destruction of sixty-three Japanese cities at a cost of half a million people dead and eight million more left homeless. Of the major Japanese cities, only Kyoto was left intact, owing to the fact that it was seen as a treasure-house of Japanese culture akin to Paris and Rome.

Modern Japan had long been unable to feed its population, and it was almost entirely without indigenous raw materials or fuel. In 1941, these factors had played a critical role in the government's decision to go to war in the first place. Now, with parts of the newly acquired empire lost to the Allies and its merchant marine all but gone, industry came to a stop. Much of the population began to starve; the destruction by air bombardment of so many homes only hastened the slide into chaos. On top of this, the war in Europe was coming to an end. It was only a question of time before the USSR entered the war to avenge its 1905 defeat and, perhaps, prevent the United States from making additional gains. Japanese attempts to prevent this, as well as negotiate an end to the conflict, were already proceeding in Moscow when the first atomic bomb was dropped.

The details of the project that led to the bomb need not concern us here.[57] Suffice it to say that, taking the value of money into account, it was the greatest of its kind in history. Considering the size of the project as well as the entirely new scientific principles involved, the speed with which it was completed was extraordinary. Such was the secrecy with which the work proceeded that Vice President Harry Truman, who had spent much of the war as a sort of self-appointed inspector of arms production, knew nothing of it. Learning of its existence when he inherited the presidency, he could only stammer: "This is the greatest thing in the world."[58]

The success of the Manhattan Project having been confirmed by the first test in New Mexico, it remained to decide whether to drop the bomb, in what manner, and on what target. Apparently there was never any question that it would be used, though whether the objective was to make an invasion unnecessary or impress the Soviets remains controversial to the present day. Still, there were some in the administration who wanted to give the Japanese fair warning, either verbally or by putting on a demonstration. This advice was rejected, and Hiroshima was selected as the first target largely because it had previously been left untouched and could therefore serve as a guinea pig. The final preparations were made on the island of Tinian, fifteen hundred miles away. So large was the bomb—it weighed no less than ten tons—that it could not be hoisted into the waiting B-29 bomber, itself the largest, heaviest, and most powerful built until then and the first to have a pressurized cabin. Instead a hole was dug in the ground, the bomb was lowered into it, the plane driven over it tail-first, and the bomb hoisted into the bay.

Shortly after the bomb had been loaded and armed, the plane commander, Colonel Paul W. Tibbets, told the members of his crew that they were about to drop the world's first atomic bomb. The trip to Japan took about six and a half flying hours and proceeded without incident. Japanese radar detected the aircraft, called *Enola Gay*, at 0700 hours, and sounded the alarm throughout the Hiroshima area. The people on the ground were, however, misled by an American weather plane that came and went; as it did so, they thought the danger was over and proceeded as usual. Enjoying very fine weather and visibility, *Enola*

Gay itself was flying at twenty-six thousand feet, almost too high to be seen and heard from the ground. At 0816 hours, the doors opened. The bomb was dropped while the aircraft, to avoid being hit by the blast, banked steeply and flew away as fast as it could.

Moments later a thousand suns shone. The city had been obliterated and as many as seventy-five thousand people lay dead or dying. With that, the first half of twentieth-century warfare was clearly at an end.

In the Shadow of the Bomb

5.1. Looking Backward

To the historians who tried to evaluate it during the early decades after 1945, the Second World War looked very different from the first. The most spectacular difference was the development and use of armored forces. In 1914, the German army—which, once it had left the railways, depended on the legs of men and animals—had failed to carry out the Schlieffen Plan and bring the war to a swift conclusion. In 1939–41, it was armored and mechanized, forces that enabled their successors to carry out sweeping operational movements, overrunning entire countries until their exploits became almost legendary. Over the next few decades, armored divisions were seen by many as the very symbol of military might; each time a coup was carried out somewhere in the world, the first sign was tanks roaming the streets. Most countries quickly followed the German example, and as a result, the experience of 1914–18 was not to be repeated; fronts rarely stayed in place for more than a few months on end.

Another critical difference consisted in the conduct of the war in the air. In 1914–18, airpower, owing to its novelty and the primitive state of technology, had been able to play only an ancillary role, whereas any blows it was able to deliver to the ground were negligible. In World War II, airpower was employed on a huge scale—never larger—and to very great effect. Many, if not all, of the German campaigns of 1939–41 had started with a blow aimed at achieving air superiority. Thereafter it was a question of interdicting enemy movements, providing close air support, and, on several occasions, carrying out airborne operations. Had it not been for the Luftwaffe, the campaigns in question would probably not have succeeded.

The role played by airpower at sea was, if anything, even greater, to the point at which it was sometimes not clear whether it was aircraft that supported ships or the other way around. To all this was added Douhet-style "strategic" bombing aimed at the enemy rear. Neither the Germans nor the Japanese really had the machines necessary for the purpose, with the result that their achievements in this field remained relatively meager. The Western Allies, however, after a slow start, let loose such a torrent of bombs in 1943–45 that many German and Japanese cities were turned into smoldering ruins.

Such developments rightly caught the imagination of military experts who tried to understand what had happened, why it had happened, and what might happen in the future. Still, at a deeper level the similarities between the two conflicts probably outweighed the differences. The most important similarity consisted of the fact that, on both sides, the belligerents were the largest and most powerful states ever seen on earth until then.

To be sure, their number and relative strength had changed; Austria-Hungary had ceased to exist; France and Britain had become much weaker; Germany, Japan, the United States, and the USSR much stronger. Still, the system of Great Powers remained intact, and the only power capable of seriously fighting any of them was another power. When Stalin during the Yalta Conference asked Roosevelt and Churchill how many divisions the pope possessed, he had a point.

Even as late as 1950, the year when the American political scientist Hans Morgenthau published his seminal *Politics Among Nations*, the state was almost the only kind of political organization he bothered to mention. And while the systems by which the various states were governed still differed as much as they did in World War II, from the totalitarian to the democratic, and from those that executed millions of their own citizens to such as for the most part safeguarded human rights even in wartime, a common thread was that each state had a government run by people who did not take a direct role in the fighting, although their task was to mobilize all the state's power and direct it against the enemy. Each had armed forces consisting of millions of uniformed men and women. Finally, in every state, there was a civilian population that provided the necessary labor and intellectual capital that the war machine demanded.

The logistic breakthroughs pioneered by German armored forces enabled the Wehrmacht to bring down medium powers such as France in a single bound. Later, the same applied to countries such as Egypt, which was defeated by Israel in 1967; or Iraq, defeated by the United States both in 1991 and in 2003. Yet powerful as they were, armored forces did not have the reach to deliver a knockout blow to continental-sized powers such as Germany or the Soviet Union, with the result that the struggle between them lasted for years.

Correctly applied, World War II–style air- and sea power could help a ground army carry out specific operations and push them to a conclusion. However, neither at sea nor in the air could there be any question of a single climactic battle that, by rendering the opponent defenseless and breaking his will, decided the issue. Even the battle of Leyte Gulf, the largest ever fought at sea, did not mark more than one stage in the destruction of the Japanese navy;[1] the fact that volumes with titles such as *Command Decisions* or *Decisive Battles of World War II* are usually divided into as many as ten chapters (and that the chapters in each book seldom overlap) speaks for itself.[2] In all three media where it was waged, and on both sides of Eurasia, the war consisted of a prolonged struggle of attrition. As such, it was marked by countless small engagements as well as a relatively small number of much larger ones.

As in 1914–18, the onset of attrition meant that sufficient time was available for the belligerents to mobilize all their resources and for the war to become total. As in 1914, the result was very rapid technological progress as both sides sought new ways to counter the other's weapons. Only on the Eastern Front could all available resources be transported and brought into contact relatively easily by land. The result was a titanic struggle that, in terms of size, easily eclipsed all the rest. Everywhere else, the role of sea power was paramount. It enabled Britain to remain in the war and survive; permitted both sides to slug it out in North Africa; allowed Japan to launch its initial offensive; and made it possible for the United States to bring its enormous resources to bear in theaters as far apart as New Guinea and the Aleutians, France, and the Philippines. Whatever the method by which the resources were brought to bear, the prolongation of the conflict tended to work in favor of the side with the larger demographic, economic, and industrial base. Conversely, those who, like the Germans and the Japanese, possessed fewer resources and were therefore forced to stake everything on the success of their initial offensives, lost.

A pilot flying a jumbo jet over a stormy ocean will get a different view of it than does a man who, sitting in a rubber boat, is tossed about by the waves. The more time passes, the stronger the tendency to see the period from 1914 through 1945 as a single conflict whose two parts were separated by a twenty years' truce. Historians may blame this or that Great Power or that for either starting the conflict or failing to prevent it; still, there is no doubt that, at bottom, its roots may be found in the competition among those Great Powers going back all the way to the eighteenth century. For almost a quarter of a millennium before 1945, the struggle, fed by the ever-growing resources of the powers themselves, expanded and expanded. Had it not been for the atomic bomb, and given a decent interval, there is every reason to believe that it would have continued to expand after 1945. And so it is to the atomic bomb, its successors, and the impact it had on war that we must next turn our attention.

5.2. From War Fighting to Deterrence

In 1939 (as in 1914) almost the entire world had been divided among a small number of Great Powers. In 1945, following a conflict that was unusually large and unusually destructive, the only two powers left that really mattered were the United States and the USSR, each of which later had the appellation *superpower* applied to it. Depending on whether they were large or small, developed or not, and their geographic location in relation to the rest, the importance of the remaining countries varied considerably. Yet the fundamental underlying fact was that, in terms of military power, no other state, however great, even came close to the superpowers in question.

And it's not that the positions of the United States and the USSR were symmetrical to each other. The latter, though it dominated most of the Eurasian continent, had suffered enormous demographic and economic losses.[3] At the time the war came to an end, the Soviet Union was engulfed in an ocean of blood and tears—a situation from which it took about fifteen years to recover fully. Militarily the communist state, like its Russian predecessor, had always been primarily a land power. This fact the subjugation of Eastern Europe did little to change; Moscow's exit to the sea continued to be blocked by the Strait of Denmark on the one hand and the Dardanelles on the other. In this respect, it differed sharply from the United States.

Like the USSR, the United States dominated an entire continent and even an entire hemisphere. Unlike the USSR, it constituted a global island and was much more dependent on sea power for both civilian and military purposes. With sea power went its now indispensable corollary, airpower; in fact long-range, strategic airpower became the field where the United States vastly outclassed everybody else.

Because it never suffered either bombardment or occupation, and because of the efficiency with which it mobilized, the United States was also the only major belligerent to get out of the war much richer than before. Between 1940 and 1944, its workforce increased by almost twenty million people. Over the same four years, GNP rose by 54 percent. The output of manufactured goods rose by 300 percent, and that of raw materials by 60 percent. By 1945, the United States, with only about 6 percent of the world's population, was accounting for half its industrial product.[4] It was this economic muscle, plus an outstanding scientific and technical infrastructure, further reinforced by many acquisitions from abroad, that enabled the United States to be the first country to build an atomic bomb, test it, and use it.

Once the bomb had been introduced, opinions on the way it would impact war quickly diverged. Politicians, military commanders, scientists (including Nobel Prize winners), academics, and journalists all took a hand in the debate.[5] Yet most of their writings have proven to have had no lasting value. Perhaps the most important contribution of all was made by a young American scholar, Bernard Brodie, who at that time was a professor at the National War College in Washington, DC.[6]

The atomic bomb, to use Brodie's own phrase, presented "the absolute weapon." Such was its destructive power, and such was the difficulty if not impossibility of mounting a defense that any large-scale war between countries that possessed it could only lead to the virtual annihilation of both. Nor did Brodie have any doubt that countries other than the United States would come to possess the bomb, and sooner rather than later. In this respect, too, he was more forward looking than his contemporaries, many of whom only woke up to what was happening when the Soviets conducted their first test. The idea that the only possible purpose the bomb could serve was to deter war from breaking out, and that military history had therefore come to a dead end, was perhaps best expressed by Walter Millis, a famous military historian who did his best work during the 1950s: "The military professional who must today preside over the design, production and employment of the giant weapons of mass destruction cannot learn much from Napoleon, or Jackson, or Lee, or Grant—who were all managers of men in combat, not of 'weapons systems' about which the most salient feature is that they must never . . . be allowed to come into collision."[7]

To the officers who had spent centuries perfecting the art of war, and who in 1939–45 had commanded millions of men in a titanic struggle, the shift from war fighting to deterrence represented something akin to a death sentence. No wonder many of them were reluctant to accept it. Brodie himself heeded Admiral Chester Nimitz', warning against leaping to the conclusion that armies and navies were now obsolete and could be consigned to the scrap heap. From then until the present day, countless similar warnings have been heard. Deterrence rests on a profound paradox. The objective is to prevent war from breaking out; the means to do so, by making it very clear to the other side that, should necessity demand, one is able and willing to fight. *Si pacem vis, bellum para.*

As it happened, the two bombs dropped on Hiroshima on August 6 and on Nagasaki three days later were the only ones in the US arsenal. As a result, the first step toward deterrence was to build more of them as quickly as possible. By the mid-1950s, such was progress in the field that the age of so-called nuclear plenty had arrived, meaning that the number of bombs available ceased to present a serious constraint for planning purposes. Yet the construction of more bombs continued. By the 1960s, the number was in the thousands, and by the 1980s it had reached the tens of thousands. Though infinitely more powerful than anything used in war up to that time, the bombs only proved destructive to medium-sized Japanese cities already well known to be quite flammable. What of larger cities, built out of cement, girders, and mortar? The successful testing of the first hydrogen bomb in 1953 solved that problem.

By the time John F. Kennedy entered the White House in 1961, the standard US "strategic" warhead was fifteen megatons—equivalent to fifteen million tons of TNT and a hundred times as powerful as the Hiroshima bomb. So large had the arsenal become that every Hiroshima-sized Soviet city was being targeted by no fewer than three hydrogen bombs. As Winston Churchill once observed, adding more explosive power would only make the rubble bounce.

But how to deliver the bomb to its target? The device that demolished Hiroshima was based on enriched uranium, weighed ten tons, and could barely fit into the largest and most powerful bomber available. The one that destroyed Nagaski weighed somewhat less but was also huge in size. The B-29 itself had been built specifically in order to reach Japan from island bases as far as fifteen hundred miles away. Still, it did not have the range to reach much of the Soviet Union, a country stretching over eleven time zones, from the bases available to the United States at the time; besides, being piston-engined and therefore rather slow, it was soon rendered obsolete as new, jet-engined fighters prepared to counter it. All this led generals to demand, and engineers to design, a series of larger, heavier, faster, and more powerful machines, including, to mention only those that were built in any numbers, the B-36, the B-47, the B-52, and the B-1.

Even so, this was only part of the story. Compared with bombers, the ballistic missiles first developed and used by the Germans in World War II had the advantage that the bases they required were much smaller and less vulnerable. Another advantage was that they did not require crews that had to be kept alive and (perhaps) extricated after the completion of the mission. Finally, their speed was much higher than that of bombers, hence they were that much harder, in fact almost impossible, to intercept.

Critics, pilots in particular, sometimes pointed out that missiles differed from bombers in that they could not be recalled after launch. That was true enough, but does not seem to have deterred any country from developing them. Their only serious disadvantage was that they could not carry as large a payload as bombers could. However, as bombs became smaller during the 1950s and 1960s, even that consideration ceased to play a serious role. By the 1970s, by the best available information, three times as much explosive power as had demolished Hiroshima could be packed into a warhead weighing only a quarter ton. The range, reliability, and accuracy of ballistic missiles grew until, by the early 1960s, the first true intercontinental ballistic missiles, or ICBMs, became available.

The general trend was that nuclear bombs became smaller and easier to handle until they could be carried not only by heavy bombers and ICBMs but by many other kinds of weapons systems as well. Eventually, fighter-bombers, tactical missiles, and heavy artillery all became delivery platforms. There was even a so-called atomic bazooka. As first MRV (multiple reentry vehicles) and then MIRVs (multiple independent reentry vehicles) made their appearance in the 1960s and 1970s, it became possible to put as many as ten warheads on a single missile. Cruise missiles, essentially versions of those first developed by the Germans in World War II, added even more destructive power.[8]

Just about every concept for delivering an atomic weapon to the target was tried by the US Army, Navy, and Air Force, and in the end, for reasons that often had more to do with interservice rivalry and the competition for resources than with real operational requirements,[9] most of them were adopted regardless of whether they made sense or not. Weapons and delivery vehicles, though, were only the tip of the iceberg.

At the height of the Cold War, American bases spread all the way from Iceland through Britain and Western Europe, the Mediterranean, Pakistan, Southeast Asia, Australia, New Zealand, Korea, and Japan. There are still hundreds in existence, some acknowledged, others not.[10] Their size varied from isolated outposts centering, say, on a radar apparatus, to enormous complexes that serviced entire fleets of aircraft, naval vessels, or missiles. Using the terminology of the time, most were not "hardened" to the point that they could expect to "ride out" a nuclear attack; but some, including in particular missile silos and headquarters, were.

To provide surveillance, reconnaissance, early warning, and a coordinated response, all the bases—as well as the numerous mobile launchers on land, at sea, and in the air—had to be linked by a vast command, control, and communications system.[11] That system itself had to be protected against a possible nuclear attack, a task made even harder by the fact that such an attack would release not only a blast but also an electromagnetic pulse (EMP) capable of neutralizing electronic components within a radius of hundreds of miles from point zero.

As the nuclear forces developed, so did doctrines for using them if necessary. Partly because the United States was the first country to build the bomb and the delivery vehicles capable of carrying it, partly because no defense appeared feasible, the early doctrines centered on the need to get in the first nuclear blow so as to destroy the other side before it could strike back. This led to a variety of campaign plans, most of them concocted by the US Air Force, with such names as Bushwacker, Dropshot, and Broiler. Each plan was designed to kill millions upon millions of people, most of them civilians unfortunate enough to live in, or near, the most important Soviet industrial cities. Each one consisted primarily of a list of such cities to be targeted. Each went into some detail by spelling out the forces allocated to demolishing them, the bases from which those forces would take off, the formations in which they would fly, the countermeasures they would take to cope with Soviet defenses, and so on.

Yet this doctrine did not survive the mid-1950s when the Soviet Union, having exploded its first hydrogen device only a year after the United States did, also approached nuclear plenty.[12] Under such conditions, launching a nuclear blow would only lead to America's own destruction as the Kremlin used its remaining forces in order to launch a counterattack. Now everything depended, or was said to depend, on building the forces to enable them to respond to such a blow—and, by so doing, deter it from being launched in the first place.[13] The concept would come to be known as mutually assured destruction, or MAD for short. The most important proponents of this shift in policy were President John F. Kennedy, President Lyndon B. Johnson, and their remarkable, if highly controversial, secretary of defense, Robert S. McNamara. Not accidentally, it was also the Kennedy administration that moved toward placing less reliance on heavy bombers and more on easier-to-conceal, easier-to-defend ballistic missiles and submarines.

Yet MAD, too, proved short-lived. The doctrine, and the forces dedicated to implementing it if necessary, might indeed be suitable to deter a full-scale Soviet nuclear attack on the United States. However, and precisely because putting it into effect would lead to an unprecedented holocaust, it did not seem capable of deterring smaller attacks on Washington's extensive overseas interests, bases, and allies. To use the terminology of the time for the second time, it did not provide "credibility." This again led to the conclusion, very welcome to the military in the endless quest for more resources, that it was necessary to have the ability, and of course the will, to counter a possible Soviet attack of any kind, anywhere in the world, not just with a massive nuclear blow (which might prove suicidal) but with forces tailored for the purpose. Precisely because they were smaller, such forces would be better able to deter; and, should deterrence fail, they could fight a "limited" war without necessarily threatening to blow up the world. The policy was called flexible response, and would be soon tested in Vietnam.

Economically speaking, and despite Secretary General Nikita Khrushchev's famous statement that "we shall bury you," the United States continued to outclass the USSR by far.[14] In 1957–61, the so-called missile gap that followed the launching of the first Soviet satellite played a role in bringing President Kennedy to power; later, however, it proved to be largely imaginary.[15] That episode apart, it was almost always the United States that, thanks to its unrivaled research and development establishment as well as its industrial prowess, pioneered the introduction of new weapons. They ranged from intercontinental bombers in the 1950s to sea-launched ballistic missiles (SLBMs), and from multiple independent reentry vehicles (MIRV) in the 1960s all the way to cruise missiles in the 1970s; to say nothing of the revolution in computers and communications needed to coordinate and target them.

Seeking allies, the United States surrounded itself with medium-sized but highly developed powers such as Britain, France, and, from the mid-1950s on, West Germany and Japan. Contrast this with the plight of the Soviet Union. Following its rift with China, which at times brought the two to the brink of war, the only allies the Soviets could truly count on were third-rate powers such as East Germany, Poland, Hungary, and North Korea. Throughout the Cold War, the situation that US secretary of defense George S. Marshall had described in 1945, in which three out of the world's major potential arms-producing regions (North America, Western Europe, and Japan) were firmly in American hands, prevailed. Yet somehow Washington convinced itself that, quantitatively and in some respects qualitatively as well, its conventional armed forces and those of its allies were incapable of matching those of the communists.[16] The implication was that, should war break out, the West would have no other choice but to use "tactical" nuclear weapons in order to stop an attack.

In time, the perceived need to counter the supposed Soviet conventional superiority with nuclear weapons without leading to escalation led to the development of numerous ideas, some of which were as hare-brained as they were dangerous. Already in the 1950s, some military men sought to dispel the "bugaboo of radiation" by convincing their colleagues that fighting a conventional war in the presence of nuclear weapons was possible, and took some steps to organize the forces accordingly.[17] Hardly more practical, some civilians hoped that it might be possible to reach agreement concerning the maximum power of nuclear warheads, limiting the kind of targets against which they might be used, and so on.[18]

Following the demise of MAD, the secretary of defense in the Nixon administration, James Schlesinger, started talking about "selective options"—the possibility of using a relatively small number of small nuclear weapons to destroy choice targets. Others thought of "escalation dominance" and "nuclear shots across the bow." Perhaps the most hair-raising idea of all was a theory called "decapitation." Its centerpiece was newly developed, unbelievably accurate delivery vehicles that entered service during the 1980s. By using them, it was hoped to eliminate the Soviet leadership by a single blow and win a war before it had actually started.

We cannot go into all the fantasies, often bearing strong sexual overtones (as when people talked of "penetration aids"), that for decades on end masqueraded as serious doctrine and sought to make the use of nuclear weapons possible. Suffice it to say that, as of the time of this writing in 2006, Brodie's analysis remains as relevant as if it had been written yesterday. A reliable defense against nuclear weapons and their delivery vehicles does not appear more feasible than it was in October 1945 when President Truman told Congress that "every weapon will eventually bring some counter defense."[19] Instead, the attempt to develop it is one more reason why the United States is teetering on the verge of bankruptcy. Though the Bush administration has developed a National Security Strategy that advocates pre-emptive attacks,[20] and though it wants to develop so-called "mini-nukes" in order to launch a strike, in reality Brodie's warning that such weapons have created an entirely new situation remains in force. There is, of course, no absolute guarantee that the United States, or some other country, will never resort to nuclear weapons, and indeed this fact itself is a cardinal factor in maintaining deterrence and securing peace. Either don't use your sword or be prepared to die on it: such has been the central logic of the last sixty years.

5.3. From Proliferation to Stalemate

As Brodie had expressly foreseen, the United States did not retain its nuclear monopoly for long. As he might also have foreseen, it did not take kindly to the idea that others might join the nuclear club. When the USSR tested its first nuclear device in September 1949, the American reaction was close to mass hysteria; was not Stalin the most evil of men, and was he not bent on destroying the United States? One outcome of the hysteria was the trial and execution of two alleged Soviet spies, Julius and Ethel Rosenberg. It also contributed to the period of intensive Red hunting that had begun gathering steam after 1945 and was destined to last until the beginning of the Eisenhower administration when, no thanks to the president, it was brought to an end.

Owing to the country's unique geographic position, military traditions, and strategic objectives, Soviet developments in the nuclear field were also unique. There was, for example, a much greater emphasis on missiles and rockets. The USSR never developed a bomber fleet even nearly as large as that of its opponent. At sea, too, the Soviet navy never deployed nuclear-capable aircraft carriers and their numerous escort vessels. Instead it focused on sea-launched rockets and cruise missiles, launched either from surface vessels or from submarines. Conversely, when the time came to introduce intercontinental ballistic missiles the Soviets ended up deploying more of them than the Americans did. Perhaps because they were less accurate, the weight of the warheads they carried was also considerably larger; a single SS-18 missile was quite capable of knocking out a medium-sized country such as France.

As already remarked, technologically speaking the Soviets tended to come second. Usually they developed new weapons only after the Americans. Sometimes they engaged in direct imitation of their ingenious rivals—as happened, for example, when Stalin gave orders to reverse-engineer the B-29. Another point on which the Soviets differed from their rivals was that they were much less voluble. They developed only one doctrine for every American ten; as a result, they were able to maintain much greater continuity and, perhaps, avoid wasting resources.

Much of what passed for American doctrine was designed to find ways of using nuclear weapons to offset a supposed Soviet conventional superiority without necessarily blowing up the world. This idea was not adopted by the Soviets, who always emphasized that the "Imperialist aggressors" were deluding themselves and that any large-scale war would be nuclear from the beginning.[21] To bolster their claim, they also claimed that their nuclear weapons and delivery vehicles were "fully integrated" with the rest of their forces—though what this meant, if it meant anything at all, remains unclear.

To follow the countless twists and turns of the two superpowers as they faced each other like scorpions in a bottle can serve little purpose and will not be attempted here. Suffice it to say that the Americans were much more aggressive, using, or threatening to use, force against third parties far more often than their opponent did;[22] the most important conflict in which they engaged, the war in Vietnam, was far larger than all the Soviet interventions combined. And although, here and there, a country that had previously been pro-American aligned itself with the Soviet Union, or the other way around, with the exception of China all those that did so were third-rate powers.

The closest the two sides got to moving away from a "war" of words and gestures toward a thermonuclear exchange was probably during the Cuban Missile Crisis of October 1962; though some key participants in that episode have argued that, even on that occasion, the chances of President Kennedy actually pushing the button were remote.[23] Next came the installation of so-called hotlines between the White House and the Kremlin as well as the 1972 Strategic Arms Limitations Treaty; the Helsinki Agreement of 1975, which provided for mutual advance notification of maneuvers; and the 1987 Intermediate Range Nuclear Forces (INF) Treaty, which made Europe into a nuclear-free zone. None of these agreements ended the arms race, but each in its time probably helped reduce tensions somewhat. In the end, without any doubt, the factor that really kept the superpowers from fighting each other was mutual fear.

The next two countries to introduce nuclear weapons were Britain and France, the former testing its first device in 1952 and the latter in

1960. Although, at the time, both were still considered "powers," both were clearly in decline. As one colony after another within their respective empires went free, their global influence contracted; in the end, it was limited almost exclusively to Europe. Both saw the bomb as a means to offset that decline and restore their prestige, but whether they could have succeeded in doing so is doubtful. Neither in terms of the number and power of bombs, nor in terms of delivery vehicles, nor in terms of the necessary command and control network, could either France or Britain even remotely compete with either the United States or the USSR. Had they ever tried to use their arsenals against the latter, then they would have been wiped off the map and their territories made into radioactive deserts.

Both Britain and France justified their programs by throwing out a screen of words, as the French did when they pretended that their *force de frappe* (deterrent force) was meant to operate in *"toutes les azymuts"* (all directions). In reality, the objective of their nuclear programs, if any, was to provide a sort of insurance policy in case the United States failed to live up to its commitment to support them against the USSR[24]—a possibility that was never far from the European mind. In the event, the Soviets never ventured to seriously test the US commitment in the first place. As a result, whether or not the existence of the British and French nuclear forces, on which so much money was spent, ever made any real difference to their owners' national strategies is debatable. Which, of course, is one reason why other NATO countries did not choose to follow their example even though some of them could have done so easily enough.

China's interest in nuclear weapons appears to date from the period immediately after the Korean War. At that time, presidents Truman and Eisenhower had apparently considered, though they ultimately did not accept, using such weapons in order to bring the conflict to an end;[25] more or less veiled American nuclear threats also seem to have played a role in the two Quemoy crises of 1955 and 1958. All this led China's leader, Mao Tse-tung, to the rather obvious conclusion that he, too, needed to have a few bombs "so that nobody will be able to touch me."[26] At first China's close ally, the USSR, assisted Mao's program by providing experts as well as some of the special materials needed to construct a gaseous diffusion plant. In 1959, however, the Soviets, afraid lest Beijing's "adventurist" policies might end in a full-scale war with the United States withdrew their support, leaving their allies nothing but a jumble of pipes.

The Chinese testing of an atomic device in 1963, followed by the testing of a hydrogen bomb four years later, formed a turning point. Until then, the four members of the nuclear club had been highly developed, relatively wealthy countries. The Chinese achievement proved that, given some external help, even some of the world's poorest, least developed countries could muster enough resources and expertise to develop the bomb; even should the help not be forthcoming, it might still be possible to steal the necessary technology. By the time Pakistan achieved nuclear parity in 1974–77,[27] almost the only countries that remained without the bomb were those that did not even attain its degree of development or deliberately refrained from joining the atomic race.

Throughout its initial period of nuclear development, and for some years thereafter, China was ruled by Mao Tse-tung, whom many considered one of the most dangerous leaders the world had ever seen. At one point he had talked of getting rid of "Imperialism" even if doing so cost hundreds of millions of dead.[28] Yet, looking back on Chinese foreign policy as it has developed since his death, if anything it has become less adventurous. The last time China used armed forces on any scale was in 1979, when the opponent was tiny North Vietnam. Even so the war only lasted for one week, involved only a small part of China's forces, penetrated to a depth of a mere fifteen miles, and ended in a withdrawal.

China's success in developing the bomb acted as a spur to India, its neighbor and rival. In terms of national development, India was not much, if at all, better off than China, and probably received even less outside assistance. Yet an Indian Nuclear Energy Committee was formed soon after independence with the prime minister, Jawaharlal Nehru, at its head. By the mid-1960s, the Indians were clearly approaching their goal;[29] indeed, it is possible that the Pakistani attack on India in 1965 represented an attempt by that country's rulers to gain Kashmir before the Indian program could bear fruit. In the event, the Indians waited another nine years before they decided to unveil their bomb, and another twenty-four years after that before they followed up their first test with others. As with China, acquisition of the bomb has made them less aggressive rather than more so, a fact that is confirmed by events on the ground. Between 1947 and 1971, New Delhi waged three wars against Pakistan and one against China. Since then, all it has done is try to pacify Sri Lanka—in vain, as it turned out—and engage in occasional skirmishes in the Himalayas.

Given the intense rivalry between the two, the Pakistani drive to acquire nuclear weapons was clearly motivated by the Indian one. After 1971, the year when India defeated Pakistan and caused it to break into two parts, its new prime minister, Zulfikar Ali Bhutto (who had previously been head of his country's nuclear energy committee), said that his countrymen would eat grass if that is what it took to build the bomb. By the late 1970s, they were clearly within sight of doing so even though, since they did not care to conduct a test, the exact time at which their program bore fruit remains unknown.[30] In the end, it was three Pakistani tests, taking place in 1998, that caused the Indians to follow suit—providing additional proof, if that was needed, that practically any country can now acquire a nuclear arsenal if it really wants to.

Currently, the four most interesting cases are those of Israel, Iraq, North Korea, and Iran. Looking back, Israel has probably possessed the bomb since before the 1967 War.[31] Because it did not want to spur the Arabs into building their own bombs, and its desire to preserve good relations with Washington, Israel has refrained from conducting an open test. Instead, it has gone out of its way to deny it possesses the bomb; arguably it was this restraint that allowed the 1967 War, as well as the Yom Kippur War in 1973, to take place. Since then, however, things have changed as the country's denials ceased to have any credibility. Probably as a result, the only large-scale armed conflict Israel has engaged in consisted of the halfhearted invasion of Lebanon. In this way, the proposition that nuclear proliferation leads to peace has held even in this case. Conversely one could argue that, had Israel's nuclear program not existed, then the 1980s and 1990s would have seen even larger outbreaks of war in the Middle East than the one that took place in 1973.[32]

Iraq's nuclear program got under way in the late 1960s. After many delays, it was reaching the point where its first, French-built reactor was about to go critical when that reactor was destroyed by Israeli bombing. Later the Iraqis tried to restart their program—with what success, is hard to say. If Western intelligence services are to be believed, at the time the First Gulf War broke out Saddam Hussein's program was well conceived, extensive, and well funded. Centering on enriched uranium rather than plutonium, it could have borne fruit in anything between six months—supposing the Iraqi dictator had contented himself with a primitive, hard-to-deliver device—and three years.[33] Given that the same intelligence services, operating in the same country, later invented weapons of mass destruction out of thin air, looking back not everybody is convinced they were telling the truth in 1991, either. Whether possession of the bomb would have made Saddam Hussein more aggressive than he was, as some claim,[34] or whether it would have the same dampening effect on him as it did on everybody else, will never be known. The man was undoubtedly very bad, but he was not mad.

North Korea, as one of the most backward, most isolated countries on earth, is also located in a rather dangerous part of the world, the so-called Iron Triangle where it is surrounded on all sides by countries much more powerful than it. All either have nuclear weapons or can produce them at short notice—to say nothing of the presence, in South Korea, of powerful American forces complete with their tactical nuclear weapons and delivery vehicles. Under such conditions, Pyongyang's apparent decision to go nuclear makes perfect sense. Its objective seems to be to guarantee the survival of a pariah regime that has practically no assets of any other kind.

To a lesser degree, the same applies to Iran. Following the 2003 war in the Middle East, Iran was surrounded by American forces, to wit the northeast (the Central Asian republics), the east (Afghanistan), the south (the Persian Gulf), and the west (Iraq). Given President Bush's national security strategy emphasizing pre-emption even against non-nuclear countries, and also in view of what happened to Saddam Hussein, whoever rules in Tehran has excellent reason to build such weapons as fast as possible. As in the case of other countries, it is not at all clear what effect the bomb, once it is completed, will have on Iranian foreign policy. Its possession may increase the mullahs' self-confidence and lead to aggression, but it may also increase self-confidence and lead to restraint. Given the historical record since 1945, the second is more likely than the first.

As the country that was the first to introduce nuclear weapons (and the only one, so far, to use it on an enemy), the United States has every incentive to prevent other countries from entering the nuclear club. As a result, each time that club expanded Washington immediately started painting apocalyptic pictures of the consequences that would follow. To a lesser but still considerable extent, this policy even applied to its closest allies, Britain and France, causing the latter to remove its armed forces from under the NATO command. In regard to nuclear issues, as to so many others, Americans see their country as uniquely chosen and uniquely moral. Yet it could certainly be argued that, long before the Bush administration produced its aforementioned National Security Doctrine, the United States had behaved less responsibly than any other country on earth. If it did not actually use nuclear weapons after Nagasaki, it has certainly threatened to do so many times and against more than one opponent. Not by accident, the term *brinkmanship* itself is an American invention.[35]

Nuclear weapons have now been around for six decades. Neither active nor passive measures to counter them or diminish their impact have made any real progress; in this respect, our situation is still what it was in 1949 when Hanson Baldwin of *The New York Times* declared such measures to be "possible and realizable."[36] At a peak in the 1980s, there were tens of thousands of nuclear warheads controlled by eight or nine countries, depending on who you believe. Yet thankfully, since Nagasaki not a single one has been detonated in anger. One result has been that many of the delivery vehicles specifically developed for carrying them, such as heavy bombers and cruise missiles, have been used only in conventional operations; the waste that doing so entails may well be imagined. As far as anybody can judge, nuclear weapons have made the world a much safer place, not a more dangerous one—as many people had feared and as many Americans in particular, seeking to prevent others from getting what they themselves already had, claimed would happen.

In fact, far from being used in another all-out war among the Great Powers as many people in the 1950s thought would happen, nuclear weapons had cast their shadow on all other forms of war as well. Therefore, it is to the development of non-nuclear, or conventional, war, that we must now turn our attention.

5.4. The Conduct of Conventional War

Since 1945 large-scale conventional, interstate war has been limited almost entirely to one part of the world. Shaped like a huge sickle, it starts in the eastern Mediterranean (the Balkans), passes through the Middle East and the Horn of Africa, extends through the Persian Gulf to South Asia, and reaches by way of Vietnam all the way to Korea. Again proceeding from west to east, the list opens with the two Balkan wars of 1992–99. It also includes the six Arab–Israeli wars of 1948, 1956, 1967, 1970, 1973, and 1982; the war between Ethiopia and Somalia; the two Gulf wars of 1991 and 2003, plus the Iran–Iraq War of 1980–88; the three Indo-Pakistani wars of 1947–48, 1965, and 1971; the 1961 Indo-Chinese War; the 1979 Chinese invasion of Vietnam; and, of course, the Korean War of 1950–53. Thus, the total number of wars waged in this region stands at eighteen. By contrast, and disregarding one or two Latin American "wars" that broke out over such things as a football match between Honduras and El Salvador, elsewhere in the world there has been only one real war: the one waged by the British and the Argentines over the Falkland Islands in 1982. However, since 1945 no first-, or second-rate powers ever engaged in more than border skirmishes against each other.

These were wars for the most part fought by third- and even fourth-rate armed forces. At the time they fought their war in 1961, neither India nor China was considered a Great Power. Here and there during those years, a Great Power—including, above all, the United States as the greatest power of all—did engage in large-scale conventional war. However, they only did so against opponents much smaller than themselves. The outcome were struggles such as Korea, the Chinese invasion of Vietnam, and the two wars against Iraq. All of which had in common that they were waged by a Great Power (in the case of the United States, a superpower) against a much smaller opponent that did not yet have nuclear weapons or, indeed, was not known to be close to acquiring them.

First-rate powers or not, the wars of the second half of the twentieth century were often as deadly and as destructive as the titanic struggles that marked its first half. Relative to the populations involved, the casualties suffered were often enormous. For example, two hundred thousand people are said to have died in the multisided struggles in the former Yugoslavia. However, even this falls far short of the eight hundred thousand who were killed in the war between Iran and Iraq and the million and a half who lost their lives in Korea. In fact, so large were losses in many of these conflicts that the relevant casualty figures are, in reality, little more than guesses.

Even so, these wars represented the exception rather than a rule. Korea, of course, was made possible solely by the fact that both sides received outside support, the north from the Soviet Union and China and the south from the United States. In the case of Iran and Iraq, what permitted them to pursue the war for as long as they did, with the intensity that they did, on the scale that they did, was the fact that both are among the largest exporters of oil on earth. By contrast, most of the remaining belligerents, lacking any considerable military industries, did not have what it took to fight for very long and did not have the administrative capacities to mobilize all their resources as the Great Powers had done in World Wars I and II. Most of their wars degenerated into low-level, though deadly, slogging matches, as happened in the case of Ethiopia and Somalia and also inside the former Yugoslavia. Or else they consisted of short, sharp thrusts—which describes most of the Arab–Israeli wars, the second and third Indo-Pakistani wars, the Indo-Chinese War, the Chinese–Vietnamese War, and the Falkland War.

Seen from the point of view of the military expert, neither the first Indo-Pakistani War nor the 1948 Arab–Israeli War had many lessons to offer. In both cases, the forces engaged were, by the standards of 1939–45, small and disorganized. For example, the largest unit fielded by the Israelis, as well as their opponents, was the brigade. The Indians and the Pakistanis didn't even manage that, but had to rest content with battalions instead. In both conflicts, the belligerents had to make do with weapons that had been abandoned by their recently departed colonial masters, plus whatever home-produced munitions they could lay their hands on; at the time the 1948 war ended, the Israeli Defense Force (IDF) had exactly four operational tanks. Qualitatively, too, they did not stand up. Springing out of the British Indian army, where they had previously served under British officers, both the Pakistani and Indian armed forces were decapitated when practically their entire officer corps packed and left for home. Having started life as an underground movement, the nascent IDF also left something to be desired in its organization, discipline, and training.[37] As an Israeli daredevil who later rose to become his country's chief of staff and minister of defense, Moshe Dayan, used to say: We're lucky that the enemy consists of Arabs, not Germans.

What applied to these two wars was almost equally true of the Korean War.[38] Initially, the order of battle on both sides was rather small. Later, it expanded greatly, and many of the forces engaged in it were as well organized and well commanded as the then current American and Soviet doctrines permitted. The war also witnessed the use of several new weapons systems, the most important of which were jet aircraft and helicopters. The latter were often employed as flying command posts but also served for liaison, supply, reconnaissance, and casualty evacuation. In Vietnam, the chop-chop of rotors was usually the signal warning medics that another load of shot-up boys was on its way.

All this is true, but it does not change the fact that, on both sides, doctrine, training, and most kinds of equipment either came directly out of World War II or were slightly improved versions of weapons used in that struggle. Both helicopters and jet aircraft had already been under development in 1939–45; some were even used in combat. As a result, the war opened with a Blitzkrieg-like North Korean offensive spearheaded by a relatively small number of those old warhorses, Soviet T-34 tanks. It continued with the American amphibious landing at Inchon, also taken straight out of World War II and commanded by the very same man (General Douglas MacArthur) who had been responsible for several of them; and it ended with a massive battle of attrition as masses of Chinese infantrymen engaged in "human wave" assaults against superior US firepower.

At the time the war broke out, both superpowers already possessed nuclear weapons—even though the United States, enjoying a head start of four years, must have possessed far more of them than the Soviets did. Fear of escalation was very much in the air, and as a result, operations never extended beyond Korea. The Americans never crossed the Yalu River or sent their forces into China. When MacArthur insisted that this should be done, his supreme commander, President Truman, fired him almost on the spot. In this respect, Korea set a pattern that, for all the efforts of the Dr. Strangeloves both in the White House and in the Kremlin to break it, was to persist to the end of the Cold War. The more closely any two belligerents were tied to the apron strings of their superpower patrons, the stronger those superpowers' control over them and the smaller the chance that they would be permitted to fight out their differences to the end. In Europe, where the superpowers' clients faced one another directly and where the enormous concentration of forces made the danger of escalation greater than anywhere else, no war was allowed to take place at all.

With the so-called Central Theater remaining peaceful, and with a wall separating the forces of North Korea from those of the south and their US allies, most interstate wars continued to be confined to the sickle that the British geographer Sir Halford Mackinder early in the twentieth century had called "the rimlands."[39] Those that drew the greatest attention largely because they involved a little country in the Middle East where three great religions are centered, were the Arab–Israeli ones. Disregarding Israel's struggle for independence in 1948, the first in the series was the 1956 Suez campaign. It fell into two parts, the Israeli drive into the Sinai and the Anglo-French seaborne descent on Alexandria and Port Said. The former only involved about two and a half divisions on either side, lasted all of six days, and was fought largely (though not entirely, as the participation of Soviet-built MiG-15 and French Mystère IV fighter-bombers showed) with the aid of such second-rate weapons as the belligerents could afford. The latter made use of the most up-to-date techniques; however, neither the British nor the French forces could stand comparison to the US or Soviet armed forces. In the end, perhaps the outstanding lesson of the campaign was that former Great Powers, now reduced to the second rank, could no longer expect to bend even a third-rate opponent in the "developing" world to their will. The more extensive the territories they overran, the greater the opposition they encountered; often that opposition originated less in their enemies' armed forces than in the conquered people themselves. Soon, moreover, the same lesson was to be applied to the superpowers as well.

The next round of Arab–Israeli wars was something else. By 1967, the Israeli air force had grown into a modern organization. It was characterized by a cohesive doctrine, excellent training, and, last but not least, motivation sans pareil; for every sortie it had generated in 1956, it was now able to generate ten. Though some of their equipment was out of date and their capacity for interarm cooperation limited, the ground forces, too, were well trained and highly motivated. On June 5, 1967, after three weeks during which the Arabs had deployed their forces along Israel's frontier, the IDF, commanded by Defense Minister Moshe Dayan and Chief of Staff Yitzhak Rabin, struck.

The campaign opened with a surprise air attack against Egyptian, Syrian, Jordanian, and even Iraqi airfields. Next, a classic Blitzkrieg spearheaded by as many as eight hundred tanks hit the combined, 350,000-strong Arab armies, scattering them as chaff is scattered by the wind. Partly because of this achievement, partly because it was compared to the American effort in Vietnam, which was already sinking (wags suggested that, in return for giving Israel companies such as General Electric and General Motors, the United States might obtain General Dayan and General Rabin), the war drew worldwide attention. The IDF's determination, willingness to act, and courage were admirable and indeed acted as an inspiration to people everywhere. However, military experts well knew that the Israeli campaign bore a stronger resemblance to those of 1940–41 than to anything else. Nor, for that matter, did what opposition the Arab armies were able to put up compare to that faced by the Wehrmacht at its prime.[40]

Fought largely with American, French, and Soviet weapons, the war transformed the Middle East. Previously it had been seen as a rather backward part of the world interesting mainly because of the Suez Canal and the oil that flowed from it. Now it was a military laboratory where both superpowers deployed and tested their most modern conventional hardware. Large-scale fighting—at peak, the Egyptians alone deployed more than a thousand guns and heavy mortars—broke out along the Suez Canal in March 1969. The Israelis relied primarily on their superb air force, which was now provided with powerful, American-built F-4 fighter-bombers as well as some of the most modern avionics. Unable to match their opponents in this respect, the Egyptians and the Syrians with Soviet aid responded by constructing the most formidable anti-aircraft systems in history. In August 1970, a cease-fire went into effect, bringing the shooting to an end and enabling the two sides to consolidate and prepare for the next round three years later.

Discounting the invasion of Lebanon in 1982, which was really only half a war (when Israeli prime minister Menachem Begin realized that it would not lead to the easy victory he expected, he went into a funk, resigned, entered his home, and never left it again), the war of 1973 proved to be the last in a series.[41] It was extremely intensive, resulting in a high expenditure of ammunition. In eighteen days, the Israelis lost a quarter of their air force as well as a similar percentage of their tanks; on the Arab side, the losses may have been four or five times as large. It was truly a war of attrition; contemporaries compared the massive armored combat that took place in the Sinai and on the Golan Heights to the battle of Kursk in the summer of 1943.

To be sure, technology had not stood still. Tanks, armored personnel carriers, and artillery all grew larger, heavier, and much more capable. Both sides made much use of precision-guided weaponry. On the Arab side, batteries of radar-controlled surface-to-air missiles as well as sophisticated anti-aircraft guns with multiple barrels prevented the Israelis from commanding the air as effectively as they had in 1967; on the Israeli side, American-supplied air-to-surface missiles were introduced during the last days of the war and helped turn the tide of battle. Probably the most important outcome of the war was that the Arabs, whether because they came within a hair of suffering total defeat or because they feared the next round might lead to Israeli use of nuclear weapons,[42] did not renew their efforts. In this respect, one could argue that the events of 1967–73 played the same role in transforming war in the Middle East as those of 1914–45 did in respect to the world at large.

Throughout the post–World War II period, incomparably the greatest naval power, and the only one whose forces possess a truly global reach, is the United States. He who has not seen one of the navy's roll on–roll off ships, with deck upon deck crammed with the machinery of war, has never really seen military power. During the 1970s and 1980s, it sometimes looked as if the USSR, guided by Admiral Sergei Gorshkov, might follow suit.[43] However, after the communist regime collapsed in 1991, the Soviet navy, too, all but disappeared from the seas. One of its main bases, that in Odessa, was lost; ten years later, lack of maintenance had reduced many of its once proud vessels to rusting hulks. Instead of threatening the world with their weapons, they did so because of the radioactivity leaking from them. Looking back, throughout the Cold War the largest amphibious operations were the 1950 American landing at Inchon and the 1956 Anglo-French landings in Egypt. Both, however, were essentially unopposed; at the former, the greatest difficulty was presented not by the enemy but by the tides.

The most important weapon that permitted the United States to exercise its dominance was, of course, the aircraft carrier. The carriers themselves were directly descended from those that had played a key role in bringing down the Japanese empire. Their number fell from ninety-eight (including escort carriers) in 1945 to twelve in 2005, yet no other country possessed a similar force. Indeed, what carriers other countries such as Britain, France, Brazil, India, Thailand and, in the last years before its collapse, the USSR did have were decidedly second rate, being either old, or small, or capable of launching only inferior aircraft that carried light ordnance. Growing from about sixty thousand tons deadweight in the 1950s to about ninety thousand at the end of the twentieth century, the carriers are the largest, most complex, and most expensive war machines ever built. Ruling the seas, yet often hesitating to approach the coast because they feared what mines, submarines, and shore-based aircraft might do, they were often used to attack countries around the world that US presidents had taken a dislike to. Hardly ever did they themselves come under fire or sustain damage, however—perhaps the clearest indication of the kind of enemies those presidents selected. This was as true during the Vietnam War in 1964–75 as it was in 2002 during the war against Afghanistan; and also, of course, during the 2003 war against Iraq.

Naval forces did play a certain part in the Arab Israeli wars and also in the 1971 war between India and Pakistan. Not only was their role ancillary, though, but at the time and later none of the navies involved was first or even second class; none of them so much as possessed a single capital vessel. The Israeli navy was long considered a stepchild by the IDF, and at the time of the June 1967 War it did not even have its own radar. Instead, it had to rely on that of the air force, a factor said to have played a role in the accidental bombing of an American spy ship, the *Liberty*. The French-built, Israeli-armed missile boats that sank their Egyptian and Syrian opposite numbers in 1973 were quite advanced for their time, and the way they were handled in battle was decidedly brilliant. Even so, given that they displaced only 250 tons, there were clear limits to what could be gleaned from their maneuvers. To learn what elephants may do, one does not look at gnats.

In the decades since 1945, the single time that oceangoing forces did clash on any scale and played a critical role was in the 1982 Falkland Islands War. The islands were separated from the South American mainland by 250 miles of deep, very cold water. Once they had been occupied by the Argentineans in a surprise move, they could only be retaken by means of an amphibious landing. To carry out that landing, the first thing the British had to do was to gain control of the sea and the air above it. The mission was entrusted to a task force that consisted of practically the entire British navy, including two medium-sized aircraft carriers (the only ones the British had), several frigates and submarines to cover them, and of course the necessary supply ships, amphibious assault ships, and landing craft. Commanded by a submarine officer, Admiral Bob Woodward, this armada gathered at Ascension Island.

Approaching its objective, it came under attack by shore-based Argentinean Super-Étendard and A-4 fighter-bombers. The aircraft in question were old, almost obsolete, dating to the late 1950s and early 1960s; some of them had even been sold to the Argentineans second-hand by the Israelis. They were, however, armed with modern, fairly sophisticated, French-built, Exocet anti-ship missiles. Operating at extreme range, their pilots proved both determined and effective, sinking several British vessels with heavy loss of life. Yet when British carrier-based aircraft started getting the better of their opponents and a British submarine torpedoed the light cruiser *General Belgrano,* the largest vessel in the Argentinean navy, the game was up.[44]

Though the number of states had risen from about sixty in 1945 to almost three times that number in 1980, the last two decades of the twentieth century witnessed only two more major interstate wars. The first, waged between Iran and Iraq, was among the largest of all. At the time the war started in 1980, both countries were flush with money from oil, whose price had been rising throughout the preceding decade. Yet Iran, having gone through a revolution in the previous year, saw its armed forces decapitated; they also suffered from deficiencies in trained personnel and maintenance as foreign, mainly American, technicians were withdrawn and the flow of spare parts for their most advanced weapons systems dried up.

Somewhat like the Japanese in 1941 launching their offensive in the hope that Britain and the United States would not fight back, Iraqi dictator Saddam Hussein used these shortcomings in an attempt to over-run an Iranian province and hold it. But the Iranians did fight back. In early 1983, it even seemed as though they might occupy the Iraqi oil-producing city of Basra. Only desperate fighting in which he was supported by virtually the entire world—which was happy to subsidize him and sell him weapons—enabled Saddam to hold out. Using poison gas among other things, his forces repulsed the Iranian human wave assaults more reminiscent of World War I than of anything that had taken place since. In the end Saddam, using Soviet-designed, Iraqi-built, surface-to-surface SCUD missile technology derived from the German V2, bombed Tehran and gained the upper hand. Yet this was less because his forces had defeated their opponents in the field than because the other side, having bled itself half to death against the Iraqi defenses, simply gave up.

Despite the fact that he has since been taken prisoner and subjected to interrogation, just what made Saddam Hussein decide to invade Kuwait in 1991 may never be known.[45] At the time, the Iraqi armed forces were touted as being the fourth or fifth largest in the world, their order of battle including no fewer than a million men with five thousand tanks. Having at length succeeded in overcoming Iran, Saddam may have deluded himself that they were up to par, qualitatively speaking. In his favor, it must be said that he was by no means the only one to overestimate their capabilities. Various American prewar estimates, designed to calculate what it would take to defeat him, exaggerated the number of anticipated casualties by as much as ten to one.[46]

Coming under attack by more than half a million first-class US, British, and French troops, the Iraqis turned out to be third rate. At the time, the Iraqi air force had as many as seven hundred reasonably modern, French- and Soviet-built combat aircraft. However, after a few of them had been shot down during the early phases of the war, they hardly dared take off again. So desperate were the Iraqis that more than a hundred aircraft escaped to Iran, the enemy they had just finished fighting; there, for all anybody knows, they still remain. Having established command of the air, the Coalition quickly destroyed Iraq's air defenses by a combination of air, cruise missile, and, it is rumored, computer attacks that rendered their electronics inoperable.

Dominating the air, the Coalition was assisted by the fact that, in all the world, no piece of territory is more barren, flatter, and less able to provide cover than the Kuwaiti desert. Given these circumstances, all the Iraqi ground forces could do was to hunker down in their over-stretched, rather lightly fortified lines, where they were subjected to weeks-long attacks by eighteen hundred aircraft of every kind and size against which they were virtually helpless. The bombardment de-prived them of supplies, communications, and intelligence. Later, it turned out that the Iraqi high command in Baghdad had not even reg-istered the movement of an entire armored corps, the US Army's VII, 150 miles to the west—yet in the whole of military history since 1945, it is impossible to find a movement that was larger or, owing to the na-ture of the terrain, more difficult to conceal. When the ground offen-sive finally got under way, it was a walkover, which was proved by, among other things, the extremely low number of Coalition casualties.

Owing largely to nuclear proliferation, the armed conflicts of the second half of the twentieth century were, without a single exception, fought either between third- and fourth-rate states or by a first-rate state against a third- or fourth-rate state. If only for that reason, in terms of size, the conflicts bore no relation to those that had taken place dur-ing the first half. In terms of quality, including the quality of weapons technology, perhaps the most pronounced tendency was continuity. As had been the case during the titanic clashes of 1914 through 1945, wars were fought by uniformed, centrally commanded, bureaucratically managed armed forces operating on land, at sea, and in the air. As had been the case in 1914–45, those forces were directed by governments and supported by civilian populations. So constructed, the forces proved remarkably able to utilize effectively any number of new weapons and weapons systems. In part, this was because many of those weapons systems and weapons were, in reality, hardly new at all.

Taking 1944–45 as our starting point, the most important distinc-tions continued to be among warfare as waged on land, in the air, and at sea. On land, the most important pieces of equipment continued to be the tank, the armored personnel carrier, and artillery. All of which of course depended on the mechanized transport of supplies—but for which twentieth-century warfare would not have been possible.[47] At sea, the most important type of ship continued to be the aircraft car-rier. Aircraft were essentially larger, faster, and more powerful versions of their predecessors. Many entirely new weapons, from attack helicopters to cruise missiles to various kinds of surface-to-surface, air-to-surface, surface-to-air, and air-to-air missiles were also used, but whether they really transformed operations in the same way, and to the same extent, as the internal combustion engine did between 1919 and 1939 is debatable.

For what it is worth, I once asked a roomful of military experts and officers, including a highly experienced three-star general who was proud of having commanded a hundred thousand men in battle, whether they could name any essential differences between the operations of General Norman Schwarzkopf in Iraq in 1991 and those of George S. Patton in France in 1944–45. They could not.

5.5. Evolution, Revolution, and Failure

Had there been an extraterrestrial observer watching military developments on Planet Earth between 1945 and 1991, the factor that would strike him most would surely be the decline in the size of the armed forces. Take the United States as the largest power (and the only remaining superpower) of all. The total number of uniformed personnel went down from 12 million to about 1.4 million. In absolute terms, this represents an 88 percent decrease; since the population has doubled, relative to the total available manpower the decline stands at 94 percent. The number of divisions went down from about one hundred (including those of Marine Corps) to fifteen, with the result that there were hardly any more formations above corps level left for generals to command. The number of major naval combat vessels went down from perhaps two thousand to fewer than three hundred. That of military aircraft produced per year went down from one hundred thousand to fewer than two hundred. Thus, in 2000, the air force was planning to procure three hundred new F-22 fighters over a period of ten years[48]— in other words, buying a number that, back in 1944, had been produced in two hours, but now took a full year. In the 1990s alone, the order of battle went down by a third as old aircraft were retired and few new ones took their place. Should this trend continue, then the old yarn about the force coming to consist of a single aircraft cannot be as far off as those who invented it believed.

Though the trajectories on which they moved differed, broadly speaking the same applied to most other developed countries as well.

West European states, Canada, and Australasia because they thought they could neither afford large armed forces nor needed them, Japan because of legal limitations imposed on it in 1945 and maintained thereafter, also saw their military establishments reduced to a fraction of what they had been during World War II. This was carried to the point that, as the twentieth century ended, they could only face the weakest opponents, and then only with US support. For example, the number of German troops went down from more than 8 million in 1944 to 750,000 in 1989 (counting both states, East and West). By 2005, it stood at less than three hundred thousand; yet Germany remains the third largest economy in the world. In the Bundeswehr, as with the forces of most other developed countries, each time a major weapon such as a tank or gun was lost, it could no longer be replaced. Indeed, instead of training with real ammunition, the troops were made to shout "peng-peng."

On the other side of the former Iron Curtain, the USSR, and to a lesser extent its East European allies, resisted the trend until the end of the Cold War. When the collapse did come, it was even more drastic. The Soviet armed forces of 3,980,000 men became a Russian force of 960,000 or so, and even these could not be properly housed, clothed, or fed. Those of the USSR's vassals either disappeared completely—as in East Germany—or were reduced to shadows of their former selves.

Back in the 1960s, something known as development theory postulated that the armed forces of many developing countries represented the most progressive part of their societies and would help pull those societies into the modern world.[49] With few exceptions, this did not happen. Instead, many of the forces in question used their weapons to seize power and rule their countries with an iron hand that was relieved, if at all, only by their own incompetence. Others were not even able to do that. Instead they degenerated into armed mobs; since then, their chief contribution to humanity has consisted of countless attempted coups on the one hand and large-scale massacres of civilians on the other. Think, in Latin America, of the military regimes that at one time or another used to run almost the entire continent and may yet return in the future if democracy fails to bring the hoped-for social and economic progress. Think, in Africa and Asia, of Sierra Leone, the Ivory Coast, the Congo, Sudan, Uganda, Burma, and many other countries made so miserable by their native armed gangs, official or otherwise.

To be sure, there were exceptions to the postwar military contraction. Most were located in or around the above-mentioned rimlands; many owed their success at least partly to outside help provided by one superpower or another. In the Middle East, countries such as Turkey, Syria, Jordan, Iraq, Iran, Egypt, and, above all, Israel were able to form sufficient military power to clobber one another very effectively when they wanted to. In Southeast Asia and the Far East, Pakistan, India, Thailand, Malaysia, Singapore, Indonesia, Vietnam, the two Koreas, Taiwan, and China did the same. With the notable exception of Israel, what most of these forces had in common was abundant manpower. Starting from scratch—many of them originated in the pre-independence resistance movements—they grew in size until they came to rival, or even eclipse, those of any other countries except the superpowers. However, after about 1985 most of them, too, started to contract. As they did so, some were able to build up so-called islands of quality, many of them came to consist mainly of low-grade infantry, suitable only for internal security duties.[50]

Fighting the world wars involved conscripting millions of men which in countries like Britain and the United States had almost always relied on volunteers. Expecting future war to be total, after 1945 most existing countries retained the draft, and most newly formed nations tried to institute it; although, in truth, surpluses of manpower and/or deficient organization meant that in most cases it amounted to only some form of selective service. Britain abolished conscription in 1963, followed by the United States in 1972. Most others waited until the end of the Cold War before following suit. Since then, however, the move toward all-volunteer professional forces has spread like wildfire. In 1996, it even reached France, the original home of the *levée en masse*. By that time Israel, which during much of the post-1945 period represented the best example of a nation in arms anywhere, was also steadily cutting down the percentage of each age group it drafted.[51] In part, this is because the Arab threat has receded until, in former prime minister Ariel Sharon's words, the most serious one is represented by Iran more than six hundred miles away. In part it is also because modern high-tech weapons demand equally high expertise to maintain and operate. Either way, conscription is no longer as useful to Israel as it once was. But for the Palestinian Intifada, which has occupied the nation's attention from 1987 on, it probably would have been abolished years ago.

Because the end of the draft meant that fewer and fewer men served, the number of uniformed women rose. As we saw, in both World Wars I and II the armed forces of several countries took in women even though, since they were volunteers and could not be sent abroad against their will or participate in combat, in reality they were only half soldiers. After 1945, the vast majority (including the Soviet female soldiers who, in 1941–45, had formed the largest single contingent of all) went home. A few countries such as Britain and the United States either retained their wartime women's corps or reconstituted them after a short interval. However, the number of women who served in them was extremely limited; barred both from the combat arms and from the most senior ranks, their position was ancillary at best.[52] During this period, and indeed in the whole of history, the only country that actually forced women to partake in military service was Israel. However, even here far fewer women were taken than men. IDF women also enjoyed numerous privileges, starting with much shorter periods of service (both as conscripts and as reservists) and ending with the fact that, unlike men, they were not obliged to fight and get themselves killed.

Around 1970, the situation changed. In part, this was the result of feminist pressures that, spreading outward from the United States, called for "equality" in every field of life. In part, it was because the armed forces of many developed countries, either because they were engaged in such unpopular wars as Vietnam or because their societies were turning increasingly pacifist, simply could no longer get the manpower they needed.[53]

Once women got a foot in the door, their presence proved extremely troublesome, and for about a quarter century after 1970 the militaries of most developed countries reverberated with the so-called gender wars. Countless court battles were fought to enable military women to obtain "equality" in everything from promotion to the kind of tasks they could be assigned, and countless military men who could not adapt to the new reality saw their careers terminated, or worse.[54] The movement spread from developed countries to the developing ones. Early in the twenty-first century, even a ruler of a Muslim country

such as Muammar Khadafi was using, or pretending to use, female body-
guards. Yet at the graduation ceremony, the officer who handed them
their insignia, as well as every one of the senior commanders attending, was male.

Looking back on this entire story, it seems that its impact has been
grossly exaggerated both by those who advocated the opening of the
military to women and by those who opposed it. Taking the United
States as our example, the number of women rose from less than 2 percent in 1965 to some 14 percent in 1980, at which point it stagnated.
One reason for this stagnation was that women tended to drop out of
the military at an earlier stage in their careers than men; armed forces,
in other words, got less mileage out of every woman they inducted and
trained than they did of their male counterparts. Women did attain
equality in many respects. However, partly because they themselves
chose to go into support positions and partly because the ground combat slots remained closed to them, they hardly ever reached the top of
the hierarchy.

About 30 percent of female members of the rank and file were single mothers who, in case they were sent abroad, faced the greatest
problems in placing their children. Female officers were married almost exclusively to male officers, and the few of them who reached
senior rank often did not have children at all. The continuing, near-
complete dominance of men is shown by the fact that, in the second
war in Iraq, less than 2.5 percent of all casualties were female.[55] In
many countries, Israel included, women were deployed not because
they could fight or were needed to do so but because they could deal
with "enemy" women at roadblocks and similar situations. Whether
this constitutes a feminist victory is, to say the least, moot—the more
so because, in every single instance, the commanders under whom
they operated were male.

The numerical decline of armed forces everywhere is explained by
two factors. First, in the case of developed countries (both those that
possessed nuclear weapons and those that chose not to build them for
the time being), there was the plain fact that a serious attack made
against them was now impossible. Hence the role of the military as the
ultimate guarantor of their existence and independence declined;
hence ministers of defense and chiefs of staff found it harder and
harder to justify them. Second, in the case of both developed and de-

veloping countries, there was the question of cost. In both 1914–18 and 1939–45, weapons were turned out by mass-production methods even though those methods were more successful in some countries than in others. In both time periods, the fact that weapons could be mass-produced reflected their relatively low cost, which helped to reduce that cost still further.

In the post-1945 world, things were very different indeed. At a time when the cost of most consumer products fell very sharply relative to income, that of weapons and weapons systems escalated. Each time it did so, fewer and fewer of them were developed, produced, and deployed. Each time fewer were developed, produced, and deployed, the cost of doing so escalated. By the early years of the twenty-first century, things had reached the point at which only one country, the United States, was still capable of fielding forces that were technologically up to date. And that country, not by accident, was sinking into a financial black hole that threatened to engulf not only it but the rest of the world, too.

Decade after decade, each successive generation of weapons systems was much more powerful than the last. To illustrate this, tanks, which in 1941 still weighed twenty to thirty tons, carried 37 millimeter guns, and had three-hundred horsepower engines, ended up weighing sixty tons, carrying 120-millimeter guns, and propelled by fifteen-hundred-horsepower engines. Such advanced weapons enabled, or at any rate should have enabled, its owners to make mincemeat of any opponents who did not modernize their forces fast enough. Particularly in the United States, which is fascinated by technology and can barely imagine any other way of conducting war,[56] hardly a year passed without some revolution in war fighting taking place. Among them were the nuclear revolution, the jet engine revolution, the ballistic missile revolution, the computer revolution, the electronic revolution, the cruise missile revolution, the revolution in outer space . . . If only because there were so many revolutions, in reality change was evolutionary. One could, indeed, argue that the endless talk about revolutions obscured, rather than clarified, what was actually happening.

Until at least 1991, there was in fact hardly any revolution at all. The most powerful new weapons, such as long- and intermediate-range ballistic missiles, were never used. Those that were used, such as medium-range missiles and cruise missiles, were hardly sufficient in number or loaded with sufficient ordnance to do great damage. At most, they did what aircraft had previously done, albeit at the cost of fewer friendly casualties. Many supposedly new weapons were either derived from those that were used in World War II, as in the case of tanks, self-propelled artillery, aircraft carriers, submarines, jet aircraft, and ballistic missiles, or else they had been on the drafting boards when that conflict ended. Other technologies, particularly electronics and space vehicles, supplemented existing forces rather than providing them with novel ways to destroy one another.

Decade by decade, gurus in and out of uniform pronounced the need for interarm cooperation as if such cooperation had not been the rule from at least 1943 on. Decade by decade, others of the same sort pronounced the death of "linear" fronts and the advent of the "battle in depth" as if history had ended in 1918 and World War II had never taken place. To justify the cost as well as the steady decline in numbers of weapons, complicated calculations were made to show that, in view of the unprecedented accuracy of the new weapons, a handful of them could "service" ten times, a hundred times, or a thousand times as many targets as their World War II predecessors could.[57]

On paper and in the circuitry of the computers on which war games were run, the figures were thought correct. In reality, they failed to take account of the critical fact that targets, provided they are of any importance, are usually defended. If only because they depend on similar electronics, offensive and defensive technologies tend to advance together. For example, the same radar beam that will detect an approaching aircraft will, given a suitable receptor, also serve the aircraft in question with warning that it is being detected and tracked. The same laser beam that enables the pilot of an F-16 fighter-bomber to target and "take out" an individual building while flying at fifteen thousand feet can also be used to guide the surface-to-air missile directed at him. The same acoustic apparatus that can discover an enemy submarine at a distance of many miles can also be used to create a phantom target and cause the torpedo to miss.

That the Coalition prevailed over Iraq in 1991 was due at least as much to its overwhelming material superiority as to any technological advantage it enjoyed. If, in 1999, NATO defeated Serbia, then this was mainly because the Coalition aircraft, operating from bases that were beyond their enemies' reach, outnumbered the Serb air force forty to one. If, in 2003, the United States defeated Iraq for the second time, then all this proved is that when an elephant steps on an ant, the ant gets crushed. The more so if, as happened in this case, it had already been crushed once before; and the more so if, as also seems to have happened in this case, the defenders, aware of what is coming at them, throw away their weapons and head for home. In this way, very often the talk about quality replacing quantity merely served to hide the fact that the enemy was very weak.

By the early 1990s, perhaps because there is a limit to the number of times people could call something a "revolution" without boring the pants off their listeners, there was a shift. Many weapons developed during the preceding decades, such as precision-guided munitions, cruise missiles, and stealth aircraft (which, in reality, were not always as stealthy or as capable as their manufacturers claimed),[58] were approaching maturity. The same applied to ground-, sea-, air-, and space-based surveillance, reconnaissance, command, control, communications, and damage-assessment systems, which together, as one expert wrote, were capable of finally "lifting the fog of war."[59]

Like a spider in a web, computers, located at the system's heart, were used to process the enormous amount of data generated, store it, and display it when and where needed. Previously, the various revolutions originated in individual new weapons. Now a so-called Revolution in Military Affairs (RMA) took hold,[60] supposedly bringing together numerous different technologies—*convergence* was the term experts used—and advancing on a much wider front. It also spawned all kinds of illegitimate offspring, such as information war, network-centric war, neocortical war, and any other number of wars as unprecedented as they were obscure.

Speaking of the second war against Iraq, and given how lopsided the balance of forces was, it is as if we had judged the Wehrmacht by its performance against Poland. Not, to wit, as it was when the Germans first invaded it, but rather as it would have become if the Germans had invaded, smashed the Polish army, withdrawn their troops, imposed ten years of sanctions, and then invaded for the second time. In the absence of a valid test—a war between two more or less equal belligerents—as of the first decade of the twenty-first century, whether there really is such a thing as a Revolution in Military Affairs is questionable.

On paper, the above-listed listed technologies should have made the armed forces that possess them—in reality, we are talking almost exclusively of the Americans and their Israeli clients—much more capable of defeating those that do not possess them than ever before. But nagging doubts remain. Did word processors and spell-checkers really make orders clearer and more succinct than they were when a master of the craft, such as Ulysses S. Grant, wrote his out in longhand?[61] Did data links really improve communications, or is it just a question of more people using more advanced circuitry to keep one another informed about nothing at all? And how about the system the US Army in Iraq used in order to call for air support? Was it really more effective than that of the World War II Luftwaffe whose dive-bomber pilots, often operating from makeshift airfields located less than thirty miles behind the front, sometimes flew as many as eight missions a day?

Much more seriously still, it is now becoming quite clear that the components of the RMA, specifically including the American missile defense shield and the Israeli-built Arrow anti-ballistic missile, will not succeed in rendering nuclear weapons impotent and obsolete. In other words, these systems will not put their owners in a position where they can threaten others with nuclear war without fear of retaliation. Of the two, the Israeli system has yet to hit its test target, a SCUD missile. As of late 2006, it was on the verge of being outclassed by a variety of surface-to-surface missiles already in the hands of, or about to be supplied to, Israel's enemies.[62] The imminent deployment of a new generation of ballistic missile by Russia may make America's system obsolete.[63] Judging by the events in Palestine and Iraq, the Revolution in Military Affairs, even assuming it did take place, has failed. It is a fact with which our children and grandchildren will have to live.

5.6. Think-Tank War

As explained in chapter 1, before the First World War the meaning attached to war as a field of study was restricted, in the main, to the construction of armed forces and their use at the tactical, operational, and strategic levels. The underlying assumption was that almost the only people who could know anything about it were uniformed members of the armed forces. As a result, except in the United States (where the four-year military academies counted as universities), war was not taught at civilian institutes of higher learning; conversely, few if any officers received a higher education. During the interwar years, some countries expanded the meaning of war by including in university curricula such subjects as industrial mobilization, and having a limited number of officers study them. Specialists such as lawyers and doctors apart, however, the idea that officers might have anything to learn by attending a civilian university simply did not catch on.

In the years after 1945, and even more so after 1965, things underwent a change. That change originated in several factors, some of which were related to war-fighting effectiveness whereas others were not. Perhaps the most important single reason was the vast expansion in civilian higher education that took place in all developed countries and, spreading outward like ripples in a pond, many developing countries as well. In the United States alone, during the two decades after 1945 the proportion of the population attending college or university doubled; most other countries did as well, or better. The number of people studying for, or possessing, higher degrees also soared, until enough PhDs were produced each year to fill a football stadium.

The larger the number of academically trained civilians at every level of society, the less secure became the position of officers as its only leading members who did not possess degrees. Without college degrees, many worried that they would neither be able to look their civilian opposite numbers in the eye nor find suitable employment after they retired. Given the prevailing system of "up or out," the latter consideration was especially important. Very often it forced officers to study regardless of whether doing so had anything to do with the demands of their military career; it also explains why military institutes of higher learning, such as the staff and war colleges, suddenly developed an interest in acquiring accreditation. While officers, particularly junior officers, were the first military personnel to feel the impact, they were not the only ones. Especially in the United States, where the cost of academic study is very high, the opportunity to engage in it, presented in the form of subsidies and college credits, also formed an important inducement for enlisted men and women to sign up.

Before 1939, in most countries the only officers who attended staff colleges were those selected for general staff service. Except in the United States, where the Army War College goes back as far as 1903, the earliest war colleges opened their doors in the 1930s, the officers who passed through them forming a still-smaller elite. During the war itself, urgent demands and heavy losses often meant that courses of study were curtailed, and many, particularly at the highest levels, were simply abolished. The personnel who should have gone through them went directly to the front; whether this led to a decline in quality is moot.[64]

The war having ended, attempts were made to correct the situation. Legions of highly experienced officers who had earned promotion without attending the necessary courses were given the opportunity—some would say, had to undergo the humiliation—of completing their desk studies. This in turn caused democratization and devaluation to set in. Gradually, in both West and East, a situation ensued where the only officers who did not attend staff colleges were those given such bad efficiency reports by their superiors as to be forced out of the service. Thus, institutions originally meant for training the elite were, too often, turned into mere diploma mills.

To justify this development, it was argued that war was becoming more complex all the time, requiring greater and greater expertise. This was true, up to a point. The more technology the armed forces introduced, the greater the need for expertise. The greater the available expertise, the more technology could be, and was, introduced. However, it was also true that, given the ever-present danger of nuclear escalation, the armed forces of many countries were underemployed. This specifically included those of one superpower, the USSR; one curious result was that, in the Soviet armed forces, almost any kind of duty ended by having the term *combat* attached to it. Ever since the first staff colleges opened their doors late in the eighteenth century, one of their goals had always been to serve as holding pools where talented officers with no prospect for immediate employment could be maintained on the cheap.[65] Now, in some cases, it seemed as if this was almost their only goal.

Ours is a world where, with some exceptions such as professional athletes and movie stars, anybody who is somebody sits behind a desk. However, many aspiring young officers are seeking more. Entering the military academies, Reserve Officer Training Courses, and officer schools, what they look for is not an opportunity to shuffle papers but adventure and the active life. Physically and mentally, they often represent the flower of the nation, bursting with testosterone (they tend to be young men), full of idealism, determined to prove themselves to themselves and to others.

For good or ill, however, few are really intellectual types.[66] Those who are, and who show it by taking their work too seriously, may experience hazing at the hands of their comrades; this, incidentally, may be one reason why female students, who are often more inclined toward desk work than males, may suffer harassment.[67] Not being intellectual types, these young officers also often make mediocre students who are more likely to take shortcuts than reflect deeply on what they are doing. The problem is compounded by the fact that, in contrast with the pre-1939 German Kriegsakademie, for example, modern staff and war colleges tend to employ instructors who are career failures; as the faculty of the Marine Corps University at Quantico used to put it, they are "children of a lesser god." They cannot act as role models. Whether what they teach is in any way absorbed by aspiring field officers can only be imagined.

Add the fact that, also in contrast with the Kriegsakademie, most present-day faculty do not have a say either in who passes or who flunks out, and the tendency of many officers to see their periods of study as exercises in ticket punching becomes understandable. Others use those periods to prepare for retirement. They take out civilian degrees in subjects as varied as international relations and education—a worthy goal, no doubt, but scarcely one that supports their professional competence. Meanwhile the armed forces of the relatively few developed countries that were engaged in war, or had recently done so, had put far less emphasis on education.

Take the case of the IDF. Consciously reacting against the long Jewish tradition of scholarship, originally it was rather anti-intellectual. For example, on the eve of the 1956 Suez campaign, Moshe Dayan, learning that a senior officer (the subsequent chief of staff Haim Bar Lev) was studying in France, retorted that the best teacher of war was war itself. Only in the mid-1980s, long after Israel had stopped fighting any enemy more powerful than the Hizbollah and the Palestinians, did these attitudes begin to change.[68] Eventually, every officer was supposed to get a degree at some stage in his or her career. One could almost conclude that armies that fight do not study, whereas those that study do not fight.

Just as the system of military education has become civilianized, parts of the system of civilian education have become militarized. There are many reasons for this, not the least of which is that, after Nagasaki, nuclear weapons have never been used. Nobody has ever commanded nuclear forces in war, nor been compelled to fight in an environment where they were present; hence officers, however well educated and trained, cannot claim to know much more about this field than civilians do. Thus, in the West at any rate, they have been unable to prevent civilian experts—from Bernard Brodie through Albert Wohlstetter, Herman Kahn, Henry Kissinger, Thomas Schelling, and Edward Luttwak—from making their views known. Being better educated, quite often they did so more coherently and more effectively than serving officers could. The outcome has been a situation whereby, in most Western countries, a so-called defense community made its appearance. It is made up of academics, consultants, civil servants, and journalists as well as serving and retired officers. All compete in gaining renown, money, office, and, if possible, influence.

In a world where technology moves at an unprecedented pace, the military seldom does its own research and development but instead contracts it out to civilian institutions—many of which are universities. The work they do ranges from the use of dolphins in tackling mines at sea to laser research and studies on foreign cultures. Quick to spot an opportunity, many universities have also set up new departments titled War Studies, Strategic Studies, and the like. Military history apart, the departments in question specialize in matters previously considered the preserve of the military, such as, say, finding the best way to train officers or determining whether a new weapons system is needed. Such institutions have proven very successful not only in attracting military personnel to enroll as students, but also in receiving contracts from traditional military institutes. Take the American Military University. It was founded in 1994 by Jim Etter, a retired Marine Corps major. Throughout the following decade, AMU has experienced explosive growth hardly paralleled by any other university.[69]

As the armed forces kept shrinking, Parkinson's Law set in. Whether in or out of uniform, more and more people felt the need to publish. In Canada, which incidentally has the highest proportion of officers to other ranks, the process reached the point at which any officer who retires almost automatically becomes a consultant to his own former subordinates. The advent of word-processing technology in the 1980s, which facilitated both writing and publishing, has accelerated the trend. Some papers are classified, but a great many are not. Whether written by civilians or by uniformed personnel, many are sent free of charge to anybody who deigns to look at them. Now that we have the Internet, even stamps are unnecessary. Military spam is as widespread, and as much of a nuisance, as any other kind. Most papers go unread by all except the author's acquaintances on whom he (or, increasingly, she) pushes them and who are unable to refuse.

The gems in the crown of military research institutes are the so-called think tanks. Perhaps the very first think tank was RAND (Research and Development), established in 1948 at the behest of General Hap Arnold, the famed World War II commander and later US Air Force chief of staff.[70] It gave employment to some of the best and the brightest in an effort to find out how best to configure and, if necessary, use the country's nuclear forces. Later, it expanded into every conceivable military problem as well as many civilian ones, from obesity to traffic congestion, and from computers to preventing substance abuse. Since then the idea has spread until, in all developed countries and some developing ones, every self-respecting ministry of defense, armed force, or service must have at least one PhD-spangled think tank at its beck and call.

Whether or not they work for the military, think tanks differ from universities—the word comes from *universe*—in that their areas of specialization tend to be narrower and their research more focused. One cannot just go off in quest of an idea, any idea, that looks interesting. Instead, there is one's field of specialization (and future grant money) to consider; to this extent, the researchers are forced to wear blinkers. Another difference is that they do not teach but spend their time (or are supposed to) either in their offices or at meetings with other interesting people such as themselves. In theory, the objective is to save valuable time. In practice, there must be many cases in which not standing in front of a class saves them not only from having their ideas questioned but also from having to properly formulate those ideas in the first place. To paraphrase the eighteenth-century English writer Samuel Johnson, next to a death sentence the best thing to focus the mind is a bunch of students. Especially if they are young, and especially if they are importunate as well.

Sometimes defined as universities without students, think tanks cannot charge tuition. Assuming they have no access to foundation money, most depend on contracts for financial support and are therefore predisposed to tell their clients what the latter want to hear. The heads of some think tanks are said to vet any material that leaves their doors in an effort to ensure that such will be the case; given the number of people for whose livelihoods they are responsible, who can blame them? Others seek to reach the same goal by employing retired officers or officers on special assignment. The outcome is that many think tanks are so close to the military's apron strings as to form part of a single complex, stifling dissent before it can even be born. To quote a Norwegian friend of mine who was in a position to know, the generals, by some mysterious process not even they understand, reach "conclusions." The job of "expert," is to justify those conclusions, elaborate on them, and, if necessary, defend them against journalists, parliamentarians, and similar nosy people.

At best, the blizzard of paper issuing from think tanks, universities, and higher institutes of military learning provides work for a great many people with degrees who would otherwise be unemployed and, perhaps, unemployable. At worst, it threatens to annihilate the world's forests and smother the globe much as old issues of *National Geographic* are said to do. Dazzled by the king's new clothes, most people see, or at any rate claim to see, all this studying as proof of modernity and progress. In reality, it is often a sign of irrelevance, decline, and impotence as many of the world's most powerful armed forces vainly try to deal with opponents so much smaller and weaker than themselves that it should be no contest. Precisely because efforts to deal with them are so often in vain, such opponents are multiplying like rabbits, and the operations on which they engage become more and more daring.

The New World Disorder, 1991 to the Present

6.1. On Nazis, Terrorism, and Counterterrorism

While in some ways it makes sense to start this chapter in 1991, there is a sense in which terrorism is as old as history.[1] There have always been groups of people who, few in number and lacking the means to engage in open warfare against those whom they regarded as their conquerors and oppressors, engaged in smaller, but still politically motivated, acts of violence instead.

The activities of the groups in question might be more organized or less so. They might succeed in establishing a sanctuary in some remote and hard-to-access part of the country, in which case it was possible to speak of guerrilla warfare, or they might not. They might receive the support (or even act as a proxy for) some neighboring country, or they might not. The activities in which they engaged might be directed either against individual opponents, such as rulers and commanders, with the aim of assassinating or otherwise neutralizing them. They might, however, also target the troops or civil servants who acted in those rulers' names, or those who cooperated with them in some other manner, or even ordinary people whose only crime was that they happened to be at the wrong place at the wrong moment.

Very often what success the terrorists enjoyed was due less to the casualties they inflicted and the damage they caused than to the psychological effects of their activities as reported by the media that be. Those reports, in turn, influenced both their own ability to draw supporters and the ability of the forces that tried to suppress them and hunt them down to avoid demoralization and retain their fighting edge.

Had it not been for their armed forces' ability to deal with this kind of warfare, the states of Europe—and later, the United States as well—could never have dominated the rest of the globe as they did. Their power to do so probably climaxed during the last years of the nineteenth century and the opening of the twentieth; as we saw, during the twenty years' truce, that domination was still very largely intact. However, both in Northwest Africa and in the Middle East, there were rumblings that suggested that it was no longer as easy to establish or to maintain as it had been in the years before 1914.

One country, Ireland, actually succeeded in shaking off its centuries-old colonial oppressor and establishing its independence. From the Philippines through India to the Middle East, many others were moving in the same direction; some of them would probably have achieved their goal even if World War II had never taken place. Living in occupied territory, without a proper industrial infrastructure, at the time they rose in revolt none of the peoples in question possessed proper armed forces, let alone a single heavy, crew-operated weapon such as an aircraft or tank. As a result, as Italy's conquest of Ethiopia showed, to the extent that non-European peoples did try to wage open warfare, they were easily, almost contemptuously, defeated.

Seen from the point of view of many peoples in Southeast Asia, all that happened during the early years of World War II was that they exchanged white masters for Asian ones. Accordingly, they did little to resist Hirohito's armies; in not a few cases, they welcomed them. This was not the case in Europe, where the Germans during their period of victory found themselves in control of any number of peoples whose traditions of nationalism and political independence were at least as well developed as their own. It is true that, from Norway to France and from Belgium to the Ukraine, in every country that came under the Nazi heel there were found people who welcomed the occupation, profited from it, and cooperated with it—even to the extent of heeding the siren call, enlisting in the Waffen SS, and risking their lives for the New Europe that Hitler promised. However, it is also true that, in every occupied country, there was resistance, which tended to become stronger as the war went on.

Supposing that Germany had "won" the war in Europe in some sense, could it have rooted out the resistance and held on to its conquests indefinitely? At least one famous military historian, John Keegan, argues that it could.[2] "Imperial forces," he says, "failed against guerrillas in the [subsequent] wars of decolonization because they were fought under the scrutiny of the world press; it might also be said that they failed because the retreating empires felt bound by a moral code that Nazism both violated and despised. There was no foreign press to scrutinize Hitler's occupation forces, and they obeyed a simple code that defiance would be punished by massacre, deportation, and the extermination camp. . . . The Germans simply killed everyone they could catch—men, women, and children, indiscriminately. The notion that the resistance had a potentiality to open the way for a conventional invasion by regular forces of the Anglo-American alliance is, therefore, wishful thinking. Anyone who entertains it should recall that Yugoslavia, the one German occupied country to mount a nationwide guerrilla campaign, lost no fewer than 10 percent of the population as a consequence."

This, of course, leaves out the most important factor of all. Imagine the war had progressed to the point that the Soviet armed forces were no longer capable of offering effective resistance. In that case, surely hostilities would have been ended by the dropping of the first atom bombs on Berlin and Vienna instead of Hiroshima and Nagasaki. At the time the Nazis finally surrendered, their own nuclear program was still so far from complete that they had not even succeeded in enriching any amount of uranium, let alone building a reactor and starting a self-sustaining chain reaction for the production of plutonium.[3] For the sake of argument, however, let us go farther than Keegan does. In the paragraphs that follow, I shall assume that Hitler's armies had succeeded in crushing the USSR as a major belligerent and had advanced to the Urals, as was his original intention. I shall also assume that this victory would have induced Britain and the United States to agree, if not to a peaceful conclusion, then to some kind of temporary truce.

Had things reached this point, then surely most of the German armed forces would have gone home. No regime, not even one as ruthless to its own population as the Nazis, can keep 10 percent of that population permanently under arms—the more so because that fraction constitutes the fittest, economically most productive part of the population. In 1942, the Wehrmacht and the Waffen SS together consisted of about eight million men. Suppose, again for the sake of argument, that demobilization would have led to a standing force twice as large as the one Germany maintained during the last months of peace: 1.5 million men instead of 750,000. Those 1.5 million would have stood guard from Narvik to the eastern tip of Crete and from Brest to Sverdlovsk. They would have had to hold down 40 million Frenchmen, 18 million Belgians and Dutchmen, some 6 million Scandinavians, 16 million Yugoslavs and Greeks, 8 million Czechoslovaks, 30 million Poles, and as many as 100 million Russians. Furthermore, though pre-1945 Germans made first-class soldiers, nobody has ever accused them of possessing a surfeit of tact. Given how heavy-handed Nazi rule was, sooner or later they would also have met resistance on the part of 40 million Italians as well as 30 million Hungarians, Romanians, and Bulgarians. The total comes to almost 300 million. Yet it was Hitler himself who, at one point, argued that Britain could not hope to keep together an empire of 350 million with a population of only 45 million;[4] in which, of course, he was soon to be proved perfectly right.

Like every occupation army that followed it, the Wehrmacht would have found most of its most powerful weapons useless, or nearly so. Like every occupation army that followed it, it would have experienced great difficulty in gaining intelligence as its enemies, fighting without uniform and often without an orderly chain of command, emerged from, and melted away into, the civilian population. The Luftwaffe fighters and bombers that had wrested command of the air and done so much to assist the Wehrmacht's ground operations in 1941–42 could not have followed every guerrilla as he (or she) made a move; conversely, the airfields from which they operated would have had to be guarded at heavy cost in manpower. The Panzer divisions that cut through their opponents like knives through butter would have been unable to follow terrorists into mountains, swamps, or densely inhabited cities.

In the case of the Wehrmacht, in order to match the mobility of the guerrillas, conducted almost all counterinsurgency operations on foot or in light, unarmored vehicles. Thus, as operations in Yugoslavia illustrated, the Germans enjoyed no great advantage over their opponents. Europe, after all, was a continent where the occupied populations had all the skills needed to manufacture light weapons of every kind, and where, owing to the system of general conscription, the number of men who had received some kind of military training during their lives ran into the millions if not the tens of millions. In all probability, the Germans would have floundered about just as subsequent conquerors did: now lashing out as hard as they could and devastating entire districts, as they actually did in several instances, now relenting and trying to strike a bargain with at least some of the insurgents as, in fact, they also did.

It is true, as Keegan says, that there would have been no foreign press to expose the Nazis, their deeds, and their misdeeds. It is also true, as Keegan for some reason does not say, that the foreign press played little if any role in the defeat the Soviet army suffered after eight years of vainly trying to hold down Afghanistan. Had it been for the foreign press alone, then the Vietnam War, too, might still be going on. Foreigners do not vote, and not a few American politicians are proud of never having set a foot outside their own country; until he was elected, one of them was President George W. Bush. Taking a more general view, the role played by the media, either foreign or domestic, in bringing about the defeat of numerous post-1945 attempts at counterinsurgency has been grossly overrated. This is evident from the fact that, at the time when the various colonial uprisings broke out, the domestic media in particular almost always provided strong support for the so-called forces of order; if they later changed their tune, then this was as much a result of changing public opinion as its cause.[5] In fact, it could be argued that exaggerating the media's role is a deliberate plot, one whose real purpose is to shift attention away from those who committed the atrocities against the occupied populations to those who reported on them.

It is true that the Nazis were ruthless (although, pace Keegan, not as ruthless as to treat men and women alike; female members of Western resistance movements, instead of being executed as men were, often ended up at Ravensbruck concentration camp instead). Even so, they were not necessarily worse than some other would-be counterinsurgents who, without acknowledging the fact, followed in their footsteps. The French in Algeria killed about a hundred people to every one they lost. They also destroyed entire villages by bombing them from the air; concerning the use of torture and the like, suffice it to say that one of their most notorious units, the foreign legion, not only had in its ranks many Wehrmacht veterans but was proud to call itself "the White SS." It was the Americans in Vietnam, not the Germans in Europe, who dropped six million tons of bombs—almost three times as many as were dropped in Germany and Japan together in World War II—and also used chemicals to defoliate vast stretches of jungle. Perhaps the main difference between the Nazis and the rest was that the former were less hypocritical. Honesty, though, is a double-edged sword. If Hitler's exposition of his intentions in *Mein Kampf* had any effect at all, surely it was to convince subject people everywhere that their only possible choice was to resist.

In saying that the struggle for liberation cost Yugoslavia 10 percent of the population, Keegan is right. That, however, is only part of the story. The war lasted four years, during which some members of the population died of natural causes whereas others were newly born. Hence, the real figure was lower than Keegan suggests; in fact, it amounted to less than 2.5 percent per year. As was also to happen in many subsequent struggles of the same kind, many, perhaps most, of the casualties were inflicted not by the German occupation forces but by internecine fighting—Serbs against Croats, communists against Chetniks. Cruel as it sounds, history shows that a tenth of the population dying in a protracted struggle is not necessarily too high a price to pay to fend off the yoke of a foreign power; for example, the USSR in 1941–45 suffered considerably more. Seen from the point of view of the generation that has to bear them, such losses are terrible indeed (although, in many cases, not so terrible as to prevent the survivors from recalling the uprising as the best time of their lives).[6] Nevertheless, demographically speaking, a country that suffers such losses will usually recover in a decade or two.

Above all, Keegan is wrong because he fails to recognize the most important factor of all: time. From beginning to end, World War II lasted only about six years. From the moment the Wehrmacht crossed into Yugoslavia, which was the first country where serious guerrilla resistance got under way, to the time the Red Army hoisted its flag over the Reichstag, only four years passed. Although some resistance movements are quick off the mark—for example, the Americans entering Baghdad in 2003 were granted only a few days' respite, if any—experience shows that most take quite some time to get up to speed.

Considering the post-1945 era only, perhaps those who hold the world record in this respect are the Palestinians in the West Bank and the Gaza Strip. They took no fewer than twenty years, before they finally began the Intifada in December 1987;[7] it is, however, possible to find some others who were almost as slow. Had the German occupation lasted much longer than it did, there is no doubt that it, too, would have met with growing resistance. And the more ruthless the repression, the more widespread and the more violent that resistance would have become.

6.2. The Record of Failure

Whether Keegan is correct in his belief that, had Germany "won" the war, Europe could not have liberated itself by resorting to terrorism and guerrilla warfare will never be known. What is known, though, is that attempts by post-1945 armed forces to suppress guerrillas and terrorists have constituted a long, almost unbroken record of failure—a record that, as events in Iraq testify, continues to the present day.

The very first failure, which took place in 1947 when the British withdrew from the Indian subcontinent, may perhaps be excused by the fact that the English hardly tried to make a military stand. That, however, was not true in the piece of land known as Palestine. A relatively small country whose borders are not too difficult to seal, in 1946 Palestine was inhabited by an estimated 1.3 million people, fewer than half of whom were Jewish. The number of armed terrorists probably never exceeded a few hundred at any one time; the heaviest weapons to which they had access were homemade bombs and submachine guns.

To oppose the terrorists, the British had no fewer than one hundred thousand troops in country although, as was also to be the case with subsequent counterinsurgents, the number of those actually available for the conduct of active operations was much smaller. Finally, these were the years immediately following the greatest war of all time. As a result, heavy weapons such as armored cars, tanks, aircraft, and warships (useful to seal off the Mediterranean shore and prevent illegal immigrants from coming in) were available in huge numbers.

From late 1944, when Jewish terrorists assassinated the British high commissioner in Egypt, the entire struggle lasted for four years. Though the number of casualties they suffered was small, the British forces found themselves hounded by their opponents. Going into a café, one could never be sure when a bomb would go off. Walking the streets, one could never be sure when a party of armed Jews would emerge from the shadows, kill, wound, kidnap, and disappear. Never being sure, British soldiers kept within the confines of their fortified compounds in Jerusalem, Ramle, Haifa, and other cities. The more they limited their movements, the less able they were to control the rest of the country where the three insurgent organizations—Hagana, IZL (Irgun Zvai Leumi), and LEHI (Lohamei Herut Israel)—did much as they pleased.

From time to time, the British struck back savagely at their tormentors. On so-called Black Saturday in June 1946, they put more than half of the entire Jewish population under curfew, arrested three thousand "leaders" and "instigators" in a single swoop, and interned them until further notice. This was all to no avail, as the subsequent destruction by a bomb of Jerusalem's King David Hotel showed. Just one year later, His Majesty's government showed its readiness to surrender by throwing the problem into the lap of the United Nations Security Council.

To a great extent, the British methods of fighting the insurgency were similar to those followed in subsequent conflicts, and so they are worth looking at in more detail. The first requirement was to establish secure zones in which the soldiers of His Majesty's forces could live in safety as they planned their operations and recuperated from them. In this, however, they were not successful. Police stations came under attack; parties of terrorists, seeking weapons, attacked bases; and even the headquarters of the British intelligence service was blown up, with heavy loss of life.

In a country whose language they did not speak, British efforts to obtain intelligence by every means from informers to wiretapping and from foot patrols to aerial reconnaissance also failed and, perhaps, were doomed to failure. An occasional terrorist might be killed or arrested, and an arms dump located. However, neither curfews, searches, nor roadblocks ever succeeded in crippling the resistance to the point that it had to suspend operations; all they did was force the terrorists to split into smaller groups so as to operate more effectively still. Perhaps the most successful of the British effort was their attempt to seal off the country's borders so as to cut the supply of weapons. However, all *this* did was to stimulate the rise of a native industry—one that, when the British Mandate ended, was already capable of manufacturing explosives and light arms as well.

Some historians claim that the British did not fight very hard, given that they had no idea what they were doing in Palestine in the first place.[8] It is true that, in 1917–18, Palestine had been conquered almost as an afterthought. As often happens, however, possession is its own rationale. Indeed by 1945, Palestine was considered a very important part of the empire; both the cabinet and the chiefs of the imperial staff were determined to hold on to it if they possibly could. In part, this was because the country provided a land bridge from the Mediterranean to Iraq, the Persian Gulf, and their oil fields. In part, it was because they thought Palestine was needed as a staging ground for heavy bombers in the event of a war against the USSR, and in part because defeat in Palestine could provide a model for further uprisings in other places.[9]

In fact, the loss of Palestine did trigger further uprisings, setting the stage for the subsequent British defeats in Malaysia, Kenya, Cyprus, and Aden.[10] Of these four, at least three counterinsurgencies were conducted with much greater ferocity, and led to far more casualties than the struggle against the Jews; in Kenya, the ratio of African to European dead stood at between fifty and a hundred to one. In terms of military organization, training, and technology, the enemies in question were even less sophisticated than the Jewish underground had been. Furthermore, whereas the British had considered the Jews "semi-European" people, in Malaysia, in Kenya, and in Aden the fight was waged against forms of life considered so low that almost anything was permissible. Yet all three, and of course Cyprus as well, ended in the withdrawal of the so-called forces of order,and the establishment of independent states. This even happened when, as in Malaysia, the British by an unequaled feat of braggadocio succeeded in disguising their defeat by talking about "victory."

Nor were the British the only ones to fail. The Dutch, assisted half-heartedly by the Australians, tried to keep Indonesia and failed. The French invested vast resources in Vietnam and Algeria—at its peak, the struggle in the latter country absorbed no fewer than four hundred thousand troops vainly trying to hold down a population estimated at eight million—and failed. No sooner did "The Savage War of Peace" end in 1962 than it was the turn of the Americans in Vietnam.[11] The Americans dismissed European failures as caused by incompetence but especially, given their sufferings in World War II, demoralization. They, on the contrary, considered themselves uniquely willing, and uniquely qualified, to carry on the mission of bringing "freedom" to the rest of the world.

In the name of that freedom, as many as 2,250,000 troops were poured into South Vietnam. At peak, in 1969, the number stood at well over half a million; probably never in history did such a mighty force assemble to put down a rebellion in such a small country. Following the American military tradition as it had been since at least the Civil War, the troops came superbly equipped this time, possessing everything from satellite communications to iced beer, heavy bombers to dancing girls. All this, in an effort to cope with opponents who dressed in black pajamas, wore shoes made of old tires, and lived on the proverbial handful of rice.

Like the British and the French in most of their colonial struggles, the Americans looked at their opponents (and at their South Vietnamese protégés) as scarcely human. In one of his visits, President Johnson himself spoke of "nailing the coonskin to the wall"; others used coarser language still, particularly when it came to describing Vietnamese women. Even more than the British and the French with their long colonial tradition, the Americans operated in a country whose language they did not know and where every civilian could well be a spy. This fact, plus the inaccuracy of many of the Americans' weapons and their sheer power, turned Vietnam into a killing field with few parallels in history.

The number of Vietnamese who lost their lives is estimated at two and a half million. Of those, countless were killed at one another's hands as both the Army of the Republic of Vietnam (ARVN) and its opponents, the Vietcong and the North Vietnamese Army, not only lashed out at one another but often carried out large-scale massacres among the civilian population. This is hardly the place to list all the desperate measures used by the Americans in an effort to achieve their aim, but suffice it to say that they included defoliant chemicals.

Of all twentieth-century guerrillas, none was more successful, or had greater influence, than Mao Tse-tung. Not only did he take control of China in 1949, but he also had what it took to express and explain his ideas. According to Mao, "people's war" falls into three stages.[12] At first it is a question of engaging in what most people would call terrorism: isolated, relatively small-scale acts of violence. The insurgent organization having built up sufficient power, it may "liberate" parts of the country and turn them into bases that the enemy forces can only enter in force and in the expectation of suffering losses; inside those bases, they continue to expand their power, and from them they mount guerrilla operations. At this stage, though, the insurgents, or revolutionary fighters as Mao prefers to call them, are still relatively weak. This forces them to operate more or less covertly, which in turn means that they need the support of the surrounding population as fish need water. There comes, however, a moment when this ceases to be the case. Thanks partly to their own effort in capturing weapons from the enemy, partly perhaps to outside support, they are able to emerge from the shadows and fight a conventional war.

The three stages Mao describes fit the war he himself waged in China as well as a few other so-called struggles of national liberation, particularly the one in Vietnam that, by 1975, had indeed developed into a conventional war. They do not, however, fit the great majority of post-1945 conflicts.

If only because insurgents can hardly establish the logistical infrastructure for operating heavy weapons, cases where guerrillas end their campaign spearheaded by artillery and tanks are rare, and indeed most never get beyond Mao's second stage. Quite a few never succeed in advancing beyond the first. The fact that they never get beyond the first and second stages means that they never succeed in conquering territory and hold on to it. To the contrary, Mao himself explained that, in case the enemy should attack their bases, it was the task of the guerrillas to carry out a withdrawal, if possible while inflicting losses, and if possible take or demolish as much of their infrastructure as they could. The main objective remains preserving their forces to fight another day.

To put it in a different way, the struggles in question hardly ever reached the point at which the "forces of order" suffer a physical collapse. Vietnam provides an excellent case in point. Over eight years,

Vietnam was devastated by bullets, by artillery shells, by bombs, by bulldozers, and by the aforementioned defoliants. Conversely, out of more than two million American troops who spent time in the theater, only about fifty-eight thousand, or 2.6 percent, were killed; taking as one's starting point the number of those who served in the US armed forces as a whole, the figure is so small as to be almost incapable of being expressed in percentage points. What war-related deaths took place in the US homeland were not even due to enemy action but occurred when the police, or National Guard, opened fire on demonstrators. When the Americans finally withdrew, they still had mountains of equipment that, hoping it would do their South Vietnamese allies some good, they failed either to evacuate (even assuming that had been possible, physically speaking) or to destroy. Those mountains, in turn, fell into the hands of the North Vietnamese Army and formed one reason why it was able to throw back the Chinese invasion in 1979.

What applies to the Americans in Vietnam applies equally to all the other "legitimate governments" or "forces of order" facing similar problems around the world. If they went down to defeat, this was not because most of their equipment had been lost or a considerable part of their personnel put out of action; instead, it was because they had become demoralized. Since failure is an orphan, the question of who was responsible for the demoralization—where the rot began—is usually moot. In the wake of practically every failed counterinsurgency campaign, it is possible to find some people who claim that it was the government that went soft. Others, to the contrary, blame society and the ordinary people of which it consists for their unwillingness to make further sacrifices; watching one's sons (recently, one's daughters, too) come home in coffins is no fun. Some believe that the armed forces were the first to throw in the towel and argue as to whether it was the officers or the rank and file who neglected their duty.[13] Very often the "unpatriotic" media are blamed for allegedly misrepresenting the war and reporters for exaggerating the atrocities that the armed counterinsurgents commit while minimizing their successes.[14]

The media, in turn, defend themselves by pointing to their duty to report the truth as they see it, as well as to the fact that their ability to influence public opinion is, in the end, limited to what that public is willing to see and hear.[15] Nor is it true, as a great many writers have claimed,[16] that the problems in question are limited to "democratic" societies. At the time the USSR invaded Afghanistan, it was no more "democratic" than Vietnam was when it invaded Cambodia. Indonesia, too, in its struggle against East Timor, and Russia in its attempt to subdue Chechnya, were not exactly model democracies. In fact, "democracy," like "media," has become an excuse for failure.

Granted, totalitarian societies can do a lot of bad things to their own citizens, silencing them, arresting them, and killing them. However, as the Italian experience under Mussolini suggests, making them fight and die willingly is not one of them. Even in totalitarian countries, bad news will spread whether the rulers permit it or not. One cannot lie to all the people all the time. The fact that information must be passed along secretly can even exaggerate its impact as people invent stories or magnify those they may have heard. The more secretive the regime and the more it muzzles the media, the less its credibility.

Thus, by and large, decision makers and others who blame the media for their defeats are talking nonsense. Indeed, as long as things go well, those decision makers like nothing better than to bask in the glory that only the media can provide.

· Such being the case, it is no wonder the record of failure did not stop with Vietnam; what changed was the fact that, whereas previously it had been the main Western powers that failed, now the list included other countries as well. Portugal's expulsion from Africa in 1975 was followed by the failure of the South Africans in Namibia, the Ethiopians in Eritrea, the Indians in Sri Lanka, the Americans in Somalia, and the Israelis in Lebanon. In 2005, Israel evacuated the Gaza Strip—proof, if proof is needed, that even one of the world's most advanced, most sophisticated armed forces operating against an extremely weak opponent could fail. In favor of the armies of some countries, such as the Philippines and Thailand, it should be said that they only failed in the sense that they did not succeed in completely eliminating the insurgents. Many others, though, had to let go of entire provinces they had long considered integral parts of their own territories, whereas others came close to disintegration.

To be sure, exceptions do exist, and two of them will be treated in considerable detail later in this chapter. Before we do so, however, it is necessary to explain the reasons why so many of the world's most powerful, most modern, and most ruthless armed forces have gone down to defeat—and, what is more, did so at the hands of forces so much smaller and weaker than themselves. The following analogy will help clarify the matter.

In private life, he (or she) who kills a little child is a criminal and his cause, whatever it may be, must be deemed unjust. Thus whether it was the child who started the fight is of no matter. The same holds true regardless of whether or not the child was armed with a knife, and regardless of what his or her motive was. Perhaps this was what the best-known Hebrew poet, Haim Bialik, meant when, having witnessed the 1905 pogrom in Kishinev, he wrote that "avenging a little child is something not even the devil can do."

At bottom, war is simply an organized fight waged for political ends. Hence, by definition, a strong counterinsurgent who uses his strength to kill the members of a small, weak organization of insurgents—let alone the civilian population by which it is surrounded and which may lend it support—will commit crimes in an unjust cause. However, very few people are so foolish as to lay down their lives in an unjust cause. Hence, almost certainly, the war will be lost. The rot may set in at the top, where a relatively small number of leaders are supposed to command, or at the bottom, where a much larger number of followers are supposed to obey. It may start in the rear, where people for the most part go about their business as usual, or at the front, where they have to fight and die. It may start among the civilian population, which may become reluctant to make the necessary sacrifices, or among the troops who refuse to throw away their lives in a bad cause.

Certainly not every person, every army, and every nation is equally susceptible to the problem. Much depends on circumstances. Some are able to withstand the moral dilemmas that "fighting" the weak creates (though whether this is to their credit is moot); others, not. The situation of the child, or the insurgent, is just the opposite. Some children are very bad, and a few are psychopaths. Some will pick up a quarrel for any reason or for no reason at all. Regardless, a child who is involved in a serious fight with an adult is justified in using every and any means available—not because he or she is right, but simply because he or she has no choice. Similarly, in an insurgency of the weak against the strong, the former will have much less cause to worry about whether or not their actions are just.

Other things being equal, and often even when they are not, a belligerent whose cause is, or is felt to be, just will find it much easier to attract people willing to fight and die for that cause—even if it means blowing themselves up.

Taking casualties, as it usually will, a strong army beating down on a much weaker insurgent will necessarily ask itself if its losses were avoidable and feel itself foolish for not having taken the measures necessary to avoid them. Taking casualties, as it certainly will, a weak insurgent group fighting a much more powerful army will do no more than suffer the ordeal it expected in the first place. Of course, the insurgents must be prepared to examine their actions and draw the appropriate lesson from them. Without the heavily articulated organization that is made necessary by the possession of complicated weapons, perhaps doing so may be easier for the insurgents than for their opponents; in this way, they make up in flexibility what they lack in strength. They are, however, spared the feeling that whatever losses they do suffer are foolish and unnecessary.

To put the same idea in a more abstract form, for the strong, every soldier, policeman, or civilian killed becomes one more reason to end the struggle. For the weak, it is one more reason to continue until victory is won.

Returning to Keegan, the critical factor in all this is precisely the one he overlooks: time. A single crime, once it has been committed, may be forgotten or at least forgiven. However, a long series of crimes, carried out over a long time span, will invariably lead to all the consequences just described.

Twentieth-century guerrilla leaders, such as the Vietnamese Ho Chi Minh[17] and his one-time right hand Dang Xuan Khu (aka Truong Chinh), understood this very well. To quote the latter: "The guiding principle of the strategy of our whole resistance must be to prolong the war. To protract the war is the key to victory. Why must the war be protracted? Because if we compare our forces with those of the enemy, it is obvious that the enemy is still strong, and we are still weak. . . . If we throw the whole of our forces into a few battles to try to decide the outcome, we shall certainly be defeated and the enemy will win. On the other hand, if while fighting we maintain our forces, expand them, train our army and people, learn military tactics . . . and at the same time wear down the enemy forces, we shall weary and discourage them in such a way that, strong as they are, they will become weak and will meet defeat instead of victory."[18]

Perhaps the person who put it most incisively was Henry Kissinger. The forces of order, he once said, as long as they do not win, lose. Insurgents, as long as they do not lose, win. To a very large extent, all this applies whether the perpetrators are white or black, traditionalist or modern, capitalist or socialist, or whatever. It also applies regardless of whether they are God-fearing Americans or atheistic communists. It even applies to arrogant, bloodthirsty, racist Nazis.

It is true that, in Nazi-occupied Europe, conditions varied greatly. A vast difference existed between occupation duty in Denmark on the one hand and the horrors witnessed in Yugoslavia and Greece on the other. Still, even in Denmark, "the model protectorate," resistance increased as time went on. The following German soldiers' lament suggests that, on the whole, things were going downhill. Far from being supermen, they were as susceptible to demoralization as anybody else:[19]

> *Vorne Russen, hintern Russen*
> *Und dazwischen wird geschussen.*
> [In front a Russ, behind a Russ
> And in between they shoot at us].

Compared with the willingness or lack of it, in men (and women) to die for their cause, virtually all questions of policy, organization, doctrine, training, and equipment pale into insignificance. It is, for example, hard to think how the United States might have won the war in Vietnam once the initial decision to engage had been made. Almost certainly neither a more intense bombing campaign, nor more battalions combing the jungle in a vain search after guerrillas, nor additional means spent winning hearts and minds, nor an invasion of the north would have done the trick. The last-named course, indeed, would almost certainly have made things much worse. Supposing the Americans had to hold down the population of North Vietnam as well, the number of insurgents would have greatly increased. China might have sent in troops, as it had in 1950.

Therefore, the real question that dominates late-twentieth- and early-twenty-first-century warfare is: Can a counterinsurgent use time in such a way as to make it work for, instead of against, him?

6.3. Case I: The British in Northern Ireland

Starting at least as early as the 1950s, the literature on counterinsurgency is so enormous that, had it been put aboard the *Titanic*, it would have sunk that ship without any help from the iceberg. However, the astonishing fact is that almost all of it has been written by the losers. It is as if we should have Saddam Hussein, sitting in his prison cell, instructing the next US commander, how he should fight the next Gulf War. Worse still, very often the authors' real objective is not to enlighten but to provide excuses by shifting the blame onto everything and everybody except themselves; hence the frequent emphasis on lack of "political direction," "coordination," and "cooperation." Even when that is not the case, many of the books and articles, being written in modern social science jargon, are simply incomprehensible. What, for example, is one to make of advice such as "seek synergy minus one interventions" or "decrease negative entropy/increase entropy"?[20]

Among the few counterinsurgency campaigns that have been successful, perhaps the most interesting is the British experience in Northern Ireland.[21] The so-called Troubles in Ireland have a very long history. They go back all the way to the Irish struggle for independence (1916–21); King William III, who won the battle of the Boyne in 1690; Oliver Cromwell, who tried to rule the island with his usual iron fist; and even King Henry II (reigned 1154–89), who was the first English monarch to campaign in the island. In January 1969, against the background of complaints that the Catholic population was getting the shorter end of the stick in everything from employment to housing, there was a fresh outbreak. As bombs went off and demonstrators fought street battles, the Troubles escalated very rapidly. The Royal Ulster Constabulary (RUC), a locally recruited police force consisting largely of Protestants, was unable to contain the violence. As a result, Prime Minister Harold Wilson ordered in the British army. From the summer of 1969 on, its troops carried the main burden of the struggle, constantly patrolling the border with the Irish Republic and maintaining a heavy presence at all the most dangerous points.

From this point, the situation went from bad to worse. In Belfast and elsewhere, mobs of young Protestant and Catholic men, many of them drunk, roamed the streets. They fought each other with weapons such as iron bars and bicycle chains, looted shops, and used Molotov cocktails to set houses on fire. In a single night's "battle" (Belfast, August 14–15, 1969), 4 policemen and 10 civilians were killed and 145 civilians were injured. Property damage was also extensive, amounting to no fewer than 150 houses thoroughly demolished. The violence, the like of which had not been seen in the region in almost fifty years, seemed to dampen the enthusiasm of both sides. However, memories proved short, and there was another outbreak of even greater violence in August of the following year. From this time on, things deteriorated as the British troops, whose number now exceeded ten thousand, vainly sought to prevent demonstrators from clashing and wreaking as much havoc as they could. Behind their backs, terrorism also escalated. In 1971, there were more than thirty-six hundred separate incidents and 174 people lost their lives. In 1972, the numbers increased to fourteen thousand and 470, respectively.[22] Not content with terrorizing Ulster, the IRA also extended its operations into the United Kingdom proper. The climax was reached on January 30, 1972, when large-scale street fighting broke out in Londonderry, ending only after British troops had killed thirteen people. The event is still remembered as "Bloody Sunday."

Then and later, the Irish Republican Army and its various offshoots contained numerous highly motivated, well-trained young men (and some women as well), many of whom found in terrorism not just a method for combating the British but a way of life as well. Then and later, the IRA could count on the support of many Northern Irish Catholics, a population that thus provided the "sea" for the "fish" to swim in. Then and later, it was quite ruthless, applying pressure to those who failed to support it and killing or torturing those it suspected of betraying it; one method for which it became famous was shooting suspects through the knees so as to cripple them for the rest of their lives. It also received considerable outside support, if not from the Irish Republic (which during most of the time that the Troubles lasted prohibited the IRA from operating on its own territory and did what it could to seal the border), then from the Irish diaspora in other countries, the

United States included. Far from limiting its operations to Ulster or the United Kingdom, the IRA launched occasional attacks against British assets in third countries such as the Irish Republic, Belgium, and Germany. Finally, over time the organization also developed an extremely sophisticated political wing. Using effective propaganda, its members received a warm welcome in a number of the world's capitals.

Had things been allowed to continue as they did in 1969–72, no doubt the British attempt to hold on to Northern Ireland would have ended in complete defeat followed by elaborate analyses as to why. If, for a change, this did not happen and the outcome did not correspond to the usual pattern, then perhaps there are some things to be learned from the way the British operated. This is hardly the place to detail all the many different things the army did during its thirty-year involvement, let alone follow the immensely complicated political process with all its twists and turns. Instead, all I can do is provide a short list of the things that the army, having used "Bloody Sunday" to reconsider its course of action, did *not* do.

First, unlike President Bush in 2001, the British did not declare war, which would have removed a whole series of legal constraints and put the entire conflict on a new footing. Instead, from beginning to end the problem was treated as a criminal one, meaning that responsibility for it rested with the fifty or so police forces (which were backed up by the army where needed) and the court system.

Second, much of the day-to-day work was left to the RUC. Its members, having been locally recruited and assigned lengthy stays at their posts, knew the area better than anybody else. Accordingly, they were often able to discriminate among the various factions inside the IRA as well as between terrorists and others; experience showed that, operating under conditions that were slightly dangerous but not too much so, its members tended to become more cohesive, not less.[23]

Third, never again did British troops fire indiscriminately into marching or rioting crowds. However violent the riots and demonstrations, the police used less violent methods to control the crowds. Among other things, this meant developing a communications and transportation system that enabled patrols caught in dangerous situations to be quickly reinforced.

Fourth, and in marked contrast with most other counterinsurgents from the Germans in Yugoslavia to the Americans in Vietnam and else-where, not once in the entire struggle did the army bring in heavy weapons such as tanks, armored personnel carriers, artillery, or aircraft to repulse attacks and inflict retaliation. Instead, the standard vehicles were modified Land Rovers; the heaviest weapons, the assault rifles infantrymen usually carry.

Fifth, never once did the British inflict collective punishments such as curfews, the cutting off of electricity and water, demolishing houses, destroying entire neighborhoods to open up fields of fire, and the like; as, incidentally, they had done at the time they were unsuccessfully trying to hold on to the same country in 1920–21.[24] As far as humanly possible, the police and the army posed as the protectors of the population, not its tormentors. In this way they were able to prevent the uprising from spreading.

Sixth and most important of all, by and large both the RUC and the army stayed within the framework of the law. Early on, what one retired officer has called "highly sophisticated and clinical, though admittedly and intentionally very frightening, methods to get vital information from evil men"[25] were used, but in 1972 the Parker Committee recommended that they be abolished. From then on, the British refrained from arbitrary imprisonment, torture, and illegal killings.

This is not to say that the British operations always smelled of rose water—no counterinsurgency (and no terrorist campaign) does. As a celebrated film, In the Name of the Father, was to show, even without breaking the letter of the law, the interrogation techniques used by the British authorities could be intimidating enough. Some of the troops sent to maintain order in the so-called sandbag areas were real killers—or at least that is how they were seen by their more civilianized, less aggressive RUC helpmeets. Here and there a soldier, unnerved by the ever-present, unseen, and unforeseeable danger ran amok, but such cases were extremely rare. More importantly, during the thirty years the conflict lasted, there were some cases when civil liberties and human rights were violated. Evidence was fabricated and heavy psychological pressure as well as false accusations were used to elicit information, leading to the conviction of men who—like the famous "Birmingham Six,"[26] the "Guilford Four," and others—were later found innocent of the charges against them. A handful of known IRA militants, having been identified and tracked in foreign countries, were shot, execution-style, in what has since become known as "targeted killings."

Even so, the tools used to kill the IRA terrorists in question were high-velocity sniper bullets, not the air-to-ground missiles and one-ton bombs that the Israelis sometimes used for the same purpose in Gaza. The fact that evidence had to be obtained by illegal means or fabricated speaks for itself; most other counterinsurgents did not bother, and still don't. On the whole, the British played by the rules. This remained true even after terrorists had murdered the seventy-nine-year-old earl of Mountbatten, the queen's uncle, as he was sailing his yacht; even after they had planted a bomb that demolished part of a Brighton hotel where the prime minister at the time, Margaret Thatcher, was due to speak; and even after they had used a van with a hole in its roof to fire mortar rounds at a cabinet meeting being held at 10 Downing Street.

As in the case of other counterinsurgents, the British were facing a loosely knit, but highly sophisticated and extremely dedicated, group of people who spent most of their time under cover, moved frequently from one place to another, and were often able to cross international borders as well. Like other counterinsurgents, they used a vast variety of intelligence-gathering methods from undercover female agents to wiretapping, and from night-vision equipment to remotely piloted vehicles (RPVs). At one point Thatcher, visiting her forces and having been briefed, suggested the use of satellites, only to have it gently explained to her that satellites, which only pass over a given area periodically and whose cameras cannot tell a Catholic Irishman from a Protestant, are not of much use in the struggle against urban guerrillas. As in the case of other counterinsurgents, too, collecting the intelligence was only the first step. This having been done, it was necessary to communicate it—while at the same time protecting the communications against interception—shift it, analyze it, distribute it, and act upon it fast enough to yield results.

All this was extremely important and has been explained countless times by assorted experts in a flood of books, monographs, and articles. Still, insofar as it is limited to tactics and techniques that were used by many others as well, it does not capture the real secret behind the British success: extreme self-control. Whatever else might happen, the British did not allow themselves to be provoked. Hence they avoided the kind of situation in which they would beat down blindly on much weaker opponents, let alone bystanders and civilians in general. By showing restraint, the British did not alienate people other than those who were already fighting them. As events were to show, the number of IRA supporters did not increase over the years. By the mid-1990s, the organization had begun to experience difficulty in recruiting new members to take the places of those who had been killed or jailed or else had left on their own accord.

Time, it is said, will wear down anything but diamonds. If that is true, then the British army proved to be a gem. Its troops, unlike those of practically everybody else, did not become demoralized. They did not take drugs, did not go AWOL or desert, did not refuse to fight, and did not turn into a danger to themselves and their officers as had happened in Vietnam, where any number of the latter were "fragged"—blown to pieces—by their own subordinates. Instead, they were as ready to give battle on the last day of the hostilities as they had been on the first—a fact that the terrorists learned to their cost.

Needless to say, all this was easier said than done. Underneath it all there was a rock-solid foundation, resulting from centuries of experience and made up of first-class training, strict discipline, high professionalism, and superb leadership. None of this would have been possible without the social cohesion for which the British regiments, organized in such a way that their personnel serve together for years on end, have long been famous. Which, in turn, may have something to do with the way British society and British life itself is constructed.

Outsiders often have great difficulty in understanding all this, which is why they focus on technicalities instead. I myself began to get an inkling of it during my numerous visits to the Army Staff College at Camberley from the late 1980s on. In late 1988, it was my privilege to talk to the incoming commander of the British forces, Northern Ireland, General Patrick "Paddy" Waters. This was a year after the outbreak of the First Palestinian Intifada. The IDF had long been considered one of the world's finest fighting machines. Now it was caught off balance by a situation it had failed to foresee—just one day before the uprising started, the "coordinator of activities in the Occupied Territories" had declared Israeli control of the Palestinians a "brilliant success."[27] The IDF reacted by lashing around incoherently, if not savagely. Over the next months, it killed hundreds, arrested thousands, imposed curfews, and blew up the houses of many suspected terrorists; acting on the specific orders of then minister of defense Yitzhak Rabin, it also used batons to break Palestinian arms and legs right and left. Hence it was unsettling to listen to General Waters, who said his objective was not to smash the IRA by killing as many terrorists as possible; instead, as long as his term of duty lasted, his mission was to make sure that as few people as possible on either side were killed.

The most important insight of all, though, did not come at Camberley but over dinner in Geneva in 1995. My partner on that occasion was a British colonel, regiment of paratroopers, who had done several tours of duty in Northern Ireland. What he said can be summed up as follows. Look at almost any one of the hundred or so major counterinsurgency campaigns that took place since 1945. To be sure, the differences among them are very great. Still, they have one thing in common: In every known instance, the "forces of order" killed far more people than they lost. Quite often they did so by an order of magnitude, as was the case in Vietnam where the Americans, engaging in what they called "body count," always emphasized how many more alleged Vietcong than marines or army soldiers died. Often they did so in such an indiscriminate manner (in counterinsurgency, whenever heavy weapons are used, the results are bound to be indiscriminate) as to make the result approximate genocide.

By contrast, he continued, the struggle in Northern Ireland had cost the United Kingdom three thousand casualties in dead alone. Of the three thousand, about seventeen hundred were civilians, either such as had been deliberately killed for supporting one faction or another or innocent bystanders who had been blown apart as bombs exploded at the time and place they happened to be. Of the remaining, a thousand were British soldiers. *No more than three hundred were terrorists,* a ratio of three to one. Speaking very softly, he said: And that is why we are still there.

6.4. Case II: Assad in Hama

Not every counterinsurgent has what the British army has: highly trained, disciplined, professional soldiers and police, and a society that values their service. Even more importantly, not every counterinsurgent has the iron nerve and sheer inertia to avoid being provoked and keep going. Nor, to be fair, is every counterinsurgent in a situation where he speaks the language of the insurgents—an immense advantage that those who speak of "information dominance" are, or should be, able to appreciate—or knows the country as well as they do. Sealing the border helps; had not the government of the Irish Republic at one point decided to do what it could to control IRA operations in its own country, it is extremely doubtful whether the Troubles would ever have been brought to an end.

At the beginning of 1982, the regime of President Hafez Assad (in Arabic, *assad* means "lion") in Syria was twelve years old. The October 1973 war against Israel, which was presented as a victory, had given Assad a certain measure of popularity; over the next seven years, rising oil prices helped keep the regime afloat. Now, however, the effect was wearing off, and Assad was meeting growing opposition that did not make the future appear at all rosy.[28] Part of the opposition came from the members of various ethnic groups. Far from being a homogeneous nation, Syria is but a potpourri of Muslims (mostly Sunnis), Christians, Druze, and Kurds. Many of the Sunnis in particular took issue with the fact that Assad, like his most important henchmen, was an Alawite. The Alawites are one of the less important Islamic sects, traditionally poor and underprivileged. Many in the Islamic world do not even see them as true Muslims. It is claimed that, instead of Allah, they worship the moon and the stars; it is as if Germany had been ruled by a Sorbic Mafia.

Furthermore, and as many others have since learned to their cost, few groups can threaten a regime as much as the Islamic priesthood, or Ulama, can. Though he had never been a great champion of liberty— no Arab leader is—in the early years after seizing power, Assad had made some concessions to them. He promoted priests, increased their salaries, and gave them limited freedom of speech as they preached in their mosques and madrassas, or religious schools. Still, the Syria that Assad inherited from his deposed predecessor was fundamentally secular, its Ba'athist ideology forming a curious mixture of nationalism, "Arab socialism," and racism that was mostly directed against the Jews in neighboring Israel.[29] In one sense, the existence of Syria itself constituted a challenge to the priesthood; the latter saw the Umma (consisting of all Muhammad's followers from the Atlantic to Indonesia), not the da'ula (national state), as its ideal. Finally, Assad's position was not made easier by the fact that a large part of his army was involved in Lebanon. Starting in 1976, originally its mission was to put an end to a vicious civil war that had broken out in that country. That proved hard to do, and the Syrians found themselves trying to run the country—which, early in 1982, was also being threatened by a possible Israeli invasion.

Opposed to Assad were the Muslim Brothers, a religious movement that has sometimes engaged in terrorism and also maintains links with similar groups. Much more than the IRA, which only aims at the "liberation" of one part of one country, the movement is strongly represented in many different Arab countries. To that extent, it is possible to speak of "international" terrorism. If Assad himself could be believed, some of the insurgents' weapons had been provided to them by the Christian militias in Lebanon, which in turn received them from the then Israeli minister of defense, Ariel Sharon.[30] By the early 1980s, the Brothers were waging a well-funded, well-organized, and effective terrorist campaign.

Initially Assad's response was similar to, though perhaps more brutal than, that of countless others before and since. His first move was to reassert his dictatorship by abolishing what few civil liberties existed. Next, he used his army and secret police to persecute, arrest, and torture thousands, going so far as to order the inmates of entire prisons stood against the wall and shot. Nothing worked, and the bombings, in which hundreds of people lost their lives, continued.

The army that Assad commanded was to the British as a mule is to a thoroughbred. The ground forces in particular were large and quite well armed, the Kremlin having provided them with some of the best equipment it had; however, the twenty-five hundred tanks and thousands of artillery barrels were designed above all for conventional warfare. The top commanders were, of course, all Assad's cronies. The officers tended to be urban lower middle class, the rank and file semi-literate lads of peasant origins; in this respect, there were certain analogies with the Italian army as it had been in World Wars I and II and also with the Egyptian army that had been so badly defeated by the Israelis in several wars.

Fighting Israel in 1973, the Syrians had been thrown out of the

Golan Heights, but they had neither disintegrated nor run. Fighting them again in Lebanon in June 1982, they were also thrown out but, outnumbered three to one, still managed to give a reasonable account of themselves.[31] Yet this was scarcely an instrument with the intellectual ability and iron discipline needed in order to wage a prolonged, careful counterinsurgency campaign.

As he saw his regime disintegrating—fearing for their lives, many officials no longer dared appear on the streets but went into hiding together with their families—and his own life increasingly threatened, the Syrian strongman resorted to desperate measures. Though clashes between terrorists and the security forces took place all over the country, the center of the rebellion was known to be the city of Hama, called "the head of the snake." Even as the repression campaign continued in full swing, a division of twelve thousand soldiers, commanded by Assad's brother Rif'at, surrounded Hama while maintaining as much secrecy as was possible under the circumstances. For what followed, we are dependent mainly on the accounts of the Syrian newspapers, not the most reliable sources in the world but useful insofar as they represent Assad's point of view. The way they told the story, the troops started combing the city house by house, making arrests. As they did so, about five hundred heavily armed mujahideen, or holy warriors, launched a counterattack. Perhaps they were deliberately provoked by Rif'at's forces. Perhaps they were hoping that the army's Sunni troops would desert from their units and, possibly, join their uprising. Either way, they emerged from hiding, took up their weapons, and engaged in open warfare, reportedly killing some 250 civil servants, policemen, and the like.

Whether or not it had been planned that way, the uprising provided Rif'at and Hafez with the excuse they had been waiting for. Neither then nor later did the Syrian army have the kind of sensors, data links, and precision-guided weapons the Americans used in Iraq. Instead, relying mainly on their most powerful weapon, heavy artillery, the Syrian troops surrounding Hama opened fire. Anywhere between ten and twenty-five thousand people, many of them women and children, were slaughtered. What followed was even more important. Asked by the media how many people his men had killed, Rif'at, far from apologizing for what he had done, deliberately gave an exaggerated number. As his reward, he was made vice president for national security; several of his fellow butchers were also promoted or decorated.[32] Later, survivors told horrifying tales of buildings that had collapsed on their inhabitants and trenches filled with corpses. They also described how, in an attempt to get at jewelry, Syrian troops did not hesitate to cut off people's fingers and ears;[33] seen from this point of view, the fact that not all terrorists were killed and that some escaped to tell the tale presented a bonus, not a failure. It has been claimed that some of the refugees later joined terrorist movements in other countries. That may be true, but it was not Assad's problem.

Hama's great mosque had been one of the best known in all Syria. Now it was razed to the ground, and later it was turned into a parking lot. Thomas Friedman of *The New York Times* wrote that "the whole town looked as though a tornado had swept back and forth for a week," and that it seemed as if Assad actually wanted people to see what he had done.[34] Another journalist, Scott Peterson of the *Christian Science Monitor*, told me that when people passed the spot, they turned away and shuddered. Some residents were so horrified by what they had seen that they did not even dare pronounce the word *Alawite;* instead, pointing at the distant hills, they spoke of "those people there."[35] In the words of Assad's Israeli biographer, Professor Moshe Maoz,[36] "the terrible crushing of the Hama revolt not only broke the military backbone of the Muslim Brothers but also served as a vivid warning to them, as well as to other opposition groups, against further acts of disobedience. And although in recent years small groups of Muslim Brothers have occasionally conducted guerrilla attacks on army units, the mujahideen ceased for the time being to be a threat to Assad."

What might have happened to Syria if Assad had not done what he felt he had to do is anybody's guess. Quite likely, the regime would have fallen. Assad himself, along with many members of the Alawite community, would have been put to death; indeed, it was probably fear of such a massacre that persuaded Bashir, who is a physician by profession, to heed his father's call and return from London, where he was building a flourishing career as an ophthalmologist, to take over the reins of government.[37] A stable regime consisting of non-Alawite Muslims might have been established, or—more likely—it would not have been. In the latter case, the outcome could have been civil war of all against all, with Turkey and Iraq, both of which have their differences with Syria over territory, water, and people (the Kurds), stirring the flames. Judging by what happened in neighboring Lebanon, a much smaller country, the number of dead might have run into the hundreds of thousands, or even more. Judging by what happened in both Lebanon and Afghanistan, the country might have turned into a stomping grounds for international terrorists of every kind. Instead, it is at least possible that the ferocious reputation Assad gained by his actions at Hama was one factor that enabled him to do what neither Israelis nor Americans could: bring the vicious Lebanese civil war to a more or less complete, more or less happy, end.

Many other counterinsurgents were not nearly as brutal as Assad, killing far fewer people than he did over much longer periods of time. Still their relative restraint did not save their societies from turning against the war and their armed forces from disintegrating. In addition, they were pilloried by the media, which may even have played a role in leading some of them toward defeat.

This was not what happened to Assad. Needless to say, the Syrian media sang the praise for the heroic "Lion" and continue to do so the present day.[38] Most foreign media condemned him, but their span of attention to the incident was short, and whatever censure they published was brief. It is true that Rif'at fell out with his brother and was forced to flee—not because he had been too harsh, but because he had designs on the presidency. Having overcome the initial difficulties, Hafez was able to underpin his standing. Internally, the regime withstood both Sharon's tanks in 1982 and the severe economic crisis of 1986–87 without coming apart.[39] Eventually, his international reputation actually rose. In 1989, he was able to negotiate the Ta'ef Agreement, thus effectively inducing the Arab states to recognize Syria's continued occupation of Lebanon. In 1991, he became a member in good standing of the Coalition that President Bush put together in order to fight Iraq. Seven years later, another US president, Bill Clinton, came to Damascus especially to meet with him; if the visitor was aware he was talking to a mass murderer, he gave no hint.[40] Until he died, Hafez Assad went on ruling Syria with an iron fist. Bashir Assad continues to do so to the present day.

Almost the entire Western literature on counterinsurgency was written by people in or out of uniform who, whatever the terrible things they may have done, claim to have liberal, democratic ideals at heart. Without question, their noble sentiments deserve respect. Nevertheless, it should not be overlooked that it was presidents Johnson and Nixon, not Hafez Assad, who tried to bomb Vietnam back into the Stone Age and almost succeeded in doing so. Whatever else may be said of the Syrian methods in restoring order to Lebanon, rarely did they resort to massive firepower. When they did, they used short, sharp bursts; as, for example, in October 1990 when they expelled (but did not kill) General Michel Aoun.[41] Even so, they did not come close to what the Americans brought to bear and, as of 2005–6, were bringing to bear day in, day out, in Iraq. Obviously, there were some things Assad knew that other would-be counterinsurgents did not. Looking back, his strategy may be condensed into five simple rules. All of them are as old as history; and all of them can already be found in Machiavelli's *The Prince* (1512–13). The following paragraphs are merely an attempt to expand on and systematize what the Italian thinker had to say.

First, there are situations in which it is necessary to resort to cruelty. If, in such situations, you are not prepared to apply it, then you are a traitor to the people who put you where you are in order that you may safeguard their liberty, their property, and their lives; at most, you are fit to be prime minister of Disneyland. Should you reach the point at which you have no choice left but to resort to cruelty, then the blow should be sudden. The more like a thunderbolt out of a clear sky it comes, the greater the effect: both because your victim will be unable to prepare, and in consideration of the all-important psychological point of view. Never threaten, and never announce what you plan to do in advance. Instead, talk softly, feign weakness, and use secrecy and deceit to hide your preparations as much as you can for as long as you can.

Second, once you have made up your mind to strike, you cannot strike hard enough. Tenderhearted people believe it is better to kill too few than too many. However applicable this may be to the justice system of a law-abiding, liberal democracy, if the alternative is civil war and, perhaps, the disintegration of the community, it is misguided. Better to kill too many people than too few. Strike so hard as to ensure you don't have to strike twice; otherwise, by showing that there is life after death, the fact that you have to do so will weaken the impact of your original blow. Besides, you must consider the effect that numerous repetitions will have on your own troops. Loyal, well trained, and hard-bitten they may well be. Still, if they are made to commit one atrocity after another (and very likely resort to alcohol or drugs in order to muster the necessary will), it will only be a matter of time before they lose their edge and, by so doing, turn into a danger to themselves and to you.

Third, considering that everything is relative, timing is absolutely vital. Everything else being equal, the earlier the blow is launched, the better—just as a blister must be lanced before it can fester and lead to gangrene. Suppose, for the sake of argument, that Rabin had understood what was going on when the First Intifada broke out in Gaza in December 1987. In that case, instead of flying to the United States to haggle about the price of some F-16 fighter-bombers Israel was about to buy, he could have ordered his troops to kill (say) five hundred Palestinians more or less on the spot and also blow up some object of high symbolic value. Assuming the troops had obeyed him, the outcome could have been, if not peace, at any rate quiet. Instead, a prolonged struggle ensued in which immense physical damage was done and several thousand Palestinian lives were lost. To the extent that it could have been avoided, Rabin might even have done his enemies a favor. To quote a Hebrew proverb: He who shows mercy to the cruel will end up being cruel to those who deserve mercy.

Of course, getting in one's blow as early as necessary is easier said than done. Inertia governs counterinsurgency operations as much as, if not more than, it does other human affairs; having watched the pot simmer for a long time, people are reluctant to admit it will end up exploding. Hence most blows are probably launched too late, not too early, in the struggle. By the time they are finally launched, people will have gotten so used to the killing that they will have little effect. Conversely, the longer you wait, the more barbaric the means you will have to use.

Many, perhaps most, of insurgents' activities take place undercover. Others are not concentrated in a single place but are widely scattered inside a country's borders and, often enough, outside them as well. Hence it is an illusion to think that you can ever "get" all or even most of your opponents at once—something not even Saddam Hussein, using gas against the Kurds, succeeded in doing. Even if you do, chances are that, like the mythological hydra, the organization will reconstitute itself.

Witness the French interception and arrest of the entire Algerian FLN leadership back in 1956;[42] just six years later, the same people were sitting across their captors at Evian and negotiating the independence of their country. To prevent this from happening, while aiming to kill as many insurgents and their leaders as possible your true target should be the spirit of the population from whom they draw their support and without whom they cannot exist. To put Mao on his head: You must refuse to admit a distinction between "active" fish and the "passive" sea in which they swim.

In other words, the true objective of your strike is not to kill people per se. Rather, it is to display your ruthlessness and your willingness to go to any lengths to achieve your objective—a war for hearts and minds, only by different means. Clausewitz once wrote that war is a moral and physical contest by means of the latter.[43] The same is even more true of the massacre that accompanies a war: If you do it right, it may even prevent a war that has not yet broken out. It is therefore essential that careful consideration should be given to the means.

Forget about infantry, it is too slow; especially when it operates in urban terrain, it is also likely to split up into small detachments and get lost. Infantry that rides armored personnel carriers cannot see a thing and will be more or less helpless facing any insurgent who chooses to shoot at it. Infantry that proceeds on foot or rides soft vehicles is too vulnerable (the war in Iraq is giving birth to an entire literature about this subject).[44] Its weapons are small, and most of them will only kill people one by one. Besides, if the enemy has similar weapons and fights back, then the process is going to be very expensive.

Airpower and missiles are much better and will save you from suffering casualties. In their case, the problem is that they are deployed from a distance; the victims, unable to see who is massacring them, will not be properly impressed by your determination. Modern airpower also has two other disadvantages. First, it is too fast. Flying high, often so high they cannot even be seen from the ground, a few fighter-bombers appear out of nowhere. They discharge their weapons and disappear; just as a colony of ants that is stirred with a stick will quickly recover, so their disappearance permits your opponents to catch their breath. Second, most of the "precision-guided" weapons it uses carry relatively small warheads and can only do limited damage to selected targets. For example, following three months' continuous bombardment by a thousand NATO aircraft, 95 percent of Belgrade was still standing. From that point of view, the Luftwaffe, though it did not have anything like the sophisticated weapons employed by NATO, did a much better job bombing the same city in 1941; the devastating blow it delivered was one from which the Yugoslavs never recovered. If inflicting real damage is your objective, as it should be, then old-fashioned, heavy "dumb" iron bombs are much superior. The problem is that only one country, the United States, still retains the kind of bomber force that can carry such ordnance in any numbers. Even that force has been reduced to one-sixth of what it used to be; in terms of ordnance-carrying capability, the replacement of the old B-52 work-horse by modern B-2 stealth bombers means that the cut is much greater still.

Everything considered, and recalling Assad at Hama, the weapon of choice should be artillery. It is true that the proponents of the Revolution in Military Affairs have not had much to say about heavy guns; Secretary of Defense Donald Rumsfeld even canceled the new "Crusader" artillery system the army had spent years and billions of dollars developing. Even the old guns, however, were sufficiently accurate to be aimed at individual targets, especially, as is desirable, if they can be made to fire point-blank. At the same time, they are sufficiently powerful to do just the kind of spectacular damage you want; to see the results, search the Internet for pictures of Hama. Unlike aircraft, they can fire nonstop for hours, even days, giving the target population no peace, shattering their nerves, and reducing their world to screaming chaos. Still, their greatest advantage is that they can be deployed in such a way that, before being blown to hell, the victims can look straight into the muzzles that are trained at them. When Napoléon famously spoke of a whiff of grapeshot, he knew what he was talking about.

Fourth, once you have started, do what you have to do openly. The media you control, you can control. The rest are your enemy. While you are busy carrying out your plans, they will gather like vultures around carrion; once you are done, they will summon their righteous wrath and denounce you as a bloodthirsty monster. Still, that does not mean you cannot harness them to your chariot. At any cost, prevent the media from messing with your operations while they are going on, both to prevent them from getting in the way and to increase the effect by giving people's imagination free play. Once you are done, though, do not try to hide your operations or explain them away. In fact, you should do exactly the opposite. Let there be no apologies, no kvetching about collateral damage caused by mistake, innocent lives regrettably lost, "excesses" that will be investigated and brought to trial, and similar signs of weakness. Instead, make sure that as many people as possible can see, hear, smell, and touch the results; if they can also taste them, such as by inhaling the smoke from a burning city, then so much the better. Invite journalists to admire the headless corpses rolling in the streets, film them, and write about them to their hearts' contents. Do, however, make sure they do not talk to any of the survivors so as not to arouse sympathy.

Last but not least, do not command the strike yourself. Instead, have a Rif'at do it for you—if at all possible, without ever giving him written orders that he may later produce to implicate you. This method has the advantage that, if your designated commander succeeds, you can take the credit. Presenting him to the world, you will make sure he looks as grim as possible, perhaps by sticking him into a blackened uniform and putting a dirty bandage on his forehead. Presenting yourself to the world, you will offer no regrets and shed no tears over the victims. Instead, you will explain why it absolutely had to be done and make sure everybody understands you are ready to do it again at a moment's notice. But what if, for one reason or another, your designated henchman fails in his mission, and resistance, instead of being broken, increases? In that case, you can always disown him and try another course such as negotiation.

On the surface, one cannot imagine the approaches, used by Assad and the British in Northern Ireland being more different, but at a deeper level, they have something very important in common. Each in its own way is designed to deal with the time-induced problem of demoralization. The former forestalls it by reducing the campaign to a sharp, powerful blow after which most of the blood-spattered troops will hopefully be able to take a shower, change into fresh uniform, and go back to their barracks. The latter exercises deliberate restraint and, doing so, inculcates them with such strict self-control as to prevent the rot from setting in, thus enabling them to sustain their morale for a long time, perhaps forever. Both methods require enormous courage and strength if they are to be consistently applied. If they are not consistently applied, then in almost all cases the result will be disaster.

6.5. Case III: The Americans in Iraq

Though the United States is supposedly an open, democratic country, the origins of its war against Iraq are unknown.[45] The more time passes and the more people publish their memoirs, the deeper the mystery; here, all we can do is guess. Perhaps President Bush and his principal advisers, Vice President Dick Cheney, Secretary of Defense Donald Rumsfeld, and the latter's deputy Paul Wolfowitz really believed Saddam Hussein was involved in global terrorism—even though the CIA Terrorism Report for 2000 had said he was not, and even though the war itself suggested that he had no links to al-Qaeda and its allies.[46] Perhaps they really believed he possessed weapons of mass destruction; although, given the crushing defeat he had suffered in 1991, how they could have thought those weapons constituted a danger to any other country is hard to understand. Perhaps they felt that, with US forces leaving Saudi Arabia and that country seemingly lurching toward civil war, the Middle East was becoming destabilized and the US needed to dominate another major oil-producing country in its stead.

However that may be, for a decade the US armed forces had talked about the Revolution in Military Affairs until they were blue in the face. During most of the twentieth century, military technology had outpaced civilian technology; as a result, the latter enjoyed what was known as the spin-off effect. Following the introduction of microchips in 1980 or so, the situation changed. From there on, owing largely to problems in procurement that grew out of the forces' unique size, inflexibility, and accountability, military technology began lagging, yet the talk about RMA continued. Still, some concrete examples of RMA began to appear in numerous new weapons, including perhaps most importantly the precision-guided JDAM (Joint Direct Attack Munitions, basically a "dumb" iron bomb fitted with a cheap global positioning system receiver like the one in the family car) entered service. So did any number of small, pilotless aircraft (variously known as remotely piloted vehicles, RPVS; or unmanned airborne combat vehicles, UAVs) as well as sensors, data links, and computer systems to control and command them. Earlier commanders had come with field glasses and maps. Now the most important piece of equipment they carried was a laptop.

Whether on land, at sea, in the air, or in outer space, the real objective of all the electronic wizardry was to enable the Americans to engage in something known as network-centric warfare. "Network-centric warfare" relies on a whole series of mysterious beings known as ARPANET, MILNET, NSFNET, CAVNET, and any number of other, even more ethereal, nets.[47] Just one net, SIPRNET (Secret Internet Protocol Router Network), uses "smart multiplexer and 512 kilobits per second (kbps) channels" to provide "high speed packet switched service" (including COMSEC keys used with the STU-III) to support "national defense C3I requirements." Among many other marvelous things, it links together no fewer than 134 different government agencies. One objective is to give commanders instantaneous access to any "lessons" those agencies, in their wisdom, may have to offer.

Another objective is to link all computers to one another so that all commanders could have the same picture of the battlefield. Next, sharing the same "real-time situational awareness,"[48] they will coordinate their moves, enabling their units to "swarm" around their objectives as bees attack a careless person who disturbs their hive. Having used their sensors to discover and identify and track the enemy before he can do the same, they will be able to operate faster than he can. Following an idea first articulated by an air force officer, the late Colonel John R. Boyd, this was known as getting inside his OODA (Observation, Orientation, Decision, Action) Loop.[49]

Iraq is a third-world country with no electronic industry to speak of. At the time it was attacked by the United States, it possessed hardly any weapons younger than fifteen years and even those were suffering from lack of spare parts and maintenance as a decade of sanctions, imposed in 1991, took its toll. The three-hundred-mile, three-week campaign that cost the Americans 138 deaths—a substantial number of which were caused by accidents and friendly fire—and ended in Baghdad was a walkover. Beyond that, anything else said about it is wasted.

Preparing for the 2003 war, the American planners expected to be welcomed by considerable numbers of Iraqi people, and this did in fact happen to a limited extent. Soon, however, it turned out that the fall of Baghdad and the toppling of Saddam Hussein did not end the struggle; instead, all they did was mark its beginning. Terrorism, originating in what it pleased Rumsfeld to call "pockets of resistance" but quickly spreading over much of the country, started almost at once. In Baghdad and elsewhere, snipers took potshots at troops of the US-led "Coalition of the Willing," inflicting casualties. Soldiers, civilian contractors, foreign aid workers, Iraqi collaborators, and civilians were all targeted; some were killed, others wounded, others kidnapped. Of those who were kidnapped, some were released in return for a ransom. Others were executed in front of the cameras; either way it was the terrorists who gained, the Americans who lost.

Soon the insurgents, whoever they were, were using a variety of light weapons, among them assault rifles, anti-tank and anti-aircraft missiles, hand grenades, machine guns of all calibers, mortars, unguided rockets (Katyushas), and improvised explosive devices (IEDs) of every size and description. As time went on, it became increasingly clear that the IEDs were the most dangerous weapons of all. Some were planted by the roadside, others carried to their targets by suicide bombers walking on foot or driving in cars. In a country as militarized as Saddam's Iraq had been, the supply of such weapons was practically endless.

As a theater in which to wage an insurgency, Iraq also has other advantages to offer. Large parts of the country constitute open desert and provide little cover. However, there are plenty of mountainous spaces, built-up spaces, and spaces that are crisscrossed by natural and artificial waterways and covered by dense vegetation. The population of twenty-four million is too large to be controlled by putting a policeman on the heels of every child (in all insurgencies, children play an important role, whether by blowing themselves up or, in case they are too young, acting as lookouts or messengers). Not only are the country's borders thousands of miles long, but some of them, notably those that separate Iraq from Turkey and Iran, run through extremely difficult terrain. They can hardly be sealed even with the aid of the most up-to date equipment. Should the insurgents one day run out of weapons, they will have no great trouble obtaining new ones.

Finally, the fact that Saddam relied on conscription has created a situation where there are hundreds of thousands (perhaps more) of men with military experience. Growing up while their country was under international sanctions, these men may not have had the opportunity to attend college. They may not be very good at flying stealth aircraft and operating computers. They are probably even worse at writing heavily footnoted papers about "network-centric warfare," and indeed many of them may never have seen a net except for the ones used to catch fish in the Euphrates. However, they do know how to use machine guns and rocket launchers, and know how to build bombs that are becoming more and more effective. The more time passed, the clearer it became that they were also mastering light infantry tactics. Above all, they died bravely—something the Americans, owing to their thousand-to-one superiority, cannot do.

Once the main units of the Iraqi army had been defeated and dispersed, most of the sensors, data links, and computers that did so much to aid in the American victory proved all but useless. In part, this was because they had been designed to pick up the "signatures" of machines, not people. But it was also because these sensors did not function very well in the densely inhabited, extremely complex environments where the insurgents operated. Myriad methods could be used to neutralize or mislead whatever sensors did work. Worst of all, sensors are unable to penetrate people's minds. As a result, almost four years after the war had started, the American troops still had no idea who was fighting them: Ba'athists or common criminals, foreign terrorists or devout believers.

As the attacks mounted, the Americans found themselves perhaps the most isolated occupation force in history—there were no areas that could be considered safe, no bowling alleys or bars or brothels where they could relax. The only way they could venture out of their fortified compounds in Baghdad and other cities was by cowering inside their armored vehicles, where they could not use their eyes and ears as soldiers should.[50] They became dependent on a vast number of local personnel, starting with cleaning ladies and ending with the politicians more or less prepared to cooperate with them and carry out their will.

Being so dependent, they were vulnerable. Every Iraqi they employed, and many they did not, was, or could be made into, a spy. Given the proper combination of pressure and inducement, many could also be made into active resistance fighters, and some could even be persuaded to blow themselves up. Whereas hundreds of thousands of Iraqis knew at least some English, hardly any American personnel could speak, read, or write Arabic (those who did were mostly Muslim Americans of Arab origins and, as such, automatically suspect). Yet in any sort of organized human activity, war included, language is the most important tool by far. In this way, what "information dominance" existed went not to the Americans but to their enemies. As a result of all this, to the extent that the war witnessed any "swarming" at all, it was done by the Iraqi guerrillas. To oppose the US gadgetry, they relied on what one US military historian called "almost intuitive situational awareness" (meaning, an intimate understanding of the society in which they live).[51] Readily available, portable and cheap, but often highly sophisticated cell phones and other communication devices gave the Iraqi resurgents a "net-centric" capability of their own.

That these operational problems would make the American task in Iraq very hard indeed was foreseen by some (although, apparently, not by those who surrounded the US president and advised him on how to run the war). What could, perhaps, not be foreseen was that the Americans would approach these issues in such a way as to make them worse still. Preparing an aggressive strike against a faraway country while inflicting all the death and destruction and misery that such a campaign entails, the Americans nevertheless called the war "Operation Iraqi Freedom." Launching their initial attack under the name "Shock and Awe," they nevertheless promised to spare as many religious shrines, cultural monuments, and civilian lives as possible. To some extent, they kept their promise. Though some bombs and missiles missed their targets, most of Baghdad was left intact. The result, however, was not what they had expected. Having been told in advance what areas would not be attacked, the fifty-something key Iraqi leaders targeted by the Americans knew what they had to do, and not one of them was hit. As to the remainder of the population, after decades of misrule and countless coups it had become inured to the prison, the torture chamber, and the execution wall taking their toll. Hence it would be surprising if that population had seen the American approach as anything but proof that the invaders were weaklings suffering from a bad conscience—which, of course, was exactly the case.

After this rather shaky start, things went from bad to worse. First the Americans embraced a longtime, voluble Iraqi exile by the name Achmed Chalabi with the aim of making him their stooge. Next, after it turned out he had no supporters in the country, they decided he was a con man (which he was) and an Iranian agent (which he almost certainly was not). They arrested him, interrogated him, and got rid of him, thus making it clear even to the last Iraqi that whatever freedom they could obtain would be like that of a dog on a leash.

Having beaten the Iraqi army, they dissolved it, then tried to build it up again with many of the same officers who had previously served Saddam Hussein. At first, they thought their best Iraqi allies would be the supposedly well-educated, supposedly secular, supposedly moderate Sunnis. Living in a country with a Shi'ite majority, however, the Sunnis had good reason to fear the kind of democracy the Americans promised; for this and other reasons, the Sunni-populated areas around Baghdad became hotbeds of armed resistance.

Frustrated by this, the Americans turned to the less educated, more religious, and more fanatical Shi'ites in the south. However, not all the Shi'ite clergymen agreed to play the role for which the Americans had earmarked them. As a result, the Americans attacked the holy cities of Kharbala and Najaf (any city the Americans attack acquires instant holiness) and flattened parts of them—only to realize that their actions might alienate more Shi'ites than those they cowed. Instead of completing the job, they drew back at the last moment. Najaf in particular was left under the control of Sheik Sistani's Shi'ite militias where, as of 2006, it still remained.

As in Vietnam, the Americans were much concerned to win what they called "the war for hearts and minds," even though it did not square very well with the censorship that the Iraqi interim government imposed. Nor did the stories of torture that leaked out of Abu Ghraib and other prisons improve the situation. In this Muslim culture, the fact that some of the torturers (as well as the officer responsible for the prison system, General Janis Karpinski) were female did not help. Also in Vietnam, a stream of statistics began to be generated concerning progress made: so and so many food packets distributed; so and so many schools and clinics reopened; so and so many miles of roads restored by engineers; and on.

Some of the statistics were probably bogus, invented by people who either wanted to sway American public opinion, to please their superiors, or to lay their hands on some of the huge sums the Pentagon was distributing.[52] Even if they reflected some kind of reality, it is doubtful whether many Iraqis thanked the Americans for rebuilding what they had previously destroyed and saving people from the starvation they themselves, by starting the war, had brought about.

This was all the more the case because the Americans were escalating the conflict. Whether done to reduce friendly casualties, or because it was what they knew best, the American forces used just about every sort of heavy weapon available to them. Sixty-five-ton Abrams tanks, armored personnel carriers, fighter-bombers, and a C-130 gunship capable of spitting out thousands of shells per minute; as well as the most sophisticated attack helicopters the world had ever seen, were applied against insurgents. Yet not even the Americans could pretend that the insurgents possessed anything heavier than mortars, machine guns, and anti-tank rockets, and homemade bombs.

As so often happens in counterinsurgency operations, the casualty figures reflected these facts. By late 2006, the number of American military killed had risen to more than twenty-seven hundred—of whom well over 90 percent had lost their lives after President Bush had formally announced an end to major combat operations. Though no formal data on the number of Iraqi dead were available, some sources put it as high as one hundred thousand. Of those, as many as four-fifths were believed to have been civilians caught in the crossfire.[53]

By way of a microcosm of the American misconceptions, errors, and, above all, inability to form a clear policy and stick to it, take the story of Fallujah. Located west of Baghdad, Fallujah's mostly Sunni population of three hundred thousand was actually expected to welcome their "liberators." In the event, this did not happen and the city quickly turned into a safe haven for terrorists, who both used it as a base for their operations and spread their own rule over it. At first, it was thought this was because the area was a stronghold of Saddam's supporters. However, Saddam's capture in December 2003 did nothing to improve the situation. Perhaps the real reason Fallujah resisted is because, for its inhabitants as for the Sunni population at large, the American promise of democracy (meaning that the country will be ruled by a Shi'ite majority) is tantamount to a death sentence. However that may be, in April 2004 the US forces, feeling that enough was enough, assaulted Fallujah from the air and the ground, only to break off their attack after a few days when it proved more costly than expected.

There followed a dubious cease-fire in which the Americans agreed not to attack the city again provided the militias that ruled it remained quiescent. That agreement, however, did not hold even for one week. For months on end, the Americans hesitated, seeking to somehow end terrorism while also threatening to attack Fallujah for the second time if their demands were not met. When they finally did attack in November, they brought in every heavy weapon they had, turning the city into a sea of ruins. This, however, was not Assad in Hama. Having been forewarned, not only did much of the civilian population flee the city, but most of the terrorists—including the most dangerous terrorist of all, the Jordanian Abu Musab al-Zarqawi—did as well. The only insurgents encountered were those who had chosen to stay and martyr themselves.

The number of militiamen killed was estimated at between one and two thousand—although some neutral observers claimed that it was much smaller. In any case, and as the continuing acts of terrorism soon proved, it was not nearly enough to shock and awe the insurgents into submission. To compound their mistakes, no sooner had the Americans flattened Fallujah than they brought humanitarian aid and started talking of rebuilding—only to break their word and pound the city again in December.

Meanwhile, what of the American troops who, ordered by their commander in chief to campaign in a faraway country most of them had hardly heard of, were fighting and dying? Partly because it has seldom resorted to conscription, partly because the rich and the influential often found ways to evade service even during periods when conscription was in force, the United States has a long tradition of fighting its wars at the expense of the poor, the disadvantaged, and the minority.[54] Moreover, owing to the way units are put together, they are not nearly as cohesive as those of some other countries; in the past, attempts to change the system have failed as commanders gave administrative requirements priority over the psychological needs of their men.[55]

Despite all this, by and large Americans, provided the task they are given is not hopeless, make good soldiers. Take the testimony of Moshe Dayan, who knew as much about fighting morale as any twentieth-century general. In 1966, a year before he led his country's army to a smashing victory over their enemies, he visited Vietnam. Though he certainly did not like everything he saw, he did call the conscripts he met "golden guys": physically fit, very well trained, and, at that time, still quite willing to do their jobs.[56]

As Vietnam dragged on without an end in sight, the atmosphere, of course, changed. In-country, the numbers of those who went AWOL, became psychiatric casualties, refused to carry out orders, or simply took to drugs to escape the hell into which their superiors had put them increased. Back home, the need to find and send in more and more servicemen (there were hardly any women), who sustained more and more casualties, led first to a great decline in popular support for the war and then to massive civil unrest. This was especially true in the universities, where the flower of the next generation were being put through their paces. Students with college deferments understandably feared the day the draft card would arrive—and so, of course, did the middle-class families in which they originated. Many universities cooperated with their students. They barred military recruiters from campus, canceled Reserve Officer Training programs, and refused to take Pentagon money to subsidize research.

Had the war gone on, then the unrest might have led to civil war—as was proved in December 1972 when a quarter million people, angered by the so-called Christmas Bombings of North Vietnam, tried to storm the Pentagon. By leaving Vietnam to its fate, President Richard Nixon saved the United States. There was, however, another side to the story. To make sure that, in case the US again went to war, public opinion would not again prevent the government from doing what it thought had to be done, Nixon also abolished the draft, replacing it with a force made up entirely of volunteers. Throughout the 1970s, the new force experienced great difficulty in attracting the qualified manpower it needed, which incidentally was one reason why it took in so many women.[57] Later, as the memory of Vietnam receded, the downsizing that took place during the 1980s and 1990s, plus a substantial pay raise granted by the Reagan administration, improved the situation. In particular, the 1991 victory over Iraq did away with the doubts that had characterized the late 1970s and early 1980s, causing them to be replaced by a feeling of hubris. Time after time, officials insisted that American troops were "the best trained, the best led, and the best equipped"[58] in the world.

To a considerable extent, the establishment of an all-volunteer force achieved its aim of decoupling the troops from the American people, thus permitting the White House to employ them where and when it saw fit. When things in Iraq started going wrong, few Americans cared about what happened to the troops in question. In New York, in Dallas, and in Los Angeles life went on as usual; as during Vietnam, many parts of the country actually profited from the war as the Pentagon, having exercised economy during the Clinton administration, started spreading money around. The troops, after all, had joined up of their own free will, as had the reservists who backed them up. In return for wages, medical benefits, and money to pay for a college education, they had sworn to risk their lives for Uncle Sam if he called on them to do so. Ignored by much of the public, used as cannon fodder by their superiors, and coming under constant attack by terrorists they could not identify, no wonder they soon came to hate the war in a way not seen since Vietnam.[59]

Before Operation Iraqi Freedom began, the army chief of staff, General Eric T. Shinseki, warned his superiors that at least two hundred thousand troops would be needed to police the country after military operations ended. As his reward, his superiors put him on the retired list; them whom the gods wish to destroy, they strike blind first. As terrorism took hold, Shinseki's figure turned out to be, if anything, a gross underestimate. Certainly only the fact that the all-volunteer force simply had no more troops available—its units and formations were spread thinly in places as removed from each other as South Korea and Bosnia—prevented Iraq from becoming a bottomless sink for manpower as Vietnam had been.[60] Probably only the fear that the draft would alienate huge parts of public opinion prevented President Bush and his advisers from trying to reinstate it. Damned if it did and damned if it did not, the Pentagon began using creative methods to squeeze greater mileage out of the available troops. It used all kinds of legal chicanery to keep them in uniform for longer than they had contracted. It also tried to circumvent its own regulations so as to push more women into combat,[61] much to the discomfiture of feminists, who suddenly woke up to the fact that war is not fun. The more exploited the troops felt, the more morale dropped. Shortchanging one's own people is hardly the best way to win a war.

By the last months of 2004, the US forces were starting to show early, but unmistakable, signs of disintegration. When Secretary Rumsfeld visited the troops, he was heckled for not providing them with proper equipment. One group of soldiers sued the Pentagon for tampering with their contracts. Several went AWOL rather than return to Iraq when ordered there for a second time, and at least one unit flatly refused to carry out orders. Back at home, the chief of the army reserve was warning his superiors that his units were cracking under the strain of providing more and more troops. To obtain the cannon fodder it needed, the Pentagon was enlisting forty-one-year-old grandmothers and even relaxed its policy against gay men and women.[62] Also back at home, and again with the universities in the lead,[63] even the most blinkered American was waking up to the fact that his country had been caught in a second Vietnam with no easy way out.[64]

Soaking up almost $450 billion a year, the mightiest war machine the world has ever seen was vainly trying to combat twenty to thirty thousand insurgents. Its ultramodern sensors, sophisticated communications links, and acres of computers could not prevent its opponents from operating where they wanted, when they wanted, and as they wanted; even to the point that, three days before Christmas, they killed nineteen US troops as they were having lunch inside their fortified base. To recall the well-known, Vietnam-era song: When will they ever learn?

6.6. Barbarians at the Gate

As the record of failure shows very clearly, for a long time after 1945, terrorism and the counterinsurgency efforts aimed at containing it were limited to "primitive," or "colonial," or "ex-colonial," or "third-world," or "developing" countries from Indochina to Yemen and from the Philippines to Peru. This, however, started changing during the late 1960s and early 1970s. Among the early harbingers of change were the IRA and its Basque counterpart, ETA. Both movements sought liberation from what they regarded as foreign rule imposed on them by forcible means centuries ago. Both operated on a considerable scale; ETA, which at one point succeeded in killing a Spanish prime minister, remains active despite attempts by the Spanish and French governments to extirpate it. The late 1960s and early 1970s also witnessed the hijacking and/or destruction of a number of Western airliners. For the most part, these attacks took place in connection with the festering Arab–Israeli and Arab–Palestinian conflict.

Next, the mid- to late 1970s saw the flourishing of left-wing terrorist groups in several European countries as well as Japan.[65] The German Baader-Meinhof Gang and the Italian Red Brigades were established by a small number of middle-class, well-educated youths (including a high percentage of women). Their objective was revolution, but they did not succeed in gaining any substantial following among the working classes whose interests they claimed to promote. As a result, they remained isolated; in Germany, indeed, the public went so far as to blame the government for not using much harsher methods than it did. Ultimately, the terrorists were put down by the police, though not before they had carried out a number of spectacular kidnappings and assassinations, including that of a prominent German industrialist, Martin Schleyer, and a former Italian prime minister, Aldo Moro. The 1980s saw attacks directed against American troops in Europe and the destruction, with heavy loss of life, of Indian and American airliners brought down by Kashmiri and Libyan terrorists, respectively. Still, by and large this was not enough to shake a complacent world.

In the event, what made the world finally take note were the spectacular attacks directed by al-Qaeda against the World Trade Center and the Pentagon on September 11, 2001. Founded some nine years earlier by Osama bin Laden, a Saudi national who had received his training while combating the Soviets in Afghanistan, al-Qaeda's original objective was to cleanse Muslim lands from the unbelievers. This is mixed with the desire to avenge all kinds of insults allegedly inflicted by the West, starting with its support for "the Jews' petty state" and ending with the "immorality and debauchery that have spread among you."[66] Its operations are organized in a way that seems calculated to illustrate the qualities of international terrorism. The men—apparently there were no women among them—originated in several different countries, especially Egypt. All were devout, not to say fanatical, Muslims, although some of them, coming from middle-class families, apparently had not started that way but had been driven to that position by their experience of living in the West and trying, vainly, to assimilate. They studied in Germany, trained in the United States and Afghanistan (where bin Laden himself was enjoying the protection of the ruling Taliban), met in Spain, and received their last-minute instructions during a gathering held amid the casinos of Las Vegas. To complete the international touch, the money they needed to live and organize was transferred to them from banks in the Persian Gulf; to communicate with one another, they used the same Internet cafés as everybody else.

The attacks on the Twin Towers and the Pentagon resulted in the death of about three thousand people and in material damage estimated in the tens of billions of dollars. More important still, they proved that the commercial and military hearts of the largest, most advanced, and most powerful country in history were vulnerable to a new form of warfare that, literally emerging from the shadows, was threatening to sweep the world. To understand the seriousness of the threat, all one has to do is to compare the measures taken, or rather not taken, to protect the Olympic Games held in Athens in 1896 with those used to secure the same event held in the same city 108 years later. In 2004, no less than 20 percent (one and a half billion dollars) of the total Olympic Games budget went for security, and indeed security personnel outnumbered athletes ten to one.[67]

Against this kind of threat, neither tanks, nor warships, nor aircraft, nor the giant "eye in the sky" the Pentagon was planning[68] to enable the last marine private in his or her foxhole to participate in "network-centric warfare," or other esoteric forms of warfare its experts kept dreaming up, are of any use at all.

As of late 2003 even that great proponent of the Revolution in Military Affairs, Donald Rumsfeld, was becoming aware of this fact—and this time, since censorship was much tighter than it had been in Vietnam, the media could not be blamed. In a memorandum to his closest aides (perhaps in an effort to show that something was being done about it) he admitted that America's defense establishment was in deep trouble.[69] Having been created to deter, and if necessary fight, others like it during the Cold War, was that establishment really the right one to take on the new threats? Or would it have to be reshaped from top to bottom? And, if so, how?[70] Three years later, judging by the mess in Iraq, the answers were still blowing in the wind.

The First and the Last

Where did war as it has been waged since 1900 come from? The answer to this question is fairly simple. In most respects, it is simply a straightforward continuation of war as it had been waged since the second half of the seventeenth century. The wars of that period, in turn, were characterized by several outstanding qualities. First, the continent that created the greatest concentration of military power by far was Europe. The last time any non-European power posed a serious danger to Europe was during the Ottoman siege of Vienna in 1683. After that, it was always European forces that invaded and occupied parts of the rest of the world, never the other way around. By 1900, as we saw, the crushing military superiority Europeans enjoyed on land and at sea enabled them to spread their rule over almost the entire globe; the only exceptions were societies that either originated in Europe, as the United States did, or adopted European ways in the nick of time, as in the case of Japan.

Second, and again starting in the second half of the seventeenth century, the political units that generated this military power and used it to fight one another each had a sovereign territory with clearly demarcated borders. Each such "power," adopting an organizational scheme that, following Clausewitz, I have called "Trinitarian," had a government whose job was to direct the war and whose members did not directly participate in the fighting. Each also had a military machine consisting of uniformed soldiers whose job was to prepare for war and fight and die in it after it had broken out. Finally, that machine was supported by a civilian population working the fields and factories to feed, supply, and, later, suffer with the troops. The laws of war as they had developed from Hugo Grotius and Samuel Pufendorf to the

Geneva Convention of 1907; the theories for its conduct as they had de-veloped from Raimondo Montecuccoli to Alfred von Schlieffen; and, indeed, the entire way war was understood and conducted reflected these facts.

Third, focusing on the second element in the "Trinity," ever since the so-called military revolution of the second half of the seventeenth century armies and navies had become larger and larger. Fed by the growing might of the powers that fielded them on the one hand, and by technological innovation on the other, their ability to kill and to de-stroy also increased. From 1800 on, the pace of innovation increased; by the second half of the nineteenth century, at the latest, a situation was created whereby any armed force that had not kept up to date no longer stood a chance against those that had.

There were, however, two caveats. First, never at any time was tech-nological superiority the sole factor that decided which side would emerge victorious and which would go down to defeat. Second, as Clausewitz noted,[1] most European armed forces did not succeed in gaining any very great, let alone lasting, technological advantage over the rest. As a result, and other things being equal, their relative power did not change; as this account has argued, in the end it was very often numbers that decided.

Among the Great Powers that waged war among themselves, the one that demanded the greatest attention was Germany. In part, this was because the German army, though not the largest, was probably the best organized and best trained of all—a fact that the rest, by send-ing their officers to study it, reluctantly acknowledged. In part it was because, in both the world wars and without entering into the ques-tion of "war guilt," it tended to attack first. In both world wars, having lost that initiative and while being greatly outnumbered by its ene-mies, it still succeeded in holding them off for years on end. Doing so, it almost always inflicted more casualties than it suffered; this was true both in absolute terms and in relation to the resources spent. Hence, and as the first four chapters of the present volume show clearly enough, the story of warfare from 1914 to 1945 is in considerable part the story of the German army, the way it acted, and the ways others re-acted to it.

How did war since 1900 develop? Both before and after 1945, per-haps the most important factor driving twentieth-century warfare was technological progress. Though there were exceptions, on the whole that progress was becoming less and less dependent on the genius of individual inventors. Instead, more and more it was generated systematically and deliberately by a growing research and development establishment; once the new devices became available, they began to be mass-produced by a vast industrial infrastructure. Throughout the twentieth century, war was transformed decade by decade, sometimes even faster. The Super-Dreadnoughts of 1914 were as superior to the Dreadnought of 1906 as the latter was to the pre-Dreadnoughts of 1905 and would, had they clashed, have swept their adversaries off the sea with contemptuous ease. The heavy artillery and tanks of 1918 would have cut through the armies of 1914 like knives through butter. During World War II, progress was faster still. New weapons, or at least new versions of existing ones, left the factories every few months; anyone who, in 1943, rode into battle aboard a 1940 tank was either a hero or a fool.

The weapons in question belonged to the "industrial age," meaning that they were standardized and mass-produced in very large numbers. The methods used for the purpose were those first developed by Henry Ford; it was, indeed, the Ford plant at River Rouge that, during World War II, produced the largest number of aircraft of all. Being standardized and mass-produced in enormous numbers, the weapons were relatively cheap and could be used to equip very large numbers of troops. Even if they were lost in battle, they weren't hard to replace. Some, particularly Soviet weapons, were made deliberately crude and left badly finished; others, particularly American-made, were so plentiful that, hostilities having ended, most of them were simply left to rust. Thus the process of numerical growth that started after 1650 continued apace so that the number of those who fought, died, and were wounded in the Second World War exceeded that in the first by far. Briefly, the more time passes and the greater the distance that separates us from those conflicts, the clearer it becomes that the two struggles constituted a single link in a long series. Like so much else in the "modern" world, that series had its origins in the second half of the seventeenth century. By comparison, the tactical, operational, and even strategic innovations that distinguish 1939–45 from 1914–18 pale into insignificance.

When did twentieth-century armed forces peak, and how did they reach the present impasse where some of the most powerful among them are helpless in front of small groups of often ill-trained, ill-funded, ill-equipped terrorists? The answer is that, on August 6, 1945, the combination of constantly improving technology with ever-growing numbers came to an abrupt end. What brought it to an end was the detonation of the first atomic bomb over Japan. Though nuclear weapons continued to grow more powerful for decades after that, none was used in anger. Certainly the holocaust that overcame Hiroshima marked the most important turning point in almost three hundred years of military history. Some, the present author included, would go much further still: Hiroshima and Nagasaki may have marked the most important turning point since men, wielding sticks and stones, first organized together and went to war against one another several tens of thousands of years ago. Until then, military history, perhaps even history as such, had been moving in one direction. Now, without doubt, it was pushed off course and started moving in another.

By this time, the main European powers had brought one another to a standstill in terms of both human and material losses and, even more importantly, the will to fight. As a result, the most important powers were no longer the ones that had dominated the world for 250 years but their larger offspring: the United States and the USSR. This in turn meant that Germany, and with it the German army, had to relinquish its previous role—something, incidentally, it did willingly enough. Whatever one may think of the rebuilt Bundeswehr, and there were times during the 1970s and 1980s when people thought very highly of it, it was not the Wehrmacht. Instead, and if only because political considerations prevented the Germans from acquiring nuclear weapons, it was the army of a second-rate power—one that, had NATO and the Warsaw Pact come to blows, would not have lasted very long.

Though numerically the armed forces of the United States were not the largest, in many ways they were the most modern. Another field in which the US led was weapons exports; as a result, its forces acted as models not only for Washington's NATO allies but for many other countries as well. Finally, and as the wars in Korea, Vietnam, and the Middle East proved all too well, the US forces were also the only ones whose reach was truly global. Throughout the period of the Cold War, America's military budget easily eclipsed that of all other countries, and as of the end of 2006 it even exceeded the sums spent by the next fourteen countries combined. The very fact that the sums in question were spent, as well as their own reach, is probably one reason why America's armed forces engaged in more campaigns, and were involved in more incidents, than anyone else. As Secretary of State Madeleine Albright once put it to Colin Powell, what is the point of having such mighty armed forces if one cannot use them?

From 1949 on, the two superpowers built up their nuclear arsenals. The hydrogen bomb followed hard on the heels of the atom bomb; both were accompanied by delivery vehicles, command and control systems, and doctrines for using them in war. Having spent decades glaring at each other, the United States and the USSR were finally forced to conclude that the old rules had changed and the only way to win the game was not to play it in the first place. Step by step, other countries followed. Either their objective was to stand up to the superpowers, as China and India did, or else they wished only to confront their own neighbors, as in the case of Israel. Since an "effective" defense against nuclear attack never materialized,[2] even with a balance of forces of a thousand to one, President Bush, for all his bluster about the "Axis of Evil," did not dare take on North Korea as he had Iraq.

Though nuclear weapons put an end to the ability of the powers that had them to battle one another in earnest, it took a long time before this fact was fully understood. Partly because it was not understood, partly because the powers in question thought they had to have the means to deal with "subnuclear" threats, and partly owing to sheer inertia, conventional armies continued to develop. Sustained by oceans of money—had they redirected 10 percent of what they spent on arms, the most powerful countries could have easily fed every man, woman, and child on the planet—military technology continued to race ahead. Even so, from the mid-1980s on, there was a sudden increase in the number of programs canceled before they had borne fruit. In the kingdom of Vulcan, something was very rotten indeed.

Whereas previously technological innovation and numerical superiority had gone hand in hand—prophets who, like Fuller and de Gaulle, advocated small, elite forces had been swept aside by the events of World War II—now they parted company. The numerical decline started earlier in the NATO countries than in those of the Warsaw Pact, and earlier in developed countries than in some developing ones. After 1985, however, even most of the latter began to see the light. By 2006, most of the world's largest armed forces were fielded by countries that did not have the scientific, technological, or industrial infrastructure to equip more than a small fraction of their troops. As a result, most of the troops in question were suitable, if for anything at all, mainly for internal security—which indeed was the reason for keeping them in the first place.

Socially speaking, perhaps the most interesting development that took place during these years was the sharp increase in the number of female service personnel. For thousands of years, armed forces had been able to fight and kill each other very effectively even though they had hardly any women in their ranks (and without experiencing any particular urge to correct that shortcoming). World Wars I and II changed this situation, but only because there existed a very great shortage of manpower, and only to a very limited extent. Though they did wear uniform, women neither became full soldiers—in the sense that they could be conscripted and utilized as their commanders wished—nor, with few exceptions, saw combat. The field where they were proportionally most numerous was the various resistance groups.[3] After 1945, too, women continued to play an important role in many guerrilla and terrorist organizations.

Two factors account for the increase in the number of uniformed female service personnel after 1970 or so. One was the rise of the feminist movement and its demand that women be made equal in every field. The other was the decline of conventional warfare and the end of conscription. The two were connected. On the one hand, armed forces, being short of male volunteers, were more prepared to take women. On the other, the fact that they would not be obliged to serve enabled women to have their cake and eat it, too—or so some of them thought. Following a millennia-long tradition, in everything from the kind of meals served to the kind of salaries provided, the military had been constructed with males in mind. Absorbing women required many changes and gave rise to endless trouble—some would say much more than they were worth. Nevertheless, as of the beginning of 2007, in no country had the presence of female soldiers even started to challenge the continued, near-absolute dominance of the military by men. Not only did the latter continue to hold practically all senior positions, but they also completely dominated the casualty lists. And if reports of

American female personnel using "sexual tactics" such as see-through lingerie and fake menstrual blood in order to pry information out of Muslim prisoners at Guantanamo are true,[4] nor did women's presence succeed in changing the character of war and humanizing it, as some radical feminists had hoped.

As most armed forces shrank, the number of major weapons systems each of them deployed declined even more. Generation by generation, those systems became much more expensive and much more complicated. Instead of being mass-produced, they had to be individually crafted like fake antiques. Instead of being given away or abandoned, as was the case after World War II, they were carefully collected, refurbished, and taken home so they could fight another day.[5] As they grew more complicated, directing them against the enemy and operating them required much more planning and more coordination, or so it was claimed. The more planning and coordination were required, the larger the number of service personnel who, instead of firing at the enemy, administered, communicated, and wrote papers either as part of their duties or while they were being educated for carrying them out. The advent of computers, laptops in particular, opened the floodgates. The size of the units available for war fighting dropped and dropped. The number of personnel allegedly needed for instructing and informing and administering and commanding and managing them grew, and grew.

Meanwhile, the world was changing. As we saw, European armed forces or their derivatives had dominated the globe from the eighteenth century on. Better organized, better disciplined, and better trained than their often ragtag opponents, and equipped with the best available technology, they easily smashed whatever levies non-European societies were able to impose on them. As Sir Hilaire Belloc once put it: "When everything is said we've got the Maxim [machine] gun, and they do not."

In 1919–39, this dominance remained largely intact; still, by that time most of the colonial peoples had realized that trying to fight in the open was the worst error they could commit. Instead of staging another Omdurman, they began developing other methods such as guerrilla warfare and terrorism. Instead of operating in the open, they engaged in hit-and-run attacks, and tried to use a combination of persuasion and intimidation to draw the civilian population to their side. Most such insurgencies were defeated, but only after a considerable time and at considerable cost. Often part of the cost was political, as countries were granted some semblance of independence or were promised it. In many places, colonial rule was no longer as complete, or as easy to maintain, as it had been.

Whether, in the face of the various resistance movements, freedom fighters, and the like, the Nazis could have ruled Europe indefinitely, as Keegan believes, or whether, given enough time, they would have gone the way almost all subsequent conquerors did, as I think, will forever remain in dispute. What can hardly be in dispute, though, is the fact that, from 1945 on, almost all attempts to deal with insurgencies have ended in failure. In 2006, the United States spent more than four hundred billion dollars on its armed forces, of which one hundred billion went to Iraq, much of it to fight the insurgency there. Yet the most important terrorists remained at large.

Seen from the point of view of most people in the so-called developed world, as long as the record of failure was limited to various exotic places where they themselves did not live, few of them cared. The most they were prepared to do was to send in peacekeeping forces, and even that was made dependent on there being few casualties or none at all. However, as of the late 1990s, there were growing signs that this respite was coming to an end; guerrilla warfare and terrorism, becoming international, were turning into an export commodity.

Does all this imply that we must resign ourselves to a world where insurgencies will typically gain their objectives? The answer is, by no means. The first, and absolutely indispensable, thing to do is to throw overboard 99 percent of the literature on counterinsurgency, counterguerrilla, counterterrorism, and the like. Since most of it has been written by the losing side, it is of little value.

Next, we should focus on the relatively small number of cases where counterinsurgency operations actually succeeded. Even disregarding small, isolated outbreaks such as the ones in Germany and Italy in the 1970s, there are such cases—campaigns in which a counterinsurgent force did succeed in coping with its enemies, bringing them to heel, and imposing something like peace. The methods used have been outlined in chapter 6. However, since counterinsurgency, and not major war, is the most important military problem facing humanity in the present and the foreseeable future, I shall take the liberty to spell them out once again.

By definition, guerrillas and terrorists are weak. By definition, their opponents are much stronger. Contrary to the accepted wisdom, and barring small movements with no popular support such as the Baader-Meinhof Gang, most guerrillas and terrorists won their struggles precisely because they were weak. It was their weakness that enabled them to hide; even more important, it was their weakness that permitted them to do what they wanted to do and what had to be done. Most, remaining weak, won their struggles long before they reached Mao's third stage of open warfare. Of those that were defeated, some suffered that fate because, emerging from hiding at too early a stage, they exposed themselves to their opponents; one very good example of this is provided by the Greek Civil War.[6] All this proves, if proof were needed, that the core of the difficulty is neither military nor political, but moral.

In principle, two methods suggest themselves. The first depends on excellent intelligence. Terrorists do not identify themselves by wearing uniforms, but rather use the natural and artificial environment to operate undercover. When everything is said and done, it is intelligence, obtained by personnel who are as familiar with the environment as the terrorists themselves, that proves decisive. Intelligence, though, is not enough. It must be backed up by the solid professionalism and iron discipline that alone make discrimination and self-restraint possible. This, in turn, will accomplish two things. First, it will prevent many more people from joining the insurgency. Second, by postponing, or perhaps even forestalling, the day when the counterinsurgents wake up, look into the mirror, and reflect on what they have become, it will also help them retain their fighting edge.

The other method will have to be used in case good intelligence is not available and discrimination is therefore impossible and, in case things reach the point where they threaten to run completely out of control. The first rule is to make your preparations in secret or, if that is not feasible, to use guile and deceit to disguise your plans. The second is to get your timing right; other things being equal, the sooner you act, the fewer people you must kill. The third is to strike as hard as possible within the shortest possible time; better to strike too hard than not hard enough. The fourth is to explain why your actions were absolutely necessary without, however, providing any apology for them.

The fifth is to operate in such a way that, in case your blow fails to deliver the results you expect and need, you will still have some other cards up your sleeve.

Each method, in its own way, demands tremendous courage and nerve—the former, if anything, even more than the latter. Clearly such nerve and such courage are not commodities every leader, every army, and every people possess. Without them, they tend to move from one extreme to another; "a sharp shift from killing to kindness," as The Washington Post, referring to US troops in Iraq, put it.[7] Now they use firepower to slaughter their enemies en masse, now they embrace them. Now they demolish, now they rebuild. Now they kill innocent people, now they pay compensation (an Iraqi life is worth twenty-five hundred dollars).[8] Now they use torture to elicit information, now they accuse the torturer of acting without orders and put him on trial; since punishments are seldom very harsh, however, the only effect is to add yet another layer of doubt and cynicism. Very often different military, intelligence, and aid organizations are in charge of the different activities. Lack of coordination ensues; the left hand does not know what the right is doing. Each time the policy shifts, the population, instead of feeling either terrified or friendly, becomes more and more puzzled at what may come next. Each time it shifts, the terrorists, interpreting the change as a proof of weakness, take heart. Over the last sixty years or so, the results have spoken for themselves.

This, of course, will not do. The attacks on the World Trade Center and the Pentagon, as well as other coups mounted by al-Qaeda and its like can leave us in no doubt; terrorism is spreading into the developed world. Precisely because so many of its proponents are able to operate inside that world, it represents a far greater threat than do any number of third-rate dictators—including, let it be added, those who have acquired, or are about to acquire, nuclear weapons. Either the developed world, with the United States at its head, shakes off its lethargy, realizes the nature of the problem (which is not the same as studying it to death), and learns to deal with terrorism, or as sure as night follows day, terrorism will deal with it. The choice, as always, is ours.

Epilogue

Ours is supposed to be an age of incessant rapid change. In view of this "fact," it is surprising that, during the two years since this book was finished, very little seems to have changed.

In Sri Lanka, in Sudan, in Somalia, in Chad, in several other places, the kind of civil war in which the members of various militias kill one another and all militias kill civilians is still raging. In Iraq, US forces are still floundering about, and the same appears increasingly true of Afghanistan as well. *Every* one of these wars is "non-Trinitarian." To the extent that they are being employed at all, in *none* of them are high-tech weapons, advanced weapons, precision-guided weapons, computerized weapons, and other ingredients of the so-called Revolution in Military Affairs capable of bringing about a decision. The king—on whom so many tens of billions of dollars have been spent and are still being spent—is naked. Yet the strange thing is that so many of his advisers, those who have brought the "Revolution" about, stubbornly refuse to admit the fact.

As of mid-2007, the case that has attracted the most attention remains the Israeli one. Between 2000, when the Israeli Defense Force (IDF) withdrew from Lebanon, and 2006, when it went to war in (but not against) that country, it underwent a technological revolution. In many ways it was inspired by, and similar to, the one experienced by the US armed forces. How could things have been different, given that it is the Americans who provide much of the hardware and pick up part of the bill? The number of tanks went down, that of computers, up. More supersophisticated and superexpensive combat aircraft and

attack helicopters were purchased. Missiles that were already very accurate were equipped with GPS and became even more so, actually
reaching the point where they were capable of being launched at a
given angle through a given window of an apartment building so as to
minimize "collateral damage" (or else maximize it, as the case might
be). Commanders who used to stay close to their troops and lead them
by calling "Follow me" were issued so-called plasma screens capable of
showing the exact location of every soldier and vehicle. And so on in
an endless chain of innovations. At the heart of every one stood the mi-
crochip; one could almost say, "Intel inside."

This is not the place to discuss the origins of the war. Suffice it to
say that, politically speaking, it was absolutely necessary. No country
can tolerate the killing of eight of its troops and the capture of two others; had Prime Minister Olmert not acted, his government would have
fallen and new elections would have taken place. As also happened in
so many other places, against a lightly armed enemy numbering no
more than three thousand to four thousand guerrillas—Hizbollah
never developed into a regular army—the Revolution in Military Affairs proved all but impotent. In more than a month's fighting, the IDF,
using some of the most sophisticated fire controls available to any army
anywhere, fired no fewer than 170,000 artillery rounds. This was twice
as many as in the October 1973 war. With the difference that, at that
time, the opponent had consisted of three Arab armies (Egyptian, Syrian, and Iraqi) with half a million men and more than four thousand
tanks.

During the first few days of the campaign, the Israeli air force did
very well against Hizbollah's long-range (50–100-kilometer) missiles,
practically destroying all of them. Later, its performance deteriorated.
In part, this was for lack of proper intelligence—though how anybody
could have been short of intelligence concerning what was happening
in a narrow strip of land, very close to the border, that Israeli forces
had occupied for eighteen years before withdrawing in 2000 remains a
mystery. In part, it was because commanders, fearful of incurring
losses, ordered pilots to fly at high altitudes, where they found it hard
to identify the elusive enemy. There was also a shortage of ammunition
suitable for busting bunkers on the one hand and burning bush on the
other. By one estimate, just 3 percent of the ordnance dropped on
southern Lebanon with the objective of halting the barrage of short-

range Katyusha rockets hit any target at all.[1] Most of the convoys coming from Syria and carrying reinforcements got through.

Above all, the air force did not succeed in waging "effect-based warfare" aimed at the enemy's consciousness, as chief of staff General Dan Halutz had hoped.[2] Instead, the longer the campaign, the less impressive did Israeli operations appear both in the eyes of outsiders and in those of the Israeli public itself. The old lesson that guerrillas rarely provide lucrative targets for airpower[3] was confirmed. As early as July 16, just four days after the opening of the campaign and with more than a month to go, the commander of the air force told the chief of staff that there were none left.[4] Dividing the money Israel spent on the war by the number of known Hizbollah dead, we find that each "precision" kill probably cost the IDF well over two million dollars.

Israeli commanders at all levels failed to use the unprecedented communications and data-processing equipment at their disposal to produce a cohesive plan and carry it out, nor was there any question of "swarming" tactics. Instead, they mobilized and deployed gradually until they had four divisions, no less. After much hesitation and many orders and counterorders, they ended up by driving parts of some of those divisions slowly and ponderously through narrow, winding mountain roads. Glued to their computers, often they had no idea of how their troops were doing or what their true condition was. Meanwhile, such were the shortcomings of the logistic and medical systems that some units had neither food nor water and some of the wounded were not evacuated.

Worse still, the commanders in question found themselves bickering with one another and contradicting one another. Constantly asking one another for permission for this operation or that to proceed, they endlessly talked to one another and to the media—often, as it turned out, with Hizbollah using sophisticated equipment to listen to their conversations. So bad was the performance of the IDF ground forces, militarily speaking, that the commander of the division responsible for the frontier with Lebanon, his superior, the commander in chief, Northern Front, and *his* superior, the chief of staff, as well as the minister of defense, were all made to resign; several other commanders handed in their resignations out of their own free will. Conversely, Hizbollah and its Syrian supporters are even now studying the lessons of the war in order, perhaps, to launch a second attack one day not very far off.[5]

The war also proved what some commentators had been saying for a long time: An army, any army, is only as good as its opponent; fighting the weak, one ends up becoming weak. For more than twenty years the IDF, "fighting" Palestinians who were armed (to the extent that they were armed at all) with very few light weapons and absolutely no heavy ones, degenerated. Making their way to arrest "suspects" in the alleys of Hebron and Nablus, IDF commanders learned how to use dogs to do their fighting for them while at the same time deploying eleven-year-old girls as human shields.

Almost all available units participated in the action. "Elite" infantry troops, including naval commandos designed and trained for entirely different purposes, eagerly volunteered to play cops and robbers with terrorists and their supporters. Tankmen and artillerists, instead of training with their weapons, patrolled the borders with Egypt and Jordan, which had not seen action for decades. Other soldiers dealt with settlers or manned roadblocks. Dealing with settlers, they were expected to behave like pussycats, suffering humiliations and pretending they just did not see. Perhaps to avenge themselves, when manning roadblocks they spent their time chicaning and humiliating Palestinian civilians on their way to hospitals or simply to work. In one notorious case, a gun-toting female soldier made an Arab woman drink some poisonous cleaning liquid the latter was carrying with her.[6] In the entire mighty IDF, which on paper counted more than half a million men and women, there was hardly a single officer left who knew how to command a unit from brigade upward. Which is not to say that, to fight the small, mobile, "swarming" Hizbollah fire teams, brigades were really what was needed.

As if to confirm section 5.2 of the present volume, all these shortcomings were covered, indeed almost smothered, by vast amounts of pseudoscientific gibberish. As I have explained elsewhere,[7] traditionally Israeli officers have not been among the most studious in the world. Plainspoken and sometimes blunt, they have gained promotion not by writing papers but by hunting Arabs and killing or capturing them. This time things were very different. If the war showed anything at all, it was how insidious the effect of "professional" lingo can be. What is one to make of a deputy chief of intelligence who, instead of looking for the facts, sees his mission as "providing decision makers with a narrative"? How does one distinguish "strategic intelligence superiority" (SIS) from "operational-tactical intelligence dominance" (OTID)? No doubt such terminology was born in "cross-rank brainstorming meetings intended to form conceptual frameworks." So thick was the nonsense, and such the resulting verbal confusion, that the need to reform officer training and education, particularly at the medium and senior levels where plans are made and orders issued, became one of the cardinal lessons to emerge from the conflict.

The objectives issued to units were often mixed up. Orders, instead of briefly telling commanders what to do and leaving the rest to them, tended to be long-winded, complex, and sometimes incomprehensible. In part, all this was due to habits formed during the six years when the Northern Front had been on the defensive, seeking nothing but peace and quiet. The outcome was an attempt to avoid mistakes at all costs. Each time an incident took place, "lessons" were drawn. Regulations, all of them aimed at preventing Hizbollah from succeeding in doing this or that, were piled on one another. At the same time initiative and independent thought were stifled. Reading some of the material, one gets the impression it was written by and for nincompoops with social science backgrounds. Many officers did in fact study social science, particularly political science, at Israel's universities. Far be it from me to discount political science as a whole—much of it is very good. However, in Israel as elsewhere, too often social scientists, trying to sound important, resort to the most obscure argot. Implanted in the minds of officers who only half understood its meaning, it seems to have done a lot of harm.

This entire sad history might make some people in other countries smile, not to say gloat; those arrogant Israelis, they may say, had it coming. But would any other armed force of any other Western country, pitted against a highly motivated and well-trained guerrilla force, have done better? Of course it is impossible to be sure. However, the mere fact that much IDF jargon was translated directly from English should be enough to raise suspicion. More seriously, "the record of failure" (see section 6.2 of the present volume), as well as ongoing events in Iraq and Afghanistan, makes one doubt that they could. In Kosovo in 1999, so terrified of casualties were NATO forces that they did not dare put a single unit on the ground; had they done so, undoubtedly many of their men would have returned home in coffins. The Americans alone excepted, few of those forces are as powerful and as sophisticated as the IDF is (at least in theory), yet all of them share the same kind of technology and are, by now, organized around it. Almost all have put their faith in the Revolution in Military Affairs, precision-guided munitions, computers, data links, sensors, and network-centric warfare.

But are these lessons being learned? Consider the newly issued US manual on COIN (counterinsurgency) operations.[8] The manual, which represents a rare instance of interservice cooperation, carries the signatures of Lieutenant General David H. Petraeus, US Army, and Lieutenant General James N. Mattis, US Marine Corps. Their main thesis seems to be that counterinsurgency has two faces. On the one hand, they tell us, it is necessary to wage an energetic military campaign aimed at finding the insurgents and killing or capturing as many of them as possible. On the other, one must take extensive civic action so as to win the "hearts and minds" of the people. This is hardly a revolutionary idea, and is one that, having failed in Vietnam, is even now failing both in Iraq and Afghanistan, as evidenced not just by continuing resistance on the part of insurgents who should have been defeated years ago but also by huge demonstrations in the center of Baghdad calling on the United States to get out.

As has been pointed out,[9] the manual, instead of looking forward into the future, quotes many of its predecessors from the 1950s on. Like others of its kind,[10] it emphasizes "extensive coordination and cooperation with a myriad of intergovernmental, indigenous, and international agencies." Unfortunately that is easier to say than to achieve. Even as these words were being written, the US Army in Iraq, commanded by none other than General Petraeus himself, announced that it was building a barrier between Shiites and Sunnis in Baghdad. Within days, however, it ran into trouble, given that Iraq's prime minister opposed the measure and "ordered" work to be halted.[11]

Here and there, the manual seeks to draw lessons from previous conflicts. However, many of these lessons are merely banal. Is it really necessary to point out that, in a "war without fronts," vehicles moving along one's lines of supply must be armed and/or escorted so as to be capable of defending against attack? Above all, there is no sign that the role of time, and thus the dynamics of the conflict, is understood. Instead, there are a few obligatory quotes from Mao. Perhaps this is because, given how badly things are going in Iraq and the progressive de-moralization of the US forces,[12] to admit the way time operates would be equivalent to conceding that the fight there is hopeless.

Ere they condemn Israel's failures, Western militaries should con-sider a number of social factors that their nations share with it and that tend to depress their own fighting spirit. First, there is rising life ex-pectancy, which results in the compulsory infantilization of young people of military age, who must be kept out of the workforce for as long as possible. Second, there is falling fertility, which makes society less willing to accept casualties. A third factor that almost everybody understands but is afraid to talk about (for fear of the consequences) is the increased presence of women in the forces: The more of them join, the less strenuous the training; the less attractive, too, those forces are to young men eager to prove themselves—instead of being pulled up to become more than they are, young men are pushed down and revert to less than they were.[13] Above all, there is the feeling that there is no threat. No Western country, almost certainly not even Israel, is about to be invaded by hordes of slogan-yelling, knife-wielding, bomb-throwing barbarians. If, when writing *The Clash of Civilizations*, Samuel Huntington had such an invasion in mind, then in all probabil-ity he was dead wrong.

In truth, the barbarians, having already passed through the gates, do not really need to invade. Inside the fortress, their number is grow-ing day by day. It is certainly true that not all Muslims are terrorists, and indeed to treat them as such would be the greatest mistake one could commit. However, it is also true that many, perhaps most, terror-ists are Muslims. Bin Laden himself is supposed to have said that the best way Muslim women can help the cause of Islam is to make sure there are more and more Muslims in the world. In the words of one prominent historian,[14] early in the twentieth century the fault line be-tween West and East was running through Bosnia-Herzegovina. Now it may be found in every European city, so much so that many of the lat-ter are having their skylines altered as more and more mosques are built in them.

To repeat the conclusions of this book, the developed world, with the United States at its head, must shake off its lethargy. It must finally get rid of the seductive but nonsensical and extremely costly illusion that is called the Revolution in Military Affairs. Instead, it must realize the nature of the problem—insurgency, guerrilla warfare, and terrorism, possibly, one day, armed with weapons of mass destruction—and learn to deal with it. Or else, as surely as night follows day, the day will come when terrorism deals with it.

Jerusalem, June 2007

Notes

Introduction

1. See on this the brilliant short piece by M. Howard, "Military History and the History of War," in Strategic and Combat Studies Institute, *Contemporary Essays*, The Occasional Number 47, Shrivenham, Swindon, 2004, pp. 45–55.

Chapter 1

1. See E. Jones, *The European Miracle*, New York, Cambridge University Press, 1987.
2. See on this C. M. Cipolla, *Guns and Sails in the Early Stages of European Expansion, 1400–1700*, London, Collins, 1965.
3. All these figures are from P. Kennedy, *The Rise and Fall of the Great Powers*, New York, Vintage, 1987, p. 149 table 6 and p. 243 table 21.
4. See on this D. Moran and A. Waldron, eds., *The People in Arms: Military Myth and National Mobilization Since the French Revolution*, Cambridge, Cambridge University Press, 2003, pp. 1–124.
5. E. Raeder, *Mein Leben*, Tuebingen, Schlichtenmeyer, 1956, vol. 1, p. 19.
6. K. Marx and F. Engels, "The American Civil War" [1863], in B. Semmel, ed., *Marxism and the Science of War*, Oxford, Oxford University Press, 1981, p. 129.
7. K.-H. Frieser, *Blitzkrieg-Legende: Der Westfeldzug 1940*, Munich, Oldenbourg, 1995, p. 35.
8. For some figures see M. G. McCoy, "Grinding Gears: The AEF and Motor Transportation in the First World War," *War in History* 11:2, April 2004, pp. 198, 200.
9. A. S. Field, "French Optical Telegraphy, 1793–1855: Hardware, Software, Administration," *Technology and Culture* 35:2, 1994, pp. 315–47.
10. See on this J. T. Sumida, "The Quest for Reach: The Development of Long-

Range Gunnery in the Royal Navy, 1901–1912," in S. D. Chiabotti, ed., *Tooling for War: Military Transformation in the Industrial Age,* Chicago, Imprint, 1996, pp. 49–96.

11. See J. Corbett, *Maritime Operations of the Russo-Japanese War,* Annapolis, Naval Institute Press, 1994 [1914], vol. ii pp. 216, 219–20, 223, 231, 237.

12. See on all this M. Palmer, *Command at Sea: Naval Command and Control Since the Sixteenth Century,* Cambridge, Harvard University Press, 2005, pp. 227, 232–36.

13. J. Corbett, *Some Principles of Maritime Strategy,* London, Longman, 1911, 231–32.

14. See on Corbett's career as a lecturer A. Gat, *The Development of Military Thought: The Nineteenth Century,* Oxford, Clarendon, 1992, pp. 216, 222.

15. S. Wilkinson, *The Brain of an Army,* Westminster, Constable, 1895.

16. See on him, Gat, *The Development of Military Thought,* pp. 105–7.

17. For an extended analysis of the lessons of the Boer War see W. McElwee, *The Art of War from Waterloo to Mons,* London, Weidenfeld and Nicolson, 1974, pp. 217–41.

18. See on this J. P. Wisser, *The Second Boer War, 1899–1900,* Kansas City, Mo., Hudson-Kimberly, 1901, p. 191.

19. See on this entire question G. Phillips, "The Obsolescence of the Arme Blanche and Technological Determinism in British Military History," *War in History* 9:1, January 2002, pp. 39–59.

20. See on this J. Luvaas, *The Military Legacy of the Civil War,* Chicago, University of Chicago Press, 1959, pp. 198–99.

21. See on this M. Howard, "Men Against Fire: Expectations of War in 1914," in S. E. Miller, ed., *Military Strategy and the Origins of the First World War,* Princeton, N.J., Princeton University Press, 1985, pp. 52–57.

22. See B. Brodie, *Sea Power in the Machine Age,* Princeton, N.J., Princeton University Press, 1941.

23. See D. C. Evans and M. P. Peattie, *Kaigun: Strategy, Tactics and Technology in the Imperial Japanese Navy, 1878–1941,* Annapolis, Naval Institute Press, 1997, pp. 50–51.

24. See his 1912 essay, "Der Krieg in der Gegenwart" (1908), in A. von Schlieffen, ed., *Gesammelte Schriften,* Berlin, Mittler, 1913, vol. 1 p. 17.

25. See his calculations as quoted in B. H. Liddell Hart, *Foch: The Man of Orleans,* London, Penguin, 1931, vol. 2 p. 490.

26. See on this D. Porch, *The March to the Marne: The French Army, 1871–1914,* Cambridge, Cambridge University Press, 1981, pp. 225–26.

27. Colonel Simansky, quoted in J. W. Kopp, "Soldiers and Civilians Confronting Future War," in Chiabotti, ed., *Tooling for War,* p. 203.

28. L. von Falkenhausen, *Flankenbewegung und Massenheer,* Berlin, Mittler, 1911.

29. Quoted in B. W. Tuchman, *The Proud Tower: A Portrait of the World Before 1914*, New York, MacMillan, 1966, p. 266.

30. A. Mahan, "The Peace Conference and the Moral Aspect of War," in *Lessons of the War with Spain and other Articles*, Boston, Little, Brown, 1899, p. 232; on the role he played in the conference see also B. Semmel, *Liberalism and Naval Strategy: Ideology, Interest and Sea Power During the Pax Britannica*, Boston, Allen & Unwin, 1986, pp. 154–58.

31. L. Wijler, "Herinneringen uit mein Leven," Herzliya, private edition, 1975, p. 11.

32. See, on her career, I. Abrams, "Bertha von Suttner and the Nobel Peace Prize," *Journal of Central European Affairs* 22:3, October 1962, pp. 286–307.

33. See on this J. Gooch, *Armies in Europe*, London, Routledge, 1980, pp. 134–35; also V. R. Berghahn, *Militarism: The History of an International Debate, 1861–1979*, Cambridge, Cambridge University Press, 1981, p. 15.

34. *L'Armee Nouvelle*, Paris, Editions Sociales, 1910.

35. See on this J. Keegan, *The Mask of Command*, New York, Viking, 1987, p. 256.

36. "Doughboy Center," available at www.worldwar1.com/dbc/origindb.htm.

37. *My Early Life; A Roving Commission*, London, Thornton Butterworth, 1930, p. 34.

38. On the link between masculinity and the high social status of armies see G. L. Mosse, *Fallen Soldiers: Reshaping the Memory of the World Wars*, Oxford, Oxford University Press, 1990, pp. 59–62.

39. See on this M. Trustram, *Women of the Regiments; Marriage and the Victorian Army*, Cambridge, Cambridge University Press, 1984, pp. 3, 91.

40. See, e.g., A. Woolacott, "Khaki Fever and its Control; Gender, Class and Sexual Morality in the British Home Front in the First World War," *Journal of Contemporary History*, 29:2, 1994, pp. 325–47.

41. See on this M. Ferro, *The Great War, 1914–1918*, London, Routledge, 1973, pp. 13–14.

42. Th. Rohkraemer, *Der Militarismus der "kleinen Leute"; Die Kriegsvereine im Deutschen Kaiserreich*, Munich, Oldenbourg, 1990, p. 76.

43. See L. Kennet, *The First Air War, 1914–1918*, New York, Free Press, 1991, pp. 13–15.

44. S. Zweig, *Die Welt von Gestern*, Frankfurt/Main, Fischer, 2000 [1941], pp. 15–17.

45. See in particular N. Angell, *The Great Illusion: A Study in the Relation of Military Power to National Advantage*, New York, Garland, 1972 [1911], pp. 25–43.

46. See on this most recently A. Watson, " 'For Kaiser and Reich': The Identity

and Fate of the German Volunteers, 1914–1918," *War in History* 12:1, January 2005, pp. 44–74.

47. A. Hitler, *Mein Kampf,* New Delhi, Jaico, 1988 [1925], p. 145.

48. Kennedy, *The Rise and Fall of the Great Powers,* p. 200 table 15.

49. See on this E. Kehr, *Economic Interest, Militarism and Foreign Policy,* Berkeley, University of California Press, 1970 [1927–28], pp. 50–75; F. Fischer, *Germany's Aims in the First World War,* London, Chatto & Windus, 1967.

50. Quoted in K. Jarausch, *The Enigmatic Chancellor: Bethmann-Hollweg and the Hubris of Imperial Germany,* New Haven, Yale University Press, 1973, p. 96.

51. R. B. Haldane, "Hegel," *Contemporary Review,* 67, February 1895, p. 232; see also B. Bosquanet, *Philosophical Theory of the State* (London: MacMillan, 1899).

52. F. Stern, "Bethmann Hollweg and the War: The Bounds of Responsibility," in idem, ed., *The Failure of Illiberalism,* New York, Columbia University Press, 1971, pp. 99ff.

53. See G. W. Gong, *The Standard of "Civilization" in International Society,* Oxford, Clarendon, 1984, p. 196.

54. Reichsarchiv, *Der Weltkrieg,* Berlin, Ullstein, 1921, series I, vol. I: p. 38 ff.

55. See M. T. Florinsky, *The End of the Russian Empire,* New York, Collier, 1961, pp. 157–58.

56. See on this J. Gooch, *Armies in Europe,* London, Routledge, 1980, pp. 145–48.

57. Quoted in G. Ritter, *The Sword and the Scepter,* Coral Gables, University of Miami Press, 1969, vol. ii, p. 205.

58. See on his exchange H. von Moltke, *Erinnerungen, Briefe, Dokumente 1877–1916,* Berlin, TAG Verlag, 1922, p. 21.

59. A. Marshall, "Russian Military Intelligence, 1905–1917," *War in History* 11:4, November 2004, p. 401.

60. A. Mombauer, "A Reluctant Military Leader? Helmuth von Moltke and the July Crisis of 1914," *War and Society* 6:4, November 1999, p. 439.

61. "Der Krieg in der Gegenwart," vol. 1 p. 11.

62. H. Thun, *Die Verkehr-und Nachrichtenmittel im Kriege,* Leipzig, Barth, 1911, pp. 184–85.

63. R. F. Mackay, *Fisher of Kilverstone,* Oxford, Clarendon, 1973, pp. 319–21.

64. C. Andrew, *Her Majesty's Secret Service: The Making of the British Intelligence Community,* New York, Penguin, 1987, p. 88.

Chapter 2

1. W. Groener, *Lebenserinnerungen,* Goettingen, Vanderbroek, 1957, p. 141.

2. See on this M. van Creveld, *Supplying War: Logistics from Wallenstein to Patton,* Cambridge, Cambridge University Press, 1978, pp. 120–21.

3. H. von Kuhl, *Der Deutsche Generalstab in Vorbereitung und Durchfuehrung des Weltkrieges,* Berlin, Mittler, 1920, pp. 205–8.

4. T. N. Dupuy, *Numbers, Predictions, and War,* Indianapolis, Bobbs-Merrill, 1979, p. 28 table 2–4.

5. According to S. C. Tucker, *The Great War, 1914–1918,* London, UCL, 1998, p. 32.

6. Quoted in M. Gilbert, *The First World War: A Complete History,* New York, Holt, 1994, p. 112.

7. T. Ashworth, *Trench Warfare, 1914–1918,* New York, Holmes & Ashworth, 1980, pp. 57, 116; J. Schindler, "Steamrollered in Galicia," *War in History* 10:1, January 2003, p. 29.

8. Unsigned, undated note, Bundesarchiv/Militaerarchiv, Freiburg i.B., H20/480.

9. Joseph Amann, *Ueber den Einfluss der weiblichen Geschlechtskrankheiten auf das Nervensystem,* Erlangen, Med. Verlag, 1868, p. 83.

10. E.g., N. Dixon, *On the Psychology of Military Incompetence,* New York, Basic Books, 1976; also Travers, *The Killing Ground: The British Army, the Western Front, and the Emergence of Modern War 1900–1918,* London, Allen & Unwin, 1987, pp. 103–4.

11. L. Renn, *Krieg und Nachkrieg,* Berlin, Aufbau, 1951 [1929] pp. 115–17; C. Zuckmayer, *Als waer's ein Stueck von mir,* Frankfurt/Main, Fischer, 1997 [1918], pp. 280–81.

12. See on this J. Keegan, *The Mask of Command,* New York, Penguin, 1987, pp. 252–53.

13. The most comprehensive account of this subject is L. F. Haber, *Gas Warfare, 1915–1945: The Legend and the Facts,* London, University of London Press, 1976.

14. See, e.g., the illustrated pamphlet by L. Raemakers, *Gassed! Another Victory for Kultur,* New York, 1916.

15. According to R. D. Mueller, "Total War as a Result of New Weapon: The Use of Chemical Agents in World War I," in R. Chickering and S. Foerster, eds., *Great War, Total War,* Cambridge, Cambridge University Press, 2000, p. 101.

16. See on this B. Holden-Reid, "Gas Wafare: The Perils of Prediction," in D. Carlton and C. Schaerf, eds., *Reassessing Arms Control,* London, MacMillan, 1985, pp. 143–58.

17. Marshall, "Russian Military Intelligence," p. 404.

18. See on her exploits and eventual fate J. Wheelwright, *The Fatal Lover: Mata Hari and the Myth of Women in Espionage*, London, Collin & Brown, 1992.

19. See on these problems B. I. Gudmundson, *On Artillery*, Westport, Conn., Praeger, 1993, pp. 36, 55.

20. W. L. Colmar von der Goltz, *The Nation in Arms*, London, Rees, 1913 ed., p. 457.

21. Figures from Oberste Heeresleitung, ed., *Taschenbuch fuer Offiziere der Verkehrstruppen*, Berlin, Mittler, 1913, p. 84; and A. M. Henniker, *Transportation on the Western Front, 1914–1918*, London, HMSO, 1937, p. 103.

22. J. Charteris, *At G.H.Q.*, London, Cassell, 1931, pp. 208–10.

23. B. H. Liddell Hart, *The Defense of Britain*, London, Faber & Faber, 1939, p. 26.

24. Figures from N. Stone, *The Eastern Front, 1914–1917*, London, Hodder & Stoughton, 1975, pp. 93–4.

25. See for these operations A. Wrangel, *The End of Chivalry: The Last Great Cavalry Battles, 1914–1982*, New York, Hippocrene, 1982.

26. According to M. J. Gregory, "Marauders of the Sea: German Armed Merchant Raiders During World War II," 2002, available at www.ahoy .tk-jk.net/MaraudersWW1/Tables.html.

27. For the figures, and why unrestricted submarine warfare did not work, see H. H. Herwig, "Germany's U-Boat Campaign," in Chickering and Foerster, eds., *Great War, Total War*, pp. 189–206.

28. See on this problem K. Doenitz, *Memoirs: Ten Years and Twenty Days*, Annapolis, Naval Institute Press, 1959, p. 4.

29. Figures from Gilbert, *The First World War*, pp. 328–29.

30. See on him C. Barnett, *The Swordbearers*, London, Eyre & Spottiswode, 1963, pp. 116, 121, 185; also Mombauer, "A Reluctant Military Leader?" especially pp. 431–40.

31. These and subsequent figures from Gilbert, *The First World War*, p. 83; J.F.C. Fuller, *The Conduct of War 1789–1961*, London, Eyre & Spottiswode, 1963, p. 171; Kennedy, *The Rise and Fall of the Great Powers*, p. 267; Stone, *The Eastern Front*, p. 231.

32. According to H. Meier-Welcker, "Die deutsche Fuehrung an der Westfront im Fruehsommer 1918," *Die Welt als Geschichte* 21, 1961, p. 166.

33. G. Hardach, "Industrial Mobilization in 1914–1918," in P. Friedenson, ed., *The French Home Front, 1914–1918*, Providence, RI, Berg, 1992, pp. 59–61.

34. G. Plumpe, "Chemische Industrie und Hilfdienstgesetz," in G. Mai, ed., *Arbeiterschaft in Deutschland, 1914–1918*, Duesseldorf, Droste, 1985, p. 181.

35. See N. Ferguson, *The Pity of War: Explaining World War I*, New York,

Basic Books, 2000, pp. 260–61; also K. Grieves, "Lloyd George and the Management of the British War Economy," in Chickering and Foerster, eds., *Great War, Total War*, pp. 369–70.

36. R. Bessel, "Mobilizing German Society for War," in Chickering and Foerster, eds., *Great War, Total War*, p. 441.

37. See for the data A. W. Kirkaldy, *Industry and Finance*, London, Pitman, 1921, vol. ii section i.

38. For some figures on this question see M. van Creveld, *Men, Women and War*, London, Cassel, 2001, pp. 127–28.

39. Josephus Daniel as quoted in Jean Ebbert and Marie-Berth Hall, *Crossed Currents: Navy Women from WWI to Tailhook*, London, Brassey's, 1993, p. 14.

40. For one excellent study of the way it worked see B. J. Davis, *Home Fires Burning: Food, Politics, and Everyday Life in World War I Berlin*, Chapel Hill, University of North Carolina Press, 2000.

41. J. M. Winter, *The Great War and the British People*, London, MacMillan, 1986, *passim*.

42. Ferguson, *The Pity of War*, pp. 336–37 and table 41.

43. Figures from B. R. Mitchell, *European Historical Statistics*, New York, Columbia University Press, 1975, pp. 108–25; Stone, *The Eastern Front*, p. 295.

44. E. Morgan, *Studies in British Financial Policy, 1914–1925*, London, MacMillan, 1952, pp. 345–49.

45. For the text of Ludendorff's letter, see E. Ludendorff, *My War Memoirs*, vol. 2, London, Methuen, 1919, pp. 724–25.

46. See on this W. McNeill, *The Pursuit of Power Since A.D. 1000: Technology, Armed Forces, and Society*, Chicago, University of Chicago Press, 1983, pp. 307–61; also M. van Creveld, *Technology and War: From 2000 B.C. to the Present*, New York, Free Press, 1990, pp. 217–32.

47. For the British one, e.g., see H. Driver, *The Birth of Military Aviation: Britain, 1903–1914*, London, Boydell Press, 1997, especially pp. 85–146.

48. See on the battle K. Macksey, *Tank Warfare: A History of Tanks in Battle*, St. Albans, Frogmore, 1976, pp. 44–73.

49. Ludendorff, *My War Memoirs*, vol. 1 p. 439.

50. H. C. B. Rogers, *Tanks in Battle*, London, Sphere, 1972, pp. 64–65.

51. See J. Weller, *Men Against Tanks: A History of Anti-Tank Warfare*, London, David & Charles, 1975, pp. 21–27.

52. M. S. Neipberg, *Foch: Supreme Allied Commander in the Great War*, Washington DC, Brassey's, 2003, p. 81.

53. The best discussion is B. Holden-Reid, *J.F.C. Fuller: Military Thinker*, New York, St. Martin's, 1987, pp. 49–54.

54. These and the following figures from E. Angelucci, *The Rand McNally Encyclopedia of Military Aircraft, 1914 to the Present,* New York, Gallery, 1990, pp. 20, 42, 66–67.

55. Figures from War Office, *Statistics of the Military Effort of the British Empire During the Great War, 1914–1920,* London, War Office, 1922, pp. 237, 352–57; and Winter, *The Great War,* p. 75.

56. See on this R. F. Weigley, "Pershing and the U.S. Military Tradition," in Chickering and Foerster, eds., *Great War, Total War,* pp. 331–45.

57. R. C. Hall, " 'The Enemy Is Behind Us': The Morale Crisis in the Bulgarian Army in the Summer of 1918," *War in History* 11:2, April 2004, p. 218.

Chapter 3

1. Kennedy, *The Rise and Fall of the Great Powers,* p. 330 table 30.

2. For the details of their cooperation see F. L. Carsten, *The Reichswehr in Politics, 1919–1933,* Berkeley, University of California Press, 1966, pp. 232–38, 275–84.

3. For the strengths and weaknesses of the Reichswehr see A. Seaton, *The German Army, 1933–1945,* London, Weidenfeld and Nicolson, 1982, pp. 1–50.

4. See, for the US, K. J. Hagan, *This People's Navy: The Making of American Sea Power,* New York, Free Press, 1991, pp. 259–80; also A. R. Millett and P. Maslowski, *For the Common Defense: A Military History of the United States of America,* New York, Free Press, 1984, pp. 361–92. For Britain, A. Herman, *To Rule the Waves: How the British Navy Shaped the Modern World,* New York, HarperCollins, 2004; also B. Bond, *British Military Policy Between the Two World Wars,* Oxford, Clarendon, 1980.

5. See E. F. Ziemke, "The Soviet Armed Forces in the Interwar Period," in W. Murray and A. R. Millett, eds, *Military Innovation in the Interwar Period,* Cambridge, Cambridge University Press, 1996, pp. 1–38.

6. See, for the essential story, B. Bond, *War and Society in Europe, 1871–1914,* London, Fontana, 1984, pp. 141–43.

7. For the aftermath of World War I and the origins of US isolationism see M. Jonas, *Isolationism in America, 1935–1941,* Ithaca, N.Y., Cornell University Press, 1966, especially chapter 1.

8. See, for the figures, R. Bridenthal, "Something Old, Something New: Women Between the Two World Wars," in R. Bridenthal and C. Coonz, eds., *Becoming Visible: Women in European History,* Boston, Houghton Mifflin, 1977, p. 426 table 18–1.

9. See his article on "Fascism" in *Encyclopedia Italianna* (1935), available at www.fordham.edu/halsall/mod/mussolini-fascism.html, especially the first paragraph.

10. See on this B. A. Shillony, "The February 26 Affair: Politics of a Military

Insurrection," in C. M. Wilson, ed., *Crisis Politics in Prewar Japan*, Tokyo, Sophia University Press, 1970, pp. 25–50.

11. Q. Wright, *A Study of War*, Chicago, University of Chicago Press, 1965 [1941], p. 1000. The most aggressive nation of all, incidentally, was Italy.

12. W. L. Shirer, *Berlin Diary*, New York, Knopf, 1940, pp. 145–46, entry for August 31, 1940.

13. See on this A. Gat, *The Fascist-Liberal Visions of War*, Oxford, Oxford University Press, 1988, pp. 43–79.

14. G. Douhet, *The Command of the Air*, New York, Arno, 1972 [1921], pp. 10–31.

15. See on him A. Trythall, *"Boney" Fuller: Strategist, Soldier and Writer*, New Brunswick, N.J., Rutgers University Press, 1977.

16. J. F. C. Fuller, *The Foundations of the Science of War*, London, Hutchinson, 1926, chapter XI.

17. See on him B. Bond, *Liddell Hart: A Study of His Military Thought*, London, Cassell, 1977; and J. J. Mearsheimer, *Liddell Hart and the Weight of History*, London, Brassey's, 1988.

18. B. H. Liddell Hart, *The Ghost of Napoleon*, London, Faber & Faber, 1933, pp. 19–44.

19. See on this A. Gat, "The Hidden Sources of Liddell Hart's Strategic Ideas," *War in History* 3:3, July 1996, pp. 293–308.

20. E. Ludendorff, *Der totale Krieg*, Munich, Ludendorff, 1935, pp. 10, 16, 87–88.

21. E.g., J. L. Wallach, *Kriegstheorien: Ihre Entwicklung im 19. und 20. Jahrhundert*, Frankfurt/Main, Bernard & Graefe, 1972, pp. 185–89.

22. See on this question Mearsheimer, *Liddell Hart and the Weight of History*, pp. 99–126, and J. S. Corum, *The Roots of Blitzkrieg*, Lawrence, University Press of Kansas, 1992, pp. 128–30.

23. See, on the way the Germans in particular did it, K. H. Wildhagen, *Erich Fellgiebel: Meister operativer Nachrichtenverbindungen*, Hannover, Wildhagen, 1970.

24. See on this period W. Murray, "Armored Warfare: The British, French, and German Experiences," in Murray and Millett, eds., *Military Innovation in the Interwar Period*, pp. 19–29.

25. On the effect Churchill's policies had on the British army see D. French, "The Mechanization of the British Cavalry Between the World Wars," *War and History* 10:3, July 2003, pp. 310–11.

26. See Bond, *British Military Policy Between the Two World Wars*, pp. 259–79.

27. Liddell Hart, *Foch*, vol. 1 p. 216.

28. See on these machines D. Crow, "The Experimentals," in D. Crow, ed., *AFVs of World War One*, Windsor, Berkshire, Profile, 1970, pp. 137–40.

29. See R. M. Habeck, *Storm of Steel: The Development of Armor Doctrine in Germany and the Soviet Union, 1919–1939*, Ithaca, N.Y., Cornell University Press, 2003, pp. 149–50.

30. On the techniques employed see OHL, *Die Angriff im Stellungkrieg*, 1918, printed in E. Ludendorff, ed., *Urkunden der Obersten Heeresleitung*, Berlin, Mittler, 1922, pp. 642–45.

31. See H. Guderian, *Panzer Leader*, New York, Ballantine, 1957 [1953], pp. 19–22.

32. See, for a comparison of the numbers and quality of the armor available to both sides, K.-H. Frieser, *Blitzkrieg-Legende: Der Westfeldzug 1940*, Munich, Oldenbourg, 1995, pp. 48–49.

33. On the process see M. Cooper, *The German Army, 1933–1945: Its Political and Military Failure*, London, Macdonald and Jane's, 1978, pp. 139–58.

34. For a perspective on the development of air doctrine see A. Stephens, "The True Believers: Air Power Between the Wars," in A. Stephens, ed., *The War in the Air, 1914–1994*, Fairbairn, ACT, Air Power Studies Center, 1994, pp. 47–80.

35. See on prewar Soviet airpower K. R. Whiting, "Soviet Aviation and Air Power Under Stalin," in R. Higham and J. W. Kipp, eds., *Soviet Aviation and Air Power: A Historical View*, London, Brassey's, 1977, pp. 47–56.

36. See, on the way it was done, M. van Creveld, S. Canby, and K. S. Brouwer, *Airpower and Maneuver Warfare*, Maxwell AFB, Air University, 1994, pp. 21–97; also, for a more general view, J. S. Corum, "From Biplanes to Blitzkrieg: The Development of German Air Doctrine Between the Wars," *War and History* 3:1, January 1996, pp. 85–101.

37. M. Gabrielle, *Operazion C 3*, Rome, Cappelli, 1965, pp. 139–40.

38. A. R. Millett, "Assault from the Sea," in Murray and Millett, eds., *Military Innovation in the Interwar Period*, p. 77.

39. See the figures in H. H. Holweg, "Innovation Ignored: The Submarine Problem—Germany, Britain, and the United States, 1919–1939," in Murray and Millett, eds., *Military Innovation in the Interwar Period*, p. 231.

40. Angelucci, *Rand McNally Encyclopedia of Military Aircraft*, pp. 51, 185, 186.

41. Frieser, *Blitzkrieg-Legende*, pp. 54–55.

42. Quoted in M. von Hagen, "The Levee en Masse from Russian Empire to Soviet Union, 1874–1938," in Moran and Waldron, eds., *The People in Arms*, p. 180.

43. See on this M. Kitchen, *The German Officer Corps, 1890–1914*, Oxford, Oxford University Press, 1968, p. 35.

44. See R.G.L. Waite, *Vanguard of Nazism: The Free Corps Movement in Post-war Germany, 1919–23*, New York, Norton, 1952, pp. 45–52.

45. See on this C. Fischer, *Stormtroopers: A Social, Economic and Ideological Analysis, 1919–1935*, London, Allen & Unwin, 1983, pp. 49–54.

46. Shirer, *Berlin Diary*, p. 327, entry for June 27, 1940.

47. See on this S. J. Zaloga, "Soviet Tank Operations in the Spanish Civil War," available at www.libraryautomation.com/nymas/soviet_tank_operations_in_the_sp.htm.

48. Habeck, *Storm of Steel*, pp. 265–66.

49. See on this R. L. Proctor, *Hitler's Luftwaffe in the Spanish Civil War*, Westport, Conn., Geenwood, 1983, especially pp. 251–64.

50. For example, J. W. Murray, *The China Quagmire: Japan's Expedition on the Asian Continent, 1933–41*, New York, 1983, does not have a word to say about this.

51. See on this encounter A. Sella, "Khalkin Gol: The Forgotten War," *Journal of Contemporary History* 18:4, October 1983, pp. 651–84.

52. The latest work on this war is W. R. Trotter, *The Winter War: The Russo-Finnish War of 1939–1940*, London, Aurum, 2002.

53. See on this F. W. Seidler, *Frauen zu den Waffen*, Bonn, Bernard & Graefe, 1998, pp. 257–61.

54. See on this Gat, *The Fascist-Liberal Visions of War*, pp. 31, 116.

55. P. W. Gray, "The Myth of Air Control—the Realities of Imperial Policing," *Aerospace Journal*, fall 2001, available at www.airpower.maxwell.af.mil/airchronicles/apj/apj01/fal01/gray.html.

56. J. Gottmann, "Bugeaud, Gallieni, Lyautey; The Development of French Colonial Warfare," in E. Mead Earle, ed., *Makers of Modern Strategy*, Princeton, Princeton University Press, 1941, p. 256.

57. See on this K. Jeffrey, "Colonial Warfare, 1900–39," in C. McInnes and G. D. Sheffield, eds., *Warfare in the Twentieth Century: Theory and Practice*, London, Unwin Hyman, 1988, especially pp. 47–48.

58. All these figures from Kennedy, *The Rise and Fall of the Great Powers*, p. 200, table 15, p. 201, table 15, p. 296, table 27.

59. *Mein Kampf*, pp. 128–29.

60. For the state of the German army on the eve of the war see M. Messerschmidt, "German Military Effectiveness Between 1919 and 1939," in Millett and Murray, eds., *Military Effectiveness*, vol. 2 pp. 218–55.

61. See V. Suvorov, *Icebreaker: Who Started the Second World War?*, New York, Viking, 1991; also J. Foerster and W. E. Mawdsley, "Hitler and Stalin in Perspective: Secret Speeches on the Eve of Barbarossa," *War in History* 1:11, January 2004, pp. 61–103.

62. M. Weygand, "How France Is Defended," address at Chatham House, May 16, 1939, *International Affairs* 18:4, July–August 1939, p. 469.

63. See G. Weinberg, *A World at Arms*, New York, Cambridge University Press, 1994, pp. 67–68.

64. Quoted in D. A. Lake, *Entangling Alliances: American Foreign Policy in Its Century*, Princeton, Princeton University Press, 1999, p. 101.

65. See on the state of Italy's armed forces B. R. Sullivan, "The Italian Armed Forces, 1918–1940," in Millett and Murray, eds., *Military Effectiveness*, vol. 2, pp. 169–217.

Chapter 4

1. See on the atmosphere of those days A. Werth, *Russia at War, 1941–1945*, London, Pan, 1964, pp. 233–38.

2. See on this W. Hubatsch, *"Weseruebung": Die Deutsche Besetzung von Daenemark und Norwegen 1940*, Goettingen, Musterschmidt, 1960, p. 47.

3. J. Piekalkiewicz, *Ziel Paris: Der Westfeldzug 1940*, Munich, Pawlak, 1986, p. 209.

4. Letter of May 3, 1940, *Documents on German Foreign Policy*, series D, vol. ix, London, HMSO, 1956, no. 192, pp. 275–77.

5. M. Domarus, *Hitlers Reden und Proklamationen*, Wuerzburg, Schmidt, 1963, vol. 2 p. 1704.

6. See, on the debate, A. Seaton, *The Russo-German War, 1941–1945*, London, Barker, 1971, pp. 142–43, 151–52.

7. See van Creveld, *Supplying War*, pp. 168–71.

8. J. von Puttkamer, *Die Unheimliche See*, Vienna, Kuehne, 1952, pp. 9–11.

9. See on this most recently J. Friedrich, *Der Brand: Deutschland im Bombenkrieg 1940–1945*, Berlin, Propylaeen, 2003, p. 74.

10. See P. Padfield, *War Beneath the Sea: Submarine Conflict, 1939–1945*, London, Pimlico, 1997, pp. 43–44.

11. J. Rohwehr, *The Critical Convoy Battles of March 1943: The Battle for HX 229/SC122*, Annapolis, Naval Institute Press, 1977, p. 198.

12. See on the chain of errors that led to the disaster P. Beesly, "Convoy PQ-17: A Study of Intelligence and Decision-Making," in M. Handel, ed., *Intelligence and Military Operations*, London, Cass, 1990, pp. 292–322.

13. The most famous study to come out of this was R. Wohlstetter, *Pearl Harbor: Warning and Decision*, Stanford, Stanford University Press, 1962.

14. See on this story J. McPhee, "Balloons of War," *New Yorker*, January 29, 1996, pp. 52–60.

15. See, on Wever, H. M. Mason, *The Rise of the Luftwaffe, 1918–1940*, London, Cassell, 1975, pp. 183–86.

16. On the battle and its aftermath see J. Erickson, *The Road to Berlin: Stalin's War with Germany,* Boulder, Westview, 1983, pp. 87–136.

17. G. M. Gilbert, *Nuerenberger Tagebuch,* Hamburg, Fischer, 1962, p. 96, entry for December 25, 1945.

18. See R. L. DiNardo, *Mechanized Juggernaut or Military Anachronism? Horses and the German Army in World War II,* Westport, Greenwood, 1991.

19. On the factors that affected air transport then and later see N. Brown, *Strategic Mobility,* London, Chatto & Windus, 1963.

20. For all these figures see the tables in R. Overy, *Why the Allies Won the War,* New York, Norton, 1995, pp. 331–32.

21. According to A. Milward, *War, Economy and Society 1939–1945,* Berkeley and Los Angeles, University of California Press, 1979, p. 333.

22. See on these problems Overy, *Why the Allies Won the War,* pp. 200–2.

23. See on this A. Speer, *Inside the Third Reich,* London, MacMillan, 1970, pp. 405–6.

24. W. Moskoff, *The Bread of Affliction: The Food Supply in the USSR During World War II,* Cambridge, Cambridge University Press, 1990, pp. 71–72; and A. Nove, *An Economic History of the USSR,* Harmondsworth, Middlesex, Penguin, 1972, p. 262.

25. Figures from M. Harrison, *Soviet Planning in Peace and War 1938–1945,* Cambridge, Cambridge University Press, 1985, p. 182.

26. Milward, *War, Economy and Society,* p. 218.

27. Ibid., p. 72 table 7.

28. According to S. Hillman, "Comparative Strengths of the Great Powers," in A. Toynbee, ed., *The World in March 1939,* London, Royal Institute for International Affairs, 1940, p. 443.

29. J. Barber and M. Harrison, *The Soviet Home Front, 1941–1945,* London, Longman, 1991, p. 155; B. R. Rosenthal, "Love on the Tractor: Women in the Russian Revolution and After," in Bridenthal and Koonz, eds., *Becoming Visible,* p. 401.

30. C. Briar, *Working for Women? Gendered Work and Welfare Politics in Twentieth Century Britain,* London, UCL, 1997, pp. 76–78.

31. A. Kessler-Harris, *Out to Work: A History of Wage-Earning Women in the United States,* New York, Oxford University Press, 1982, p. 276; US Department of Labor, *Industrial Injuries to Women,* Washington, DC, 1947, Government Printing Office, 1947, p. 4 table 1.

32. See Thomas R. H. Havens, "Women and War in Japan, 1937–1945," *American Historical Review* 80, 1975, pp. 913–34.

33. D. Winkler, *Frauenarbeit im Dritten Reich,* Hamburg, Hoffman and Campe, 1977, pp. 110–19, 123.

34. See, for the evidence, M. van Creveld, *Men, Women and War*, London, Cassell, 2003, pp. 134, 136, 140–41.

35. Overy, *Why the Allies Won the War*, passim.

36. The estimate is reproduced in War Office, ed., "German Army Documents Dealing with the War on the Western Front from June to October 1944," n.p., no editor, 1946.

37. See Th. Bauer, *History of the Industrial College of the Armed Forces, 1924–1983*, n.p., Alumni Association of the Graduates of the Industrial College of the Armed Forces, 1983, chapter 1.

38. See, for a good account of the development of the various instruments and the way they interacted, A. Price, *Instruments of Darkness*, London, MacDonald & Jane's, 1977.

39. See M. J. Neufeld, *The Rocket and the Reich*, New York, Free Press, 1995, pp. 272–75.

40. See M. Bar Zohar, *The Hunt for the German Scientists*, New York, Hawthorn, 1967.

41. See F. W. Lanchester, *Aircraft in Warfare: The Dawn of the Fourth Arm*, London, Constable, 1916.

42. See on this F. H. Hinsley and A. Strip, *Codebreakers*, Oxford, Oxford University Press, 1993, pp. 1–13.

43. See P. Beesly, *Very Special Intelligence: The Story of the Admiralty's Operational Intelligence Center, 1939–1945*, London, Hanish Hamilton, 1977, pp. 160–63.

44. M. van Creveld, *The Transformation of War*, New York, Free Press, 1991, pp. 171–72.

45. J. W. Dower, *War Without Mercy: Race and Power in the Pacific War*, New York, Pantheon, 1986, p. 299.

46. Halder, *Kriegstagebuch*, Stuttgart, Kohlhammer, 1962, vol. 2, pp. 335–37, entry for March 30, 1941.

47. See, on the German side, the figures in O. Bartov, *The Eastern Front, 1941–54: German Troops and the Barbarisation of Warfare*, London, MacMillan, 1985, pp. 12–21.

48. A. Beevor, *The Fall of Berlin, 1945*, New York, Penguin, 2003, pp. 28–32, 409–12.

49. See, in general, D. Graham, *Tug of War: The Battle for Italy, 1943–1945*, New York, St. Martin's 1986.

50. See above, p. 134.

51. R. Overy, "World War II: The Bombing of Germany," in Stephens, ed., *The War in the Air*, p. 118.

52. See on it, most recently, Biddle, *Military Power*, pp. 108–31.

53. Seaton, *The Russo-German War*, p. 566.

54. R. M. Leighton and R. W. Coakely, *Global Logistics and Strategy*, Washington, DC, OCMH, 1955, vol. I, p. 638.

55. See, for a brief account of US submarine warfare, Padfield, *War Beneath the Sea*, pp. 337–421.

56. Dower, *War Without Mercy*, pp. 61–71.

57. The definitive work on that subject is R. Rhodes, *The Making of the Atomic Bomb*, New York, Touchstone, 1988.

58. Ibid., p. 690.

Chapter 5

1. See on this most recently Th. J. Cutler, *The Battle of Leyte Gulf*, Annapolis, Naval Institute Press, 2001.

2. K. R. Greenfeld, ed., *Command Decisions*, New York, Harcourt Brace, 1965; H. A. Jacobsen, ed., *Decisive Battles of World War II*, New York, Putnam, 1965.

3. See Nove, *An Economic History of the USSR*, p. 285.

4. Figures from Keegan, *The Battle for History: Re-Fighting World War II*, London, Hutchinson, 1995, pp. 95–96; W. Ashworth, *Short History of the International Economy Since 1850*, London, Longman, 1952, p. 268.

5. Much the best summary of that debate, albeit that it only goes as far as 1980, remains L. Freedman, *The Evolution of Nuclear Strategy*, New York, St. Martin's, 1980.

6. B. Brodie, *The Absolute Weapon*, Princeton, Princeton University Press, 1946, pp. 24, 28, 34, 46.

7. W. Millis, *Military History*, Washington, DC, Service Center for Teachers of History, 1961, p. 16.

8. See on this particular subject R. K. Betts, ed., *Cruise Missiles: Technology, Strategy, Politics*, Washington, DC, Brookings, 1981.

9. For the game of budgetmanship as it is played in the Pentagon see R. A. Stubbing, *The Defense Game: An Insider Explores the Astonishing Realities of America's Defense Establishment*, New York, Harper & Row, 1986; also E. N. Luttwak, *The Pentagon and the Art of War*, New York, Simon & Schuster, 1984.

10. See most recently C. Johnson, *The Sorrows of Empire: Militarism, Secrecy, and the End of the Republic*, New York, Metropolitan Books, 2004, pp. 151–86.

11. The best discussion of this rather esoteric, highly secret subject remains B. G. Blair, *Strategic Command and Control: Redefining the Nuclear Threat*, Washington, DC, Brookings, 1985; and P. Bracken, *The Command and Control of Nuclear Forces*, New Haven, Yale University Press, 1983.

12. See on this story D. Holloway, *Stalin and the Bomb: The Soviet Union and Atomic Energy*, New Haven, Yale University Press, 1994.

13. The most detailed exposition of MAD, written by two of those who helped implement it during the Kennedy and Johnson administrations, remains A. C. Enthoven and W. K. Smith, *How Much Is Enough? Shaping the Defense Program 1961–1967*, New York, Harper & Row, 1971.

14. See Kennedy, *The Rise and Fall of the Great Powers*, p. 436 table 44, for some figures.

15. See D. Ball, *Politics and Force Levels: The Strategic Missile Program of the Kennedy Administration*, Berkeley, University of California Press, 1980, pp. 58, 88, 172–73, 234–39.

16. See, on these efforts, T. Gervassi, *The Myth of Soviet Military Superiority*, New York, Harper & Row, 1987; also A. Cockburn, *Threat: Inside the Soviet Military Machine*, New York, Vintage, 1983, pp. 441–60.

17. See on this A. Bacevich, *The Pentomic Era: The U.S. Army Between Korea and Vietnam*, Washington, DC, National Defense University Press, 1986.

18. The most prominent among them was H. A. Kissinger, *Nuclear Weapons and Foreign Policy: The Need for Choice*, New York, Harper & Row, 1957, chapter 6.

19. Quoted in Brodie, *The Absolute Weapon*, p. 28.

20. "The White House, National Security Strategy of the United States," 2002, available at www.informationclearinghouse.info/article2320.htm.

21. See, on Soviet nuclear doctrine, J. F. and W. F. Scott, *The Soviet Art of War: Doctrine, Strategy, and Tactics*, Boulder, Colo., Westview, 1982, pp. 165–66, 174, 211–15; J. Erickson, "The Soviet View of Deterrence: A General Overview," *Survival* 26, November–December 1982; as well as the older work by H. S. Dinerstein, *War and the Soviet Union: Nuclear Weapons and the Revolution in Soviet Military and Political Thinking*, New York, Praeger, 1962.

22. "To the Brink and Back 330 Times," *Time*, January 17, 1977, pp. 25–26.

23. E.g. McG. Bundy, *Danger and Survival: The Political History of the Nuclear Weapon*, New York, Random House, 1988, p. 616.

24. See on the French reasoning D. S. Yost, "France's Deterrent Posture and Security in Europe," *Adelphi Papers*, No. 194, London, International Institute of Strategic Studies (IISS), 1984, part I, pp. 4–10; also D. A. Ruiz-Palmer, "French Strategic Options in the 1990s," *Adelphi Papers*, No. 260, London, IISS, 1991, pp. 15–16.

25. See D. Callingaert, "Nuclear Weapons and the Korean War," *Journal of Strategic Studies* 11, June 1988, pp. 177–202; also R. J. Foot, "Nuclear Coercion and the Ending of the Korean Conflict," *International Security* 13:3, winter 1988–89, pp. 92–112.

26. Quoted in H. Gelber, "Nuclear Weapons and Chinese Policy," *Adelphi Papers*, No. 99, London, IISS, 1973, p. 9.

27. See the Dutch government report on this interesting episode as reprinted in Subrahmanyam, ed., *Nuclear Myths and Realities*, New Delhi, ABC Publishing, 1981, appendix I, pp. 165–89.
28. According to N. S. Khrushchev, *Khrushchev Remembers*, London, Sphere Books, 1971, p. 255.
29. See the statement by the head of India's nuclear program, Homi Bhaba, quoted in P. K. S. Namboodiri, "Perceptions and Policies in India and Pakistan," in K. Subramanyam, ed., *India and the Nuclear Challenge*, New Delhi, Lancer International, 1986, p. 222.
30. See Spector, *Nuclear Ambitions: The Spread of Nuclear Weapons 1989–1990*, Boulder, Westview, 1990, pp. 64–65, 89–93.
31. See on this S. Peres, *Battling for Peace*, London, Weidenfeld & Nicolson, 1995, p. 167.
32. For some Arab speculations as to what such a war might be like see S. Shazly, *The Arab Military Option*, San Francisco, American Mideast Publications, 1986.
33. See, for the details, Federation of American Scientists (FAS), "Iraqi Nuclear Weapons," 1998, available at www.fas.org/nuke/guide/iraq/nuke/program.htm.
34. See on this S. J. Cimbala, "Nuclear Weapons in the New Order," *Journal of Strategic Studies* 16:2, June 1993, especially pp. 187–88.
35. Freedman, *The Evolution of Nuclear Strategy*, pp. 86–87.
36. "Strategy for Two Atomic Worlds," *Foreign Affairs* 28:3, October 1949, p. 383.
37. See on this M. van Creveld, *The Sword and the Olive: A Critical History of the Israel Defense Force*, New York, Public Affairs, 2002, pp. 77–81.
38. See on it C. A. MacDonald, *Korea: The War Before Vietnam*, New York, Free Press, 1986.
39. See on his theories G. Sloan, "Sir Halford Mackinder: The Heartland Theory, Then and Now," *Journal of Strategic Studies* 22:2/3, June–September 1999, pp. 15–38.
40. See, for this war, M. B. Oren, *Six Days of War: June 1967 and the Making of the Modern Middle East*, Oxford, Oxford University Press, 2002.
41. The best recent account of the war is A. Rabinovich, *The Yom Kippur War: The Epic Encounter That Transformed the Middle East*, New York, Schocken, 2004.
42. For what Syrian president Hafez Assad, *père*, had to say about this subject in the 1970s and 1980s see M. van Creveld, *Nuclear Proliferation and the Future of Conflict*, New York, Free Press, 1993, pp. 112–14.
43. The best study of the Soviet navy in its prime is N. Polmar, *The Naval Institute Guide to the Soviet Navy*, Annapolis, Naval Institute Press, 1991.

44. See on these operations M. Middlebrook, *Task Force: The Falkland War, 1982,* Harmondsworth, Middlesex, Penguin, 1987, especially pp. 125–66.

45. The most detailed analysis is H. A. Hassan, *The Iraqi Invasion of Kuwait,* London, Pluto, 1999.

46. See on this Biddle, *Military Power,* pp. 1 and 240, footnote 1.

47. See, on the continuing role of trucks and the effects this had on land warfare, van Creveld, *Supplying War,* pp. 254–56.

48. Glenn W. Goodman, "Ruling the Skies," *Armed Forces International,* June 1999, p. 30.

49. For a good example of how development theory was supposed to work see M. Lissak, "Military Roles in Modernization: Thailand and Burma," in A. Perlmutter and V. P. Bennet, eds., *The Political Influence of the Military: A Comparative Reader,* New Haven, Yale University Press, 1980, pp. 440–80.

50. For the process as it affected the most important of the armed forces in question, those of China, see You Li, *In Quest of High-Tech Power: The Modernization of China's Military,* Canberra, ACT, ADFA, 1996.

51. For the latest figures see Y. Levy, *The Other Army of Israel: Materialist Militarism in Israel,* Tel Aviv, Yediot Achronot, 2003 [Hebrew], p. 238.

52. See on this M. van Creveld, *Men, Women and War,* London, Cassell, 2000, pp. 180–88.

53. See on the process, as it applied to the United States, J. Holm, *Women in the Military: An Unfinished Revolution,* Novato, Calif., Presidio, 1992, chapter 15; and J. H. Stiehm, *Arms and the Enlisted Woman,* Philadelphia, Temple University Press, 1987, p. 55.

54. The literature on this question is enormous; see L. B. Francke, *Ground Zero: The Gender Wars in the Military,* New York, Simon & Schuster, 1997.

55. CNN figure, December 1, 2004, available at www.cnn.com/interactive/world/0401/chart.iraq.fatalities/frameset.exclude.html.

56. See on this H. Brown, *Thinking About National Security: Defense and Foreign Policy in a Dangerous World,* Boulder, Westview, 1983, pp. 225–33.

57. For some calculations pertaining to this subject see D. T. Kuehl, "Airpower vs. Electricity: Electric Power as a Target for Strategic Air Operations," *Journal of Strategic Studies* 18:1, March 1995, pp. 250–60; also I. Ben Israel, "The Revolution in Military Affairs and the Operation in Iraq," in S. Feldman, ed., *After the War in Iraq: Defining the New Strategic Balance,* Brighton, Sussex Academic Press, 2003, p. 69 table 6.5.

58. See on this Anon., "New Radar Could Defeat Stealth Technology," *Free Republic,* June 15, 2001, available at www.freerepublic.com/forum/a3b29f6c505a3.htm.

59. W. Owen, *Lifting the Fog of War,* New York, Farrar, Straus & Giroux, 2000.

60. See on this entire subject T. Benbow, *The Magic Bullet? Understanding the*

Revolution in Military Affairs, London, Brassey's, 2004; C. Gray, *The American RMA: An Interim Assessment,* Occasional Paper No. 28, 1997; S. Metz and J. Kieviet, *Strategy and the Revolution in Military Affairs: From Theory to Policy,* Carlisle Barracks, US Army Strategic Studies Institute, 1995.

61. See on them Keegan, *The Mask of Command,* pp. 199–200.

62. Arutz Sheva, "Arrow System Malfunctioning in Test," August 27, 2004, available at www.freerepublic.com/focus/f-news/1200979/posts; D. Bachur-Nir, "Israel Neglecting Missiles," *Yediot Achronot* [Hebrew], January 12, 2005.

63. AP, "Russia Developing Nuke Missiles, Putin Says," November 14, 2004, available at www.billingsgazette.com/index.php?id=1&display=rednews/2004/11/18/build/world/40-russian-nukes.inc.

64. See on this subject the reflections of the chief of staff of the German army, General Kurt Zeitzler, in H. Guderian and K. Zeitzler, "Comments on P-41s–P41hh," in US Army Historical Division Study MS #P-041, Washington, DC, Office of the Chief of Military History, 1953, p. 34.

65. See on this A. de Philippe, *Etude sur le service d'etat major pendant les guerres du premier Empire,* Paris, Hachette, 1900, p. 6.

66. See on this the classic study by M. Janowitz, *The Professional Soldier: A Social and Political Portrait,* New York, Free Press, 1960, p. 135.

67. See Francke, *Ground Zero,* pp. 202–5.

68. See van Creveld, *The Sword and the Olive,* pp. 315–16.

69. See its website atwww.military.com/Education/SchoolDisplay?school=80.

70. For a brief history see RAND Overview, available at www.rand.org/about/history/.

Chapter 6

1. For a comprehensive history see R. A. Asprey, *War in the Shadows: The Guerrilla in History,* New York, W. Murray, 1994.

2. Keegan, *The Battle for History,* p. 23.

3. See D. Irving, *The German Atomic Bomb,* New York, Simon & Schuster, 1967; also J. J. Fischer, *Hitler und die Atombombe,* Asendorf, Mut, 1987.

4. See on this N. Rich, *Hitler's War Aims,* New York, Knopf, 1973, p. 8.

5. See, for a somewhat detailed case study of this problem, E. V. Larson, *Casualties and Consensus: The Historical Role of Casualties in Domestic Support for U.S. Military Operations,* Santa Monica, RAND, 1996.

6. See on this J. Smith, *The Russians,* London, Sphere, 1976, pp. 369–71.

7. On the reasons for this see M. van Creveld, *Defending Israel: A Controversial Plan Towards Peace,* New York, St. Martin's, 2004, pp. 60–61.

8. E.g., T. Segev, *One Palestine, Complete,* New York, Metropolitan, 2000, pp. 198–201.

9. See A. Nachmani, "Generals at Bay in Post-War Palestine," *Journal of Strategic Studies* 4:6, December 1983, pp. 66–83.

10. For a brief history of the British attempts to hold on to their empire see L. James, *Imperial Rearguard*, London, Brassey's, 1988.

11. For the origin of the war see R. H. Spector, *Advice and Support: The Early Years of the U.S. Army in Vietnam, 1941–1960*, New York, Free Press, 1985.

12. See Mao Tse-tung, "Strategic Problems in the Anti-Japanese Guerrilla War," in *idem, Selected Works*, ii, New York, International Publishers, 1954 [1938], vol. II pp. 134–45.

13. For the idea that Vietnam was lost by the US officer corps see R. A. Gabriel and P. L. Savage, *Crisis in Command: Mismanagement in the Army*, New York, Hill & Wang, 1978, pp. 51–96.

14. See, for instance, W. C. Westmoreland, *A Soldier Reports*, New York, Dell, 1976, pp. 81–83, 89, 553–58.

15. R. B. Sims, *The Pentagon Reporters*, Washington, DC, National Defense University Press, 1983, especially pp. 139–50.

16. See most recently G. Merom, *How Democracies Lose Small Wars: State, Society and the Failures of France in Algeria, Israel in Lebanon, and the U.S. in Vietnam*, Cambridge, Cambridge University Press, 2004.

17. Ho Chi Minh, "Revising Working Methods," quoted in Douglas Pike, *PAVN: People's Army of Vietnam*, Novato, Calif., Presidio, 1986, p. 219. Thanks are due to Professor Achmed Hashim of the Naval War College for bringing this reference, as well as the next, to my attention.

18. Truong Chinh, *Primer for Revolt*, New York, Praeger, 1963, pp. 11–12.

19. See Th. J. Schulte, *The German Army and Nazi Politics in Occupied Russia*, Oxford, Berg, 1989, p. 260.

20. T. S. Thomas and W. D. Casebeer, *Violent Systems: Defeating Terrorists, Insurgents, and Other Non-State Adversaries*, INSS Occasional Paper, No. 52, Colorado Springs, US Air Force Academy, 2004, pp. 72, 76.

21. Much of what follows is based on M. Dewar, *The British Army in Northern Ireland*, London, Arms and Armor Press, 1985.

22. Figures from T. Taylor, "United Kingdom," in Y. Alexander, ed., *Combating Terrorism: Strategies of Ten Countries*, Ann Arbor, University of Michigan Press, 2002, pp. 201, 202 tables 1 and 2.

23. On the involvement of the RUC in the struggle see J. D. Brewer, *Inside the RUC: Routine Policing in a Divided Society*, Oxford, Clarendon, 1991, especially pp. 118–54.

24. See on this C. Calwell, *Notes on Imperial Policing, 1934*, London, HMSO, 1934, pp. 1012, 1034.

25. Dewar, *The British Army in Northern Ireland*, p. 55.

26. See for some of the details concerning the "Birmingham Six," Wikipedia, available at http://en.wikipedia.org/wiki/Birmingham_Six.

27. Van Creveld, *The Sword and the Olive*, p. 342.

28. The following is based on M. Maoz, *Assad: The Sphinx of Damascus,* New York, Grove Weidenfeld, 1988, pp. 149–63.

29. Surprisingly, the only English-language book about the subject is by its founder, M. Aflak, *The Ba'ath and the Heritage,* n.p., n.p., 1976.

30. See P. Seale, *Assad of Syria: The Struggle for the Middle East,* London, Tauris, 1988, p. 336.

31. See R. A. Gabriel, *Operation Peace for Galilee: The Israeli-PLO War in Lebanon,* New York, Hill & Wang, 1984, pp. 119–21.

32. Statement by Syrian Human Rights Committee, February 18, 1999, available at www.shrc.org/English99/reports/18021999.htm.

33. Statement by Lebanese Liberation Party, 2000, available at www.21a.org/lebanon/ee/terrorsy/htm.

34. Th. L. Friedman, "Hama Rules," *New York Times,* September 21, 2001.

35. Scott Peterson, "How Syria's Brutal Past Colors Its Future," June 20, 2000, available at search.csmonitor.com/durable/2000/06/20/pls3.htm.

36. Ibid., pp. 162–63.

37. See on this J. Dunnigan, "Why Syria Is Still Saddam's Friend," *DLS,* May 2, 2004, available at www.strategypage.com/dls/articles/200452.asp.

38. See the website the Syrian government maintains in his memory: www.assad.org.

39. See on this S. Even, "Arab Regime Stability and the Allocation of Resources: Three Case Studies," in P. Rivlin and S. Even, *Political Stability in Arab States,* Tel Aviv, Jaffee Center for Strategic Studies, Memorandum No. 74, 2004, pp. 31–34.

40. B. Clinton, *My Life,* New York, Knopf, 2004, p. 886.

41. For a pro-Aoun account of these events see G. C. Gamboll, "Michel Aoun," *Middle East International Bulletin* 3:1, January 2001, available at www.meib.org/articles/0101_1d1.htm.

42. See on this episode A. Horne, *A Savage War for Peace: Algeria 1954–1962,* London, MacMillan, 1977, pp. 159–60.

43. C. von Clausewitz, *On War,* M. Howard and P. Paret, eds., Princeton, Princeton University Press, 1976, p. 127.

44. See R. Rieckhoff and D. Hochman, "How the Pentagon Has Failed U.S. Troops," *International Herald Tribune,* August 31, 2004; E. M. Kennedy and B. & A. Hart, "Pentagon Still Fails the Troops," *Boston Globe,* February 3, 2005.

45. See, for what it is worth, W. Murray and R. H. Scales Jr., *The Iraq War,* Cambridge, Belknap, 2003, pp. 15–44.

46. According to the agency, the last time Saddam had targeted a Western asset (President G. H. W. Bush) was in 1993; Center for the Coordination of Counterterrorism, "Overview of State-Sponsored Terrorism," 2001, available at www.state.gov/s/ct/rls/pgtrpt/2000/2441.htm. See on this question also Y. Schweitzer, "The War in Iraq and International Terrorism," in Feldman, ed., *After the War in Iraq*, p. 49.

47. See for these and other nets D. J. Gruber, *Computer Networks and Information Warfare: Implications for Military Operations*, Colorado Springs, Colo., Air War College, 2000, pp. 9–10.

48. S.J.A. Edwards, *Swarming on the Battlefield*, Santa Monica, Calif., RAND, 2000, p. xvii.

49. See on Boyd and his OODA Loop, Benbow, *The Magic Bullet?*, pp. 83–85.

50. See S. Wilson, "Fear Hamstrings Quest for Intelligence in Northern Iraq," *Washington Post*, December 11, 2004.

51. "U.S. Historian Cities Lack of Iraq Post-War Plan," *Washington Post*, December 25, 2004.

52. For some such figures see B. Graham, "Generals See Gains from Iraq Offensives," Washingtonpost.com, December 6, 2004.

53. J. Tirman, "100,000 Dead in Iraq," October 30, 2004, available at www.alternet.org/waroniraq/20352 (based on a Johns Hopkins University study).

54. J. A. Barber, "The Social Effects of Military Service," in S. Ambrose and J. A. Barber, eds., *The Military and American Society*, New York, Free Press, 1972, pp. 205–18.

55. See on this M. van Creveld, *Fighting Power: German and U.S. Military Performance, 1939–1945*, Westport, Greenwood, 1982; also Anon., "Unit Cohesion and Why Personnel Rotation Policies Hurt the Army's Readiness for Combat," 1998, available at www.d-n-i.net/fcs/comments/c210.htm.

56. M. Dayan, *Vietnam Diary*, Tel Aviv, Dvir, 1977 [Hebrew], p. 62.

57. M. Binkin and S. J. Bach, *Women in the Military*, Washington, DC, Brookings, 1977, pp. 62–63.

58. E.g., B. Whitman, deputy assistant secretary for public affairs, quoted in American Forces Information Service, March 10, 2003, available at www.defenselink.mil/news/Mar2003/n03102003_200303105.html.

59. See E. Grossman, "Tensions Rise Across Iraq as Troops Are Told to Cut It Out," *Inside the Pentagon*, November 4, 2004.

60. For some figures concerning the strength of the forces and the number of troops deployed abroad see M. Kilian, "Fears Grow of Military Spread Thin," *Chicago Tribune*, December 3, 2004.

61. E. Donnelly, "The Army's Gender War," *National Review*, January 7, 2005, available at www.nationalreview.com/comment/donnelly200501070750.asp.

62. S. Hananel, "Soldiers Challenge Enlistment Extensions," Yahoo! News, De-

cember 6, 2004; P. Garwood, "U.S. Army Reservists Escape Court-Martial," Yahoo! News, December 6, 2004; B. Graham, "General Says Army Reserve Is Becoming 'Broken' Force," *Washington Post*, January 6, 2005; E. Nieves and A. S. Tyson, "Fewer Gays Being Discharged Since 9/11," Washington post.com, February 12, 2005.

63. A. Dubilet, "Harvard Law Bars Military Recruiters," *Daily Pennsylvanian*, December 3, 2004.

64. J. F. Harris and C. Muste, "56 Percent in Survey Say Iraq War Was a Mistake," *Washington Post*, December 21, 2004, available at story.news .yahoo.com/news?tmpl=story&cid=1802&e=3&u=/washpost/20041221/ ts_washpost/a14266_2004dec20.

65. See, for a good survey of the period in question, W. Laqueur, *The Age of Terrorism*, Boston, Little, Brown, 1987 ed.; also, for the European movements, Y. Alexander and D. Pluchinsky, *Europe's Red Terrorists: The Fighting Communist Organizations*, London, Cass, 1992.

66. "Fatwah Urging Jihad Against the Americans," *Al Quds al-Arabi*, February 23, 1998, available at www.ict.org.il/articles/fatwah.htm; and O. bin Laden, "Letter to America," *The Observer*, November 24, 2002, available at observer.guardian.co.uk/worldview/story/0%2C854725%2C00.html.

67. R. Woodward, "Athens Prepares for Olympic Party Under Unprecedented Security Blanket," TurkishPress.com, September 11, 2004, available at www.turkishpress.com/news.asp?id=24227.

68. T. Weiner, "Pentagon Envisioning a Costly Internet for War," *New York Times*, November 13, 2004.

69. Rumsfeld memo to General D. Meyer, "Global War on Terrorism," 27.10.2003, available at www.usatoday.com/news/washington/executive/ rumsfeldmemo.htm.

70. Rumsfeld memo, October 16, 2003, available at Yahoo! News, October 22, 2003.

Chapter 7

1. Clausewitz, *On War*, p. 195.

2. See, for the latest on this, AFP, "Top U.S. Scientists Urge Halt to Funding for Missile Defense," Yahoo! News, April 7, 2005.

3. For some figures on this see L. Polizzi, "Le donne nella guerra de Liberazione," in F. Battistelli, ed., *Donne e forze armate*, Milan, Agneli, 1997, p. 130; and B. Jancar, "Yugoslavia's War of Resistance," in N. Loring Goldman, ed., *Female Soldiers, Combatants or Noncombatants?*, Westport, Greenwood, 1982, pp. 85–102.

4. C. D. Leoning and D. Priest, "Detainees Accuse Female Interrogators," *Washington Post*, February 10, 2005.

5. See on this, in reference to the 1991 Gulf War, H. Pagonis, *Moving Mountains: Lessons in Leadership and Logistics from the Gulf War*, Cambridge, Harvard University Press, 1991, pp. 151–58.

6. An excellent case in point was the Greek Civil War of 1947–49; see on this L. E. Cable, *Conflict of Myths: The Development of American Counterinsurgency Doctrine and the Vietnam War*, New York, New York University Press, 1986, pp. 9–32.

7. B. Graham, "A Sharp Shift from Killing to Kindness," *Washington Post*, December 4, 2004, p. A4.

8. C. Asquith, "What Iraqis Receive for their Losses," *Christian Science Monitor*, February 23, 2004, available at www.csmonitor.com/2004/0223/p11s01-woiq.htm.

Epilogue

1. Figures from O. Shelah and Y. Limor, *Captives of Lebanon*, Tel Aviv, Yedioth Ahronoth, 2007 [Hebrew], pp. 159, 240–47. Essentially similar data may be found in R. Tira, *The Limitations of Standoff Firepower-Based Operations on Standoff Warfare, Maneuver, and Decision*, Tel Aviv, INSS, 2007, p. 44.

2. General Dan Halutz as quoted in Z. Schiff, "The Foresight Saga" *Haaretz* [Hebrew], August 18, 2006.

3. See J. S. Corum and W. R. Johnson, *Airpower in Small Wars*, Lawrence, University Press of Kansas, 2003, p. 8.

4. Shelah and Limor, *Captives of Lebanon*, p. 120.

5. For what they may have learned, see M. van Creveld, "Make a Deal with Syria and Weaken the Iran-Hezbollah Axis," *Forward*, January 26, 2007, available at www.forward.com/articles/make-a-deal-with-syria-and-weaken -the-iran-hezboll/.

6. G. Alon and A. Harel, "Female Soldier Accused of Forcing Palestinian Woman to Drink Poison" *Haaretz* [Hebrew], June 23, 2003.

7. Van Creveld, *The Sword and the Olive*, pp. 261–63, 315–16.

8. The manual is available online at 66.218.69.11/search/cache?p=coin+ manual&fr=yfp-t-501&toggle=1&ei=UTF-8&u=www.fas.org/irp/doddir/ army/fm3-24fd.pdf&w=coin+manual+manuals&d=JgXJM_mdOl w0&icp=1&.intl=us.

9. By E. N. Luttwak in "Dead End: Counterinsurgency Warfare as Military Malpractice," *Harper's*, February 2007.

10. E.g., R. Trinquier, *Modern Warfare*, New York, Praeger, 2006 [1964].

11. Q. Abdul-Zahra, "Construction on Baghdad Barrier Halted," Associated Press, April 23, 2007, available at news.yahoo.com/s/ap/20070423/ap _on_re_mi_ea/iraq_neighborhood_barrier.

12. B. Bender, "West Point Grads Exit Service at High Rate; War Redeployment Thought a Major Factor," *Boston Globe,* November 4, 2007, available at www.boston.com/news/nation/washington/articles/2007/04/11/west_point_grads_exit_service_at_high_rate/. Thanks to Larry Kummer for pointing me to this article.

13. For what women's presence has done to training, see. S. Guttmann, *The Kinder, Gentler Military: Can America's Gender-Neutral Fighting Force Still Win Wars?*, New York, Scribner, 2000.

14. N. Ferguson, *The War of the World: Twentieth-Century Conflict and the Descent of the West,* New York, Penguin, 2006, p. xli.

Index

About the Author

MARTIN VAN CREVELD, professor of history at Hebrew University, Jerusalem, is one of the best-known experts on military history and strategy. He has written seventeen books, which have been translated into fourteen languages; most notable among them are *Supplying War: Logistics from Wallenstein to Patton, Command in War,* and *The Transformation of War.* Professor van Creveld has consulted to the defense departments of numerous governments, including that of the United States. He was the second civilian expert ever to be invited to address the Israeli General Staff, and has lectured or taught at practically every institute of strategic military study. He has appeared on CNN, the BBC, and other international networks and has been featured in many magazines and newspapers, including *Newsweek* and the *International Herald Tribune.*